Women and the Economi

California Series on Social Choice and Political Economy
Edited by Brian Barry, Robert H. Bates, and Samuel L. Popkin

Women and the Economic Miracle

*Gender and Work
in Postwar Japan*

Mary C. Brinton

UNIVERSITY OF CALIFORNIA PRESS
Berkeley · Los Angeles · London

University of California Press
Berkeley and Los Angeles, California

University of California Press, Ltd.
London, England

© 1993 by
The Regents of the University of California

First Paperback Printing 1994

Library of Congress Cataloging-in-Publication Data

Brinton, Mary C.
   Women and the economic miracle : gender and work in postwar Japan
/ Mary C. Brinton.
      p.   cm.— (California series on social choice and political
economy ; 21)
   Includes bibliographical references (p.   ) and index.
   ISBN 0-520-08920-0
   1. Women—Employment—Japan. I. Title. II. Series.
HD6197.B75   1992
331.4'0952—dc20   91-30670
                                                                        CIP

Printed in the United States of America
9 8 7 6 5 4 3 2 1

Contents

Tables

Figures

A Note on Japanese Names

Japanese names appear in the text in Japanese order, with the family name preceding the personal name. To avoid confusion, I have followed this practice throughout, whether Japanese scholars have published in Japanese or in English. The bibliography follows American custom, with authors listed in alphabetical order by family name.

Acknowledgments

"Someone once said that he had very great difficulty in writing poetry; he had plenty of ideas but could not get the language he needed. He was rightly told that poetry was written in words, not in ideas" (Mead 1934: 148). Books, like poems, are born of ideas but executed in words. Such execution frequently requires not only the perseverance of the author but the support of many institutions and individuals as well. I am very grateful to the Japan Foundation, the Social Science Research Council, and the Sanwa Bank Foundation for financing my stay in Japan during 1983–85 and for helping defray expenses incurred during preparation of the initial draft of this book. The National Science Foundation and the Graduate School of the University of Washington provided extra funds for the survey research I carried out. A fellowship from the Spencer Foundation in 1987–88 allowed me to take time off from teaching in order to carry out additional research necessary for revising the manuscript. The support of the University of Chicago Social Sciences Divisional Research Fund and the Center for East Asian Studies is also gratefully acknowledged.

The support and encouragement of several people were critical to me in the early stages of the project. Michael Hechter provided guidance by giving positive feedback only for "intellectually ambitious" work, and tried to keep me on track whenever I strayed into too much detail. Yamagishi Toshio was always miraculously available when I needed him in either Japan or the United States for help and a good argument, whether about theoretical or empirical issues. His support

xv

as harsh critic and good friend was invaluable to the execution of the project. Tom Pullum and the late Tad Blalock provided methodological feedback. Special thanks go to Karen Cook, who stepped in when I most needed her. Thanks also go to Steve Harrell, who almost convinced me that I am part anthropologist.

The best part of doing the research for this book was the opportunity to live in Japan and share one and a half years of my life with many wonderful people. Although I lived alone in Tokyo while I was doing this research, moments of loneliness were very few indeed. This was due to a set of Japanese friends and acquaintances that seemed to grow larger every week, and that succeeded in creating a warm environment I had never expected to find in a foreign country. In a country where many *gaijin* (foreigners) feel like unwelcome intruders, I am grateful to all the people who took the time to get to know me as an individual.

Among those who expressed concern to me that the project would fail, I am lucky to count many who felt that only with *their* help could I succeed to any reasonable degree. Of course they were right. Several people said that I needed help and expert advice to prepare and carry out my own survey, then proceeded to provide such assistance. Horiuchi Mitsuko of the Japanese Ministry of Labor took my project under her wing as soon as I arrived in Japan and promptly learned how to explain it more concisely than I could to anyone who would listen. She introduced me to many people in the Ministry of Labor, academic circles, and Tokyo metropolitan government offices who gave me valuable, practical advice on the survey construction. My institutional affiliation at Keiō University gave me a home base from which to conduct the mailing of the survey, and a place to hang my hat (even if it was among economists). Shimada Haruo enlisted his students to help in coding the survey data precisely when I mistakenly thought I could handle things by myself. He was right. Two others who offered help when I most needed it—in dealing with the printing company, hiring people to stuff envelopes and code data, getting keypunching done, and writing up results for my first article in Japanese—were Suzuki Ryū, of Sophia University and the Social Science Research Institute of Japan, and Nakayama Keiko, then at Niigata University and the Waseda Social Science Research Institute and now at the University of Shizuoka. Sano Yōko and Nishikawa Shunsaku helped with various aspects of the research and made me feel at home at Keiō.

Fukuzawa Jōji provided not only the best sushi in Tokyo but also many unexpected glimpses into Japanese life. His presence sprinkled more than a little humor into the serious task of surviving as a foreign researcher in Japan.

My greatest thanks for being able to survive in Tokyo, though, go to Murakami Yasusuke and Murakami Keiko and their sons, who were my "family" away from home. They served me more green tea, roast beef, and good advice than I can ever hope to repay.

My colleagues at the University of Chicago provided stimulating criticism and much support while this book was being written and revised. In particular I would like to thank Gary Becker, Charles Bidwell, Jim Coleman, John Craig, and Bob Willis for their interest in the work. I am indebted to Bill Parish for reading an earlier draft of the entire manuscript and providing very helpful criticism. The comments of Marty Whyte, at the University of Michigan, were also above and beyond the call of duty. I also want to thank Gay-Young Cho for her unflinching editing, and Moonkyung Choi, Lingxin Hao, Sunhwa Lee, and Hang-yue Ngo for their support. David Baird labored over the figures for the book. Finally, thanks go to Arai Hiroko, Lillian Bensley, Frederick Brinton, Barbara Brooks, Karen Hegtvedt, Jeff Kingston, Margaret Levi, Barbara Metch, Tony Maier, Namiki Hiroshi, Osawa Machiko, Tanaka Kazuko, and Michael Uehara for equal parts distraction and help in getting this book done.

ONE

Introduction

What do Americans and other Westerners think of when they hear the phrase "women in Japan"? For many people, the immediate image is that of kimono-clad, tea-serving, compliant women who do not play any role in the modern economy. This image is erroneous. Japanese women now participate in the economy at levels similar to women in Western industrial nations. Yet to conclude that there is equivalence between women's roles in the economies of Japan and the industrial West would be to replace one misleading image with another. The main goal of this book is to provide more realistic—and necessarily more complex—images of women's role in the postwar Japanese economy.

While Western impressions of Japanese women's roles may be poorly informed, Japan nevertheless represents a seeming contradiction: high rates of participation in the economy, yet sharp gender differentiation in wages, employment status, and occupational roles. The past few decades of experience in Western industrial nations, both capitalist and socialist, have suggested that a high female labor force participation rate does not necessarily mean the rapid extinction of sharply delineated sex roles in the economy or the disappearance of the male-female wage gap. But Japan demonstrates this more clearly than any other industrial society. No matter how we choose to measure gender stratification in the labor force, Japan represents the most marked deviation from other countries. This is true despite the fact that Japan has entered the ranks of advanced industrial economies. About 58 percent of Japan's people live in cities of over 100,000, compared to

76 percent of the U.S. population, and although the agricultural sector remains slightly larger than in the United States and a number of other industrial nations, the vast majority (over 90 percent) of Japanese workers are in the manufacturing and service sectors of the economy. The size of the service sector in Japan is comparable to that of West Germany and is slightly smaller than those of the United States, Great Britain, and France.[1] But the contrast between the roles of men and women in the Japanese economy is greater than in the West. Why should this be of interest to Western social scientists, policymakers, and the public at large?

Japan's phenomenal rate of economic growth in the past quarter-century and its increasing dominance in world markets have transformed it into a model of a successful postindustrial society in many people's minds. So it is critical that we ask whether Japanese sex roles represent an epiphenomenon, a legacy of Japan's relatively late entrance into the industrial world. Alternatively, do the Japanese social and economic institutions so admired by Westerners for their cohesion and efficiency actually produce and maintain strong sex roles in the economy? Have these institutions produced an even stronger case of the contradiction, already apparent in the West, between high rates of female participation in the economy on the one hand and economic inequality between men and women on the other?

I argue that this is the case. Japanese women's roles are not the epiphenomenal result of late industrial development per se. Nor are these roles simply the product of a strong sex-role ideology in Japanese culture. Rather, they are closely tied to the development of social and economic institutions in postwar Japanese society. These social and economic institutions did not "just happen." They are the result of purposive action. As Robert Cole, a long-time scholar of Japanese industrial relations, points out in reference to Japan's infamous "permanent employment system": "Although there are some aspects of an unconscious persistence of custom in the evolution of permanent employment, for the most part it represents a conscious act of institution building" (Cole 1979: 24).

---

[1] The proportion of the labor force employed in the service sector (industries other than agriculture, mining, forestry and fishing, manufacturing, and construction) is 59.6 percent in Japan, 71.2 percent in the United States, 72.2 percent in Great Britain, 66.2 percent in France, and 57.2 percent in West Germany (International Labor Organization 1988). Note that the statistics reported in this book are for West Germany prior to its unification with East Germany.

The Japanese educational system and labor market have developed historically in ways that disadvantage women in economic terms. This book is concerned principally with these institutions and with the family. Because my argument is about how these institutions structure the opportunities and constraints for Japanese men's and women's economic roles, the story I tell is not one based on a conspiracy of men against women or capitalists against workers. The story is about why Japanese institutions such as schools and work organizations operate in the ways they do, and how men and women respond rationally to the choices and constraints inherent in these institutions. The aggregate result is a high level of gender differentiation and stratification in the economy.

JAPAN AND WESTERN INDUSTRIAL ECONOMIES COMPARED

Japanese women participate in the labor force at a similar rate to women in Western industrial nations, as the following percentages of participation (all for 1987 unless otherwise indicated) show:[2]

Sweden	81.1
Norway	63.7
Denmark (1986)	57.5
Canada	56.2
United States	54.2
Japan	*48.6*
Australia	48.3
United Kingdom (1986)	48.2
France	45.8
West Germany	42.0

With 49 percent of adult females in the labor force, Japan stands between the high rates of North America and Scandinavia and the somewhat lower rates of Western Europe. This apparent typicality masks three important phenomena that set Japan apart: (1) Japanese

[2] International Labor Organization 1988; Ministry of Labor, Japan, 1988. Countries were chosen on the basis of geographical representation and comparability of data. Figures are calculated as (total number of women in the labor force/total female population aged 15 and above) x 100, with the following exceptions: (1) for Norway, the denominator is the total female population aged 16 and above; (2) for Sweden, population and employment figures are reported for age 64 and under, which inflates the rate of participation in the labor force relative to other countries, because the 65+ age group, not included in the Swedish figure, has a very low rate of economic participation.

women, relative to men, are much more likely than their Western counterparts to be piecework laborers or workers in family-run enterprises; (2) there is a greater tendency in Japan than in other countries for white-collar jobs to be "male" and blue-collar jobs to be "female"; and (3) the male-female wage gap is greater in Japan.

EMPLOYMENT STATUS

Employment status is an important indicator of gender stratification that has generally been ignored in research in the United States because the overwhelming majority of the U.S. labor force consists of employees.[3] In economies such as Japan's, employment status is a more salient aspect of work. Fully one-quarter (14,640,000 people) of the Japanese labor force are self-employed workers or workers in small family-run businesses. This is a greater proportion than in any other industrial country, although France and Australia also show high rates of self-employment. If men and women are distributed differently among the employee, self-employed, and family enterprise sectors, this is an important indicator of gender stratification. For example, working in a small family business involves more flexible working hours than working as an employee in a large corporation. But it also involves a dependence on the continuation of the family unit. It is typically unpaid labor, so it does not imply the economic independence that can arise from wage labor. Self-employment is also an important category to examine in and of itself. In Japan this category is comprised both of independent shopowners (the classic "petite bourgeoisie"), who tend to be men, and piece-rate workers who work out of their living rooms assembling modern or traditional consumer goods. The latter are overwhelmingly women.

Table 1.1 shows the sexes' distribution by employment status (employee, self-employed, and family enterprise worker) in a number of industrial economies. In all countries but Japan, female workers are more likely than male workers to be paid employees. For example, in the United States, 94 percent of employed women and 90 percent of employed men are employees. Japan displays the largest gap between the proportions of men and women who work as employees, and the gap is in the *opposite* direction: men are more likely than women to

---

[3] Recent observers argue that more self-employment is emerging in the U.S. economy, involving 8–14 percent of the labor force (Steinmetz and Wright 1989).

TABLE 1.1
EMPLOYMENT STATUS OF WORKERS
IN INDUSTRIAL ECONOMIES

	Employee (%)	Self-employed (%)	Family enterprise worker (%)
Japan			
Women	68.6	12.1	19.3
Men	79.5	17.8	2.7
Nonagricultural population only			
Women	75.6	11.6	12.9
Men	84.7	13.5	1.7
Sweden			
Women	94.8	4.6	0.7
Men	87.2	12.5	0.2
United States			
Women	93.7	5.7	0.6
Men	89.8	10.1	0.1
United Kingdom			
Women	93.3	6.7	Not reported
Men	85.0	15.0	Not reported
Denmark (1986)			
Women	92.3	3.3	4.4
Men	86.2	13.7	0.1
Norway			
Women	92.3	4.1	3.6
Men	85.8	12.7	1.4
Canada			
Women	91.2	6.8	1.9
Men	88.7	10.9	0.4
West Germany			
Women	88.8	4.7	6.6
Men	88.1	11.2	0.6
Australia			
Women	87.0	11.7	1.2
Men	81.6	17.9	0.6
France			
Women	86.1	6.7	7.2
Men	82.0	16.9	1.1

SOURCES: International Labor Organization 1988; Ministry of Labor, Japan, 1988.
NOTE: All figures are for 1987, except where indicated. Figures represent the percentage of workers in each employment status. Workers designated in the International Labor Organization statistics as "unclassifiable by status" are not included in the table.

be employees. When industrial economies are compared, Japanese women make up the lowest proportion of employees relative to men.

The comparatively low percentage (69 percent) of Japanese women workers who are employees is complemented by the high percentage who labor as family enterprise workers in small family-run businesses or farms. Fewer than 3 percent of all Japanese male workers (and fewer than 2 percent of those not employed in agriculture) work in family-run enterprises. This proportion is slightly higher than in other industrial countries. But almost one-fifth of the Japanese female labor force work as family enterprise workers. This is about three times the rate in France and West Germany and more than twenty times the rate in countries such as the United States, Sweden, and Australia. The high rate in Japan cannot be explained solely by the presence of a larger agricultural sector. Table 1.1 demonstrates that even in the nonagricultural population, Japanese women exhibit a much higher rate of family enterprise employment than women in other countries. Japanese women also have a high rate of self-employment compared to women in most other industrial countries, and the difference between the proportions of Japanese men and women who are self-employed is not as great as in many countries. But the content of the work performed by the two sexes is radically different. Over one-third of Japanese female self-employed workers are laboring on a piece-rate basis (called "home handicraft" labor in the Japanese census). This involves tasks such as sewing or putting together electronics parts at home and delivering the work to a firm, often a subcontractor for a larger firm. This is hardly the image of an independent entrepreneur that the term "self-employment" brings to mind. In contrast to the high proportion of piece-rate work among the female self-employed in Japan, fewer than *half of one percent* of self-employed males are piece-rate workers. About one-third of male self-employed workers have employees working for them, but fewer than 15 percent of self-employed females do. Restricting the gender comparison to self-employment in the manufacturing sector presents an even sharper picture: 94 percent of self-employed women are piece-rate workers, as opposed to 3 percent of men.

OCCUPATIONS

The location of women relative to men in the occupational structure is also distinctive in Japan vis-à-vis Western industrial nations. Figure 1.1 shows the percentage female in each occupational group in six

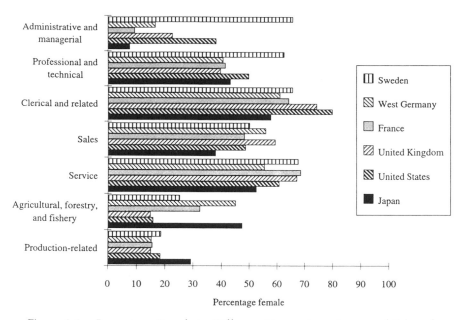

Figure 1.1.   Percentage Female in Different Occupations, Japan and Selected Western Countries

SOURCE: International Labor Organization 1988.

NOTE: Administrative/managerial occupations and clerical occupations are assigned the same percentage female in Sweden, because figures for these groups of occupations are reported together in the *Yearbook of Labor Statistics* for the country.

industrial countries. The most striking characteristic of Japanese women's participation in white-collar work (administrative and managerial, professional and technical, clerical, sales, and service) is their extremely low representation in administrative/managerial positions. Only 8 percent of managers are women. France also shows a low rate of female managers (9 percent), while the rates of other countries range from 17 percent in West Germany to 66 percent in Sweden. (Since figures for administrative/managerial and clerical workers are reported together in Sweden, it is misleading to place too much emphasis on the high proportion of female managers there.) Japanese women participate in professional and technical occupations at a rate similar to that in other industrial countries. In clerical, sales, and service occupations, however, Japan shows the lowest rates of female participation compared to other industrial countries.

Figure 1.1 also shows that Japanese women are more likely than women in other countries to be heavily involved in agriculture and manufacturing (production) relative to their male counterparts—48 percent of Japanese agricultural workers are women. This compares to much lower rates in the United States, Great Britain, France, and Sweden, and a slightly lower rate in West Germany. Japanese women are represented in production-related work (manufacturing, transportation, and other blue-collar jobs) at a rate approximately twice that of women in other countries. The unusual concentration of Japanese women in manufacturing is especially apparent when we consider part-time workers. The postwar increase in married women's participation in the labor forces of industrial countries is partially constituted by part-time work, and Japan is no exception. But it *is* exceptional in the industrial distribution of female part-time workers: nearly one-half of such workers were engaged in manufacturing jobs in 1980, compared to only 9 percent in the United States. In contrast, in the United States and other industrial countries, 50 to 60 percent of female part-time workers are employed in clerical or service occupations; in Japan, such occupations constitute only about 30 percent of the female part-time labor force. The proportion of Japanese female part-time workers in professional and technical occupations is also negligible, at 3 percent in 1980, whereas the figure for the United States is 15 percent.

WAGES

International comparisons of wage data are notoriously difficult because of comparability problems, but a few illustrative figures may be given. The overall female/male wage ratio for full-time workers in the mid 1980s ranged in Western industrial nations from a low of 68.2 (weekly rate) in the United States to highs in the 84–89 percent range (hourly) in France and northern Europe (International Labor Organization 1988). Wages in Japan are typically reported as monthly rates, and the female/male ratio in 1987 was 57.6, substantially lower than in any other industrial country (Ministry of Labor, Japan, 1988).[4] So not only are women more underrepresented as employees and as white-collar workers in Japan, but their wage levels lie farther below men's than is the case in Western capitalist economies.

[4] In East Asia, Japan and South Korea show the lowest female/male wage ratios (International Labor Organization 1987).

PROBLEMS IN THE COMPARATIVE
STUDY OF WOMEN'S ECONOMIC ROLE

These international comparisons show that in considering women's participation in industrial economies, much is obscured by focusing only on the level or amount of participation as in the figures given on p. 3 above, where Japan appears typical in the context of other nations.[5] When we examine the type of work women engage in relative to men—measured by employment status, occupation, and wage levels—the broad similarities among industrial countries become fuzzier and contrasts emerge. Nowhere is this more apparent than in the comparison between Japan and other industrial countries.

The economic and social institutions of capitalism exhibit variations across societies owing to historical and cultural disjunctures. American sociologists and economists have tended to ignore this in their studies of women's economic role. It has been easier to see and document the broad similarities in the historical trajectory of women's economic participation than to discern deeper cultural differences. This is true because of some very good methodological reasons and some rather bad theoretical reasons.

Methodologically, it is only recently that social scientists have had access to reliable time-series labor force statistics from a range of countries. So it is natural that the main focus of interest in comparing countries has been the aggregate *level* at which women participate in the economy. The issue of how to measure cross-culturally the *type* of economic participation in which women are engaged is conveniently avoided if the comparable statistical base across countries and over time is limited to labor force participation rates. But greater female labor force participation in one economy compared to another may or may not correspond to better wages or working conditions for women relative to men. Women's labor force participation may increase because wartime circumstances create a demand for their labor or because an increasing rate of divorce propels them into the work force.

[5] In an empirical analysis of female labor force participation in 61 countries, Moshe Semyonov found that "all characteristics that favored women's labor force participation also enhanced discrimination" (1980: 544), or the concentration of women in low-status occupations. Further, as the number of economically active females increases in a society, the odds in favor of men rather than women belonging to high-status occupations significantly increase. Thus, women's entrance into the public sphere per se is not at all coterminous with, and may even inhibit, their equal distribution with men across occupational status categories. As Semyonov points out, this finding is consistent with theories of economic discrimination that suggest declining rewards for minority group members as their supply increases.

The jobs they perform may involve poor working conditions, low economic compensation, or no economic compensation at all. An increase in women's labor force participation and a decrease in gender stratification in the labor force are not the same and should not be collapsed into one concept. An example from Japanese experience illustrates this well.

During the high-growth period of the Japanese economy that lasted from the early 1960s until the first oil shock in 1973, the demand for labor increased. In particular, as larger numbers of male junior high school graduates continued on to high school and then to university, a shortage of unskilled labor developed. This created a demand that women in their mid thirties to forties could naturally fill. Because the majority of these women had left the labor force while they were raising children, they had little work experience. Moreover, their educational level was generally below that of men. These conditions created a "fit" between the demand for cheap, unskilled labor and its supply. Large numbers of women entered the labor force as part-time workers. In 1960, 43 percent of all part-time workers were women; by 1986, this figure had shown a remarkable increase to 70 percent.[6]

The working conditions and wages of these part-time women workers are inferior to those of regular employees. A much-cited report by the International Labor Organization in 1984 found that Japan was the only industrial nation where female wages actually *fell* relative to male wages during the previous year. Subsequent reports have shown little improvement. The decrease in the hourly wage level of Japanese women relative to men is partially a result of the huge increase in the relatively unskilled female labor force.

This example shows that a comparison of the simple rate of female labor force participation in Japan and other countries masks the complexities of women's work situation. The labor force participation rate can rise as a result of women entering the labor force in subsidiary positions.

While one of the major problems in comparative studies of women's economic role has been obtaining cross-cultural data to construct good measures, this is not the only issue. A *theoretical* stumbling block has also lain in the path of people studying women's economic role in capitalist industrial societies. American social science remains guided

[6] Phrased as the percentage of all working women who are part-time workers, the figure was 9 percent in 1960 and 23 percent in 1986 (Office of the Prime Minister, Japan, *Rōdōryoku chōsa*, 1988).

by a strong underlying belief that Western Europe and the United States are cut out of similar developmental fabric, and that the more recently industrializing societies will follow suit in their educational systems, social organization of work, and family patterns. Small cultural variations may persist, of course, but the social and economic institutions and the demographic patterns arising from them are predicted to be common to the industrialization process. This viewpoint has inhibited a strong push from the side of social science theory to consider the cross-cultural variations among women's roles in different capitalist economies more carefully.

Those who argue that societies converge with industrialization would say that, as a latecomer to industrialization, Japan will gradually come to resemble all other industrial societies. However, recent studies of East Asia, particularly Japan, argue instead that societies may follow different paths to industrialization, and may therefore exhibit differences in social structure and organizational forms once they get there (see Bae and Form 1986; Hamilton and Biggart 1988; Kalleberg and Lincoln 1988; Morgan and Hirosima 1983). While a myriad of activities ranging from complex business transactions to the equally complex education of children have to be carried out in any industrial society, the organization of these activities varies across societies. Western social scientists have been slow to recognize that the organization of men's and women's roles in East Asian economies may not be on the rapid route to convergence with the West.[7] Many social scientists regard the sex-role revolution and the decline of the "breadwinner system" as concomitant phenomena of industrialization per se (Davis 1984). But Japan continues to represent a puzzle. Because it has maintained a sharply delineated sexual division of labor and is at the same time one of the leading industrial economies of the world, it is a crucial case for study.

WOMEN'S DUAL ROLE IN THE JAPANESE ECONOMY

A central argument of this book is that Japanese women have played a dual role in the postwar economic success of their country. The first

---

[7] There are some exceptions to this. A cogently argued recent example concludes: "The West and Japan provide quite different models of development and demographic transition. Japan illustrates that egalitarian sex roles and nuclear family structure are not necessary to achieve low fertility. Some would argue that Japan is a special case in many ways. Yet for many nations in Asia the Japanese model may be a more appealing and successful strategy of modernization, inasmuch as it retains many traditional Eastern institutions" (Morgan, Rindfuss, and Parnell 1984: 34).

role is as direct participants in the economy: they have supplied inexpensive labor to employers. The Japanese economy is segmented into a formal sector, consisting of medium-sized and large firms with paid employees, and an informal sector, made up of very small, family-run firms with some paid employees and some family members (who are typically unpaid workers). Women are likely to be full-time employees in the formal sector when they are young and part-time employees (particularly in the smaller-sized firms) or family enterprise workers when they are older. Women's direct role in the economy is therefore strongly influenced by their age. They work when young in certain sectors of the economy at the low wages of youth, and when middle-aged they work in other sectors of the economy, again generally at the low wages of youth.

Women's second role in the postwar Japanese economy has been as indirect participants: they have nurtured higher-priced male labor, the labor of their husbands and sons. To explain the nature of women's direct economic participation and the additional, more indirect economic role they play in shaping and investing in men's human capital, I argue that we need to understand the nature of the *human capital development system* in Japan—the social processes that govern the formation and use of "human capital," the skills and abilities of people. This entails a close examination of how those processes came to be embedded in the family, the educational system, and the workplaces of postwar Japan.

So far I have been careful to refer to "Japanese women's roles in the economy" rather than to "Japanese women's social status" or "the status of women in Japanese society." This is intentional. This book is about women's roles in the economy and does not deal with other dimensions of women's status, such as access to political power or to cultural symbols and resources. Yet in defining not only a direct economic role for women but a second, indirect role as "investors" in the human capital of men, the family explicitly enters into the discussion. This is because of its ubiquitousness: marriage and childbearing are nearly universal among Japanese women. Men's and women's valuation of the roles of wife and mother is high, and women are the principal caretakers of all household responsibilities save the primary breadwinner role. Particularly important is their investment in the "quality" of children, especially sons. A full examination of women's participation in the Japanese economy therefore needs to include women's role in the development of male human capital. While most of the empirical materials of the book deal with the nature of women's direct participation in the economy, women's indirect economic role is important in the guiding theoretical framework: women play an important part in Japan's human capital development system by investing heavily in the human capital of the males to whom they are attached. This is anathema to most Western women, especially Western feminists. What does it mean for Japanese women's own view of themselves? What implications do Japanese women's dual economic roles have for their status in society? I shall return to these questions in my conclusion.

WESTERN STUDY OF THE JAPANESE "ECONOMIC MIRACLE"

If the variations in women's economic role in industrial societies have not been well mapped by social science researchers, neither has Japanese women's role in the modern economy been well mapped in the rapidly expanding body of writings on Japan. In the past decade, the eyes of the world—especially the industrialized Western nations and the rapidly industrializing nations of East Asia—have turned to Japan as a successful model of industrialization, economic growth, and stability, both in politics and in labor relations. James Abegglen's classic *The Japanese Factory* appeared in 1958. After a ten-year hiatus, during which Japan exhibited unprecedented economic growth, Western social scientists began to produce studies of Japanese industrial relations at a rapid pace.[8] These studies contributed a great deal to our understanding of the origins and functioning of the Japanese permanent employment system, whereby workers are hired into firms directly out of school and remain with the same firms for the duration of their working lives. Japanese management practices were brought to the attention of a broad Western audience both inside and outside academia. Japan's high economic growth rate and increasing share in foreign trade also prompted the publication of dozens of popular books aimed at a broad audience. At first, these were almost uniformly in praise of the Japanese management system (e.g., Ouchi 1981; Vogel 1979). A

---

[8] Representative examples include Abegglen and Stalk 1985; Caves and Uekusa 1976; Clark 1979; Cole 1971a, 1971b, 1973, 1979; Crawcour 1978; Dore 1973; Kalleberg and Lincoln 1988; Levine and Kawada 1980; Kalleberg and Lincoln 1985; Lincoln, Hanada, and McBride 1986; Lincoln and McBride 1987; Marsh and Mannari 1976; Rohlen 1974; Takezawa and Whitehill 1981; Vogel 1975.

few years later, a rash of highly critical "Japan-bashing" books (e.g., Kamata 1983; Van Wolferen 1988; Woronoff 1980, 1983) decried various aspects of the same system.

A striking feature of both the scholarly and popular treatments of Japanese industrial relations is their overwhelming focus on the small proportion of the labor force that is covered by permanent employment policies. (Such a policy is constituted by the tacit assurance by the employer, in the absence of a formal contract, that the employee will have guaranteed employment through retirement). This emphasis on permanent employment excludes at least 70 percent of the male labor force from discussion, and omits closer to 85 or 90 percent of the female labor force.[9] The result is a very biased view of Japanese labor and industrial relations. Nearly all of the workers cushioned from the ripples of change in the economy are male, and they are employed in the government sector or in the large, stereotypical firms— the Mitsubishis, Sonys, and Toyotas—with which Americans are now so familiar.

Recent critical Western writings on the Japanese management system emphasize the inequalities in the system. But these writings have been journalistically rather than analytically oriented, and they have rarely focused on the position of women. There is a need now to analyze the "underside" of the permanent employment system closely. Leading scholars in the field of Japanese studies have pointed to the need for more research focusing on female workers, temporary employees, and workers employed in small firms (Cole 1979). But American social scientists with Japanese expertise have almost universally chosen other issues to study.[10] By and large, the perception of Japanese and Western observers that Japanese gender roles are clear-cut, and that considerable sex discrimination exists in Japanese labor markets,

[9] Because permanent employment is not based on a legal contractual arrangement, we must rely on estimates to give a sense of the numbers of people involved. My estimates are based on the proportions of men and women who work as "regular employees," rather than temporary employees or day laborers, in large firms (of 1,000 or more employees) or the government sector. If anything, these estimates will overstate the extent of permanent employment because not all workers classified as full-time are necessarily immune to the danger of being laid off by the employer.

[10] This may be partially a by-product of the gender composition of the small group of Americans who are Japan specialists. It is important to keep in mind that the field of Japanese studies developed largely in response to World War II, and many of the senior scholars in the field are men who received language and area-studies training via the military. The entrance of more women into the field is a relatively recent phenomenon. It thus is not surprising that most work on women in Japanese society has been produced in the last ten years or so.

seems to have exerted a dampening rather than an energizing effect on research. Embedded in the pages of one of the best studies of Japanese work organizations is the simple statement, "Japanese companies do not promote women" (Clark 1979). On a more cynical note, a well-known American scholar of the Japanese economy produced no rebuttals (although he had perhaps hoped for some) at an international conference in 1984 with his comment that "the function of Japanese women is to work at low wages, produce 1.9 children, and work at low wages again." It is hard to imagine a more succinct summary of women's dual role in the economy.

A number of anthropologists, as well as several interdisciplinary groups of scholars, have produced vignettes of Japanese women's lives. We have a few writings in English on the legal aspects of Japanese women's employment. Research on women in selected occupations—including geisha, government bureaucrats, and office workers—has appeared in the past few years.[11] And some popular accounts of women's roles have been produced by Western journalists stationed in Japan. Taken as a group, these writings provide much in the way of valuable detailed descriptions of women workers, but little in the way of analysis of why women play the economic roles they do.

Japanese scholars' own investigations of women's economic participation represent a different genre of research: quantitatively sophisticated studies, mainly of the level of female labor force participation itself. This research is represented in English by a few sociologists and by several neoclassically oriented labor economists (see Kawashima 1983; Osawa 1984, 1988a, 1988b; Shimada and Higuchi 1985; Shinotsuka 1982; Yashiro 1981). Tanaka Kazuko (1987), a sociologist, has utilized a life-cycle approach to labor force participation similar to that of labor economists. She examined the labor force participation

[11] Takie Sugiyama Lebra (1984) offers rich ethnographic material on women's lives, and Robert Smith (1987) provides an overview of the status of women in Japanese society. Alice Cook and Hiroko Hayashi (1980) focus on how Japanese law deals with women's employment. Frank Upham (1987) includes a chapter on the passage of the Equal Employment Opportunity Law and litigation in sex discrimination cases. For work on women in different occupations, see Dalby 1983; Lebra 1981; Osako 1978; Lebra, Paulson, and Powers 1976. Glenda Roberts's dissertation (1986) is a wonderful ethnography of women workers in a lingerie factory. A journalist's exploration of women's roles is offered in Condon 1985. Susan Pharr's account provides the best picture of women in politics (1981). Research on rural women includes Bernstein 1983 and Smith and Wiswell 1982. Dorinne Kondo (1990) focuses on the construction of the self in small Japanese family businesses. The most comprehensive account of women in the labor force is Saso 1990, which compares women's roles in the contemporary Japanese economy to the roles of women in the economies of Britain and Ireland.

decisions of several cohorts of Tokyo women at different points in their
lives, as they balanced family and work responsibilities. Also on the
sociological side, work in the status-attainment tradition has been carried out by Tominaga Ken'ichi, Naoi Atsushi, and several other scholars.[12] In labor economics, a number of Japanese scholars have studied
women's labor force participation, usually with aggregate-level government data.[13]

In summary, most of the English-language literature on gender stratification in Japan falls into two categories: descriptive, qualitatively
rich vignettes of individual Japanese women, and quantitatively sophisticated work either by labor economists working in a human capital tradition or by sociologists working in a status-attainment
tradition. Upon initiating the current study, this distribution of research perspectives left me feeling unsatisfied, for both theoretical and
methodological reasons.

On the one hand, the micro-level, descriptive literature is useful in
being able to tap into how individual Japanese women think, feel, and
behave. But this literature offers no sustained analysis of *why* patterns
of gender stratification are systematically reproduced in Japanese society. On the other hand, the labor economics and status-attainment
literatures give the outlines of labor force participation patterns and
relate them to standard demographic characteristics of individuals
(such as age, education, marital status) and households (employment
status and income of household head, number of children, etc.). This
produces an aggregate picture in which individual motivations and
behaviors are blurred. Blurred, too, are the characteristics of Japan's
particular social-institutional context. It is certainly of great interest to
see how women's level of participation in the economy has changed
over time. But looking at the *quantity* of participation obscures the
type of participation and inhibits careful analysis of the position of
women in the stratification system.

The bifurcation of the literature on Japanese women's work patterns
into rich descriptive accounts and aggregate labor force descriptions

[12] This work has been published mainly in a series of reports in Japanese based on the
Social Stratification and Mobility (SSM) surveys carried out by Tominaga's group.

[13] See Higuchi 1982, 1983; Higuchi and Hayami 1984; Sano 1972; Yashiro 1983. The
work of Anne Hill (1983, 1984) has both built upon and stimulated Japanese economists' efforts to understand the nature of female labor force participation in Japan. Hill
was the first American scholar to analyze Japanese female economic participation in the
paid and unpaid sectors of the economy.

has another unfortunate result. Existing research fails to consider individual men and women in the social context of Japanese society and in the accompanying opportunity structures and constraints implied by Japanese social institutions. (Lebra 1984, a beautifully written text on contemporary Japanese women, is one exception to this.) Stated bluntly, the cultural myopia of some of the principal traditions of American sociology and economics seems to be repeated in the English-language literature on Japanese women's work patterns. Let us consider this cultural myopia for a moment.

A number of bodies of literature in sociology and economics have dealt both theoretically and empirically with the male/female wage gap and other male/female employment differences in the United States. In sociology, these include the status-attainment tradition and various approaches emphasizing the structure of labor markets. In economics, the human capital tradition dominates, and is supplemented by labor market approaches. A number of other literatures in the two fields deal with male/female employment: the sex-role socialization literature, literature on screening and statistical discrimination in employment, and Marxist-feminist literature on capitalism and patriarchy.

Current theories, especially human capital theory in economics, lift the individual-level processes producing large-scale stratification patterns outside of social-institutional constraints and the structure of human relationships. In other words, these theories tend to abstract the individual from the surrounding social context. They are therefore culturally quite narrow. The social-institutional context and the normative patterns of human relations vary among industrial societies. These variations need to be—and can be—theoretically formulated. This is important if we are to understand women's current roles in different industrial economies and how those roles will change in the future.

Gender stratification is systemic. It is the result of a sequence of choices made across the life cycle of an individual, choices that are structured by the institutions and the people with whom one has contact. It is critical to develop a theory of gender stratification that combines principles of voluntaristic social action (how individuals make choices) and a structuralist perspective (how those choices are constrained by the environment). Adjudicating a balance between an explanation of gender stratification based on individual, voluntaristic action and one based on the institutional structures of society is a

central purpose of this book. The tension and complementarity between these two types of explanation will surface many times in the
succeeding discussions.

JAPANESE "UNIQUENESS"

In Japan, the first non-Western nation to industrialize successfully,
Westerners see a unique, exotic culture. Given this, it is easy to analyze
social phenomena in terms of the country's exceptionalism. Readers
committed to this view may regard my analysis of gender in the Japanese economy as having too much of the sociologist in it and not
enough of the anthropologist. That is, they may feel that I do not place
enough emphasis on the uniqueness of sex roles and sex-role ideologies
in Japan vis-à-vis the West. My analytical approach stems from the
belief that while exegesis of cultural uniqueness makes for fascinating
reading, it ultimately does not advance theoretical understanding.
American sociology has become so turned in on itself that the important role of comparative work in testing and modifying theory is obscured. Sociological and economic work on gender stratification, where
the emphasis on highly quantitative studies of the U.S. population em-
bodies strong, often unstated, assumptions about the social-institutional and normative environment, represents a particularly strong case in
point. Stepping outside American society to view how the same basic
social institutions operate in a different industrial society (Japan) is
necessary for the development of a general theory of gender stratification in industrial societies. To the extent that Japan is "unique," its
uniqueness lies in the way in which the institutions of capitalist industrial society operate in that cultural context. The same is true of the
United States and other countries.

STRUCTURE OF THE STUDY

The opposing tendencies to see Japan either as a follower of Western
societies or as completely "special" and "unique" are simplistic views.
The only route to a more balanced and deeper view is to compare
Japan closely with another culture or cultures. Chapters 2 and 3 examine Japan and the United States. Chapter 2 shows that women have
always played somewhat different roles in the two economies. Japanese
women's more disadvantaged role is closely linked to employment
practices that place heavier emphasis on seniority and work experience

than American employment practices. Chapter 3 extends the analysis of the employment system to a theory of human capital development systems. These systems vary across industrial societies and have a strong influence on the extent and perpetuation of gender stratification. The family, the educational system, and the work organization in Japan together constitute a particular type of human capital development system that contrasts with that of the United States. Coupled with Japanese norms governing marriage timing and interpersonal relationships, this system produces strong barriers to women's advancement as direct participants in the economy and provides support for their indirect participation as nurturers of husbands and sons.

The two-country comparison of chapters 2 and 3 focuses on the historical incorporation of women into the economy, the dominant employment practices, and the structure of the human capital development system in each country. While it would be instructive to include more countries, this would make the comparisons unwieldy. The United States is a good companion case to Japan. It has neither a radically high nor a radically low female labor force participation rate, and in this respect it is representative of other industrial countries. Employment practices and the other institutions—education and the family—that constitute its human capital development system are arguably less representative of the full range of industrial economies than a Western European case might be. But because the distinctiveness of American institutions highlights the distinctiveness of Japanese institutions, our understanding of how both societies operate can be deepened by the comparison. Admittedly there is a personal stake at work as well: as an American, my research on Japan is inevitably shaped by implicit comparisons with the United States. An intuitive base of knowledge about one's own culture forms part of the conceptual guide for any researcher's investigation.

Chapters 4–7 focus exclusively on Japan. Chapter 4 examines changes in work organization in twentieth-century Japan, with particular emphasis on the postwar period. I argue that the employment system in large firms was structured by conscious policy decisions in the sphere of private enterprise and in government. These decisions have had the consequence of constructing and perpetuating a subsidiary economic role for women. In chapter 5, I introduce my own study of 1,200 men and women in three Japanese cities in the mid 1980s. This study facilitates detailed examination of how and why the two sexes fare differently in the labor market. The data also permit a comparison of the experiences of a younger and an older group of people, in order to see how much gender stratification patterns have or have not changed in recent years. In chapter 6, I turn to education, arguing that Japan's educational system and the way it is articulated with the labor market are also the outcomes of policy decisions, decisions that have had very different effects for men and women.

The exclusively Japan-focused chapters describe the recent historical trajectory of educational institutions and the labor market, and examine how men's and women's lives are played out in these institutions. The intersection between the household and the economy is also a central emphasis, in terms of the separateness of men's and women's roles and the centrality of Japanese women's roles as household financial managers, nurturers, and educators. In chapter 7 I examine the implications of rapid social change in Japan for women's economic roles during the final decade of the twentieth century, and evaluate whether Japan, if not a "follower" of Western gender stratification patterns, is a "leader" of other East Asian countries.

A NOTE ON METHODOLOGY

Issues of methodology constitute some of the most significant barriers to an understanding of Japan, to communication about Japanese society among social scientists, and to communication between the social scientist and the lay person. These barriers are unfortunate and bear some comment here.

Early in the process of researching this book, it became clear that primary data collection would be necessary in order to have a good set of observations on the contours of individual Japanese men's and women's lives—their family backgrounds, educational and work histories, attitudes and expectations about their children, and so forth. First of all, these data would provide valuable descriptive information. Second, they would provide the grist with which to carry out quantitative analyses and test hypotheses about how Japanese social institutions structure the roles of men and women in the economy. This latter purpose was eminently more pressing. Because there are no public data consortia in Japan, the social scientist faces an odd situation: Japan is arguably a data-rich research environment and a data-poor environment at the same time. One can obtain published statistics on virtually anything—private research firms and the government collect and publish a great deal of information and conduct many surveys of social attitudes and behaviors. There is thus a relative abundance of *descriptive* material. But it is nearly impossible to obtain the individual-level data (what social scientists call "raw" data) necessary for the labors of causal, statistical analysis.[14]

The consequent need to collect primary data produces advantages and disadvantages for one's research agenda. The design and execution of my project to collect data from 1,200 people in three cities were predictably time-consuming and frustrating, but this was compensated for by the joy of being able to ask exactly the questions I wanted. (I also included in my survey enough descriptive questions to compare my sample of 1,200 individuals with published statistics on the national and urban populations of Japan.) My quantitative data set thus has the typical dual characteristics of containing a wealth of original questions designed for testing hypotheses, while at the same time representing the limitations of a small-scale survey research effort. Appendix A describes the survey and sampling design and discusses the representativeness of the sample.

This book reflects a commitment to methodological eclecticism, a commitment that developed not in the classroom (in either my role as student or teacher) but in the field. Although I ostensibly went to Japan to collect survey data, I also collected a great deal of other material in the course of living there for a year and a half. As a sociologist, I wanted to immerse myself in Japanese life as much as possible and develop acquaintances and friendships. I also came to regard—probably as a matter of survival—even the briefest of encounters, be it with a taxi driver or a bank teller, as an opportunity to learn more about the society. For the first time it became apparent to me what it means to live as a sociologist. I found that if one is able to keep one's sociological glasses in place, any event, any social or business encounter, becomes data or food for generating hypotheses or confirming hunches and moving on to the next sociological puzzle. Induction and deduction took turns in shaping this study.

Although I originally intended to do a small number of interviews of my survey respondents, midway through my stay in Japan I reconsidered this plan. I came to feel that the comments made to me under natural circumstances, while not necessarily statistically representative of the attitudes, or *ishiki*, held throughout Japanese society, neverthe-

---

[14] No matter how their collection is funded, data are essentially treated as the property of individuals in Japan. And most of the data collected by the government to produce reports are destroyed a few years after the publication of results.

less had high reliability. As a young, highly educated, single woman living alone in a foreign country, I represented something of a curiosity to people. My Japanese is close to fluent, but (fortunately or unfortunately) not so perfect as to elicit the concern or suspicion reportedly inspired by some Westerners raised in Japan. I was comfortably *outside* the social system but was able to communicate with people *inside* it, in their own language. I posed no threat. In a sense, this was the ideal sociological situation. Young men talked to me about the conflict between their own aspirations and those their parents had for them. Young women facing the pressures of society and their parents talked to me about whether they could possibly hope to get a good job, and, if they did, whether they would be able to find someone willing to marry them. Middle-aged parents and employers talked to me about their expectations of the younger generation. And married men and women talked to me always about their expectations of the opposite sex, over endless cups of tea or *sake*, as the case may be. The natural give and take of relationships and the importance of *continuing, enduring* relationships over time in Japanese society made the exchange of ideas, as well as of worries and joys, more frank and honest than would be true had I selected a group of strangers from among my survey respondents and interviewed them.[15]

One of the reasons for using ethnographic or fieldwork techniques in studying Japanese society lies in the fact that there is tremendous consensus about a range of social and demographic behaviors in the society. I was frequently struck by the fact that I heard such similar comments and opinions from a variety of people—from sushi makers, small business owners, and taxi drivers to government bureaucrats and middle-level managers in major Japanese corporations and banks. The degree of social consensus in Japanese society can of course be overemphasized. But it nevertheless is a social fact in itself. I have tried wherever possible to test this impression of consensus regarding certain attitudes and behaviors critical to women's labor market position against a quantitative manifestation of consensus in attitudes and behaviors. (For instance, is the statistical variation in women's age at marriage as low as one would expect, based on people's common perceptions? Yes!) Here again, the process of induction from people's

---

[15] In all cases, I have made a special effort not to provide any information that would lead to a person's identification, and all my friends and acquaintances knew that there was some chance that their comments might occasionally serve as background material for the "real" analysis of quantitative data.

comments has led me to some investigations into quantitative data that deductive theory would most likely not have yielded.

In sum, I constructed a division of labor among methodologies. The three-city survey provides rich data on life histories and, secondarily, on attitudes. Interactions with people in my daily life, as well as monitoring of newspapers, television, and other mass media, helped me tap into attitudes in a way that would probably not have been possible in interviews or surveys conducted with a random sample of strangers. And government statistics and newspaper reports on attitudes and behavior regarding women's labor force participation, sex roles, family life, education, corporate life, and so on, provide the broad context for this book and the hypotheses I test. I have tried as much as possible to bridge the gap between quantitative and qualitative techniques, motivated by the belief that good social science comes not just in the form of constructing regression equations but also in listening to what people have to say about their own lives.

TWO

Women in the Japanese and U.S. Economies

Industrialization alters women's role in a country's economy in a number of general ways that are quite independent of culture. The shifts from an agrarian to an industrial economy and then to a service-oriented economy create a curvilinear historical pattern of women's labor force participation: high rates of participation prior to industrialization, a decline in the early stages of industrialization, and an upswing with the rise of the service sector (Pampel and Tanaka 1986). This common pattern means that it is not surprising that advanced industrial countries should have similar levels of female participation in the labor force.

In creating a divide between the home and the workplace as loci of production, industrialization forges a separation of work into private and public spheres (Degler 1980; Rosaldo 1974). Sharp age stratification in women's work typically emerges in the early phases of industrialization: young, unmarried women enter factory work in the market economy in large numbers, and married women with young children engage in childrearing and home production of various commodities. Along with the development of a strong market economy, married women's role in the production of goods therefore declines as family farms and businesses are replaced by large-scale commercial farming and factories (Boserup 1970; Pampel and Tanaka 1986; Tilly and Scott 1978). Women's ability to alternate energies throughout the day between childcare and commodity-production activities such as spinning, weaving, and soap making becomes less and less feasible as production activities move to the factory. The net result is a decline in women's measurable participation in the economy.

This pattern shifts again as a society moves into the later stages of industrialization and postindustrialization.[1] For example, changes in industrial structure involving the expansion of the service sector in the post–World War II period created a greater demand for labor in the United States and other Western countries (Goldin 1983; Smith and Ward 1984, 1985). The addition of these jobs to the low-wage labor market for women in domestic work and piecework has had the historical effect of raising women's wages, thereby drawing more women into the labor market. Employers' demand for more labor has been complemented by strong forces on the labor supply side pushing married women into the work force. The decline in fertility rates with industrialization and urbanization has led to a decrease in the average number of years women spend in childrearing and the care of young children. More time has been freed up for work and leisure activities outside the home. As a result, the female labor force participation rate has risen. But the fact that the level of female labor force participation changes in a predictable fashion with industrialization does not necessarily mean that women are absorbed into the economy in the *same way* in every industrial society.

The first part of this chapter explores the historical changes in women's role in the Japanese economy in comparison with the U.S. economy. The current national differences do not disappear if we compare the United States of twenty or thirty years ago with contemporary Japan, an exercise that seems reasonable if one views Japan as "lagging behind" the United States. The divergencies persist, and a major reason is the variation in the dominant employment practices of the two countries. This subject is taken up in the second part of this chapter.

JAPANESE WOMEN'S LABOR FORCE PARTICIPATION IN HISTORICAL CONTEXT

Women historically played an important role as agricultural workers in Japan, as they have in other countries as well. With the beginning of industrialization in the Meiji period (1868–1912), women entered

---

[1] I am tempted to say, "into the later stages of capitalism," as our purpose is to figure out how well theories fit the case of Japan, a capitalist society. But research on China (Stacey 1983; Wolf 1985), the Soviet Union (Lapidus 1978), and other societies convinces one that significant sex segregation in occupations and sex differences in

TABLE 2.1

DISTRIBUTION OF JAPANESE WORKERS
BY INDUSTRY, 1920–1980

	Distribution of all workers by industry (%)			Distribution of female workers by industry (%)			Percentage of all workers that are female
	Primary	*Secondary*	*Tertiary*	*Primary*	*Secondary*	*Tertiary*	
1920	56.2	21.9	21.8	67.5	17.7	14.8	36.4
1950	48.3	22.0	29.7	61.3	13.2	25.5	38.6
1980	11.0	33.6	55.4	13.7	26.2	60.1	37.9

SOURCE: Office of the Prime Minister, Japan, *Kokusei chōsa* (Population census), 1920, 1950, 1980.
NOTE: Primary industry is comprised of agriculture, forestry, and fishing. Secondary industry is comprised of mining, construction, and manufacturing. Tertiary industry is comprised of utilities, transportation and communication, sales, finance, insurance and real estate, services, and government.

the labor force as factory operatives, particularly in light industry. By 1895, women factory workers are estimated to have outnumbered men by a factor of 1.6 (Yokoyama 1898). The main characteristic of this female labor force was that it consisted primarily of young, unmarried women who worked for several years before marriage and then returned to their rural homes and got married. The typical female manufacturing worker was in the textile industry, was the daughter of a farm family, and was employed only on a temporary basis. In most cases, employment was governed by a contract signed between the employer and the young woman's father or brother. "Until the end of the nineteenth century, parents or brothers received money advanced against wages to be earned so this was, in effect, a method of trading in human beings. The system gradually disappeared in the early twentieth century, but for a long time when a young woman became a factory worker the decision required a resolution similar to that of selling herself into prostitution, as the social status was nearly as low," Hazama Hiroshi observes (1976: 30).

---

wages are not restricted to capitalism. Thus it would be a mistake to imply that gender stratification is limited to capitalist economies. Nevertheless, my empirical basis of comparison with Japan will mainly be other capitalist societies in East Asia and in the West.

Figure 2.1.   Labor Force Participation of Japanese Women, 1955–1987
SOURCE: Office of the Prime Minister, Japan, *Rōdōryoku chōsa* (Survey of the labor force), various years.

Despite the participation of women as paid laborers in the manufacturing sector early in Japan's industrialization, the majority of female workers were employed in agriculture up until 1954. As heavy industry expanded during the early twentieth century, a greater share of manufacturing came to be dominated by the metal, chemical, and machinery industries, where workers were generally male. In 1920, slightly over two-thirds of female workers were employed in the primary sector (agriculture, forestry, and fishing), another 18 percent in the secondary sector (mining, construction, and manufacturing), and 15 percent in the tertiary sector (utilities, transportation and communication, sales, finance, insurance and real estate, services, and government). This is shown in Table 2.1. With industrialization, women moved out of the agricultural sector and into the secondary and tertiary sectors, but not until the mid 1950s did the percentage of employed women who worked in agriculture fall below 50 percent. This mirrors the transformation of Japan from a primarily agricultural economy to an advanced industrial economy with a large service sector.

Figure 2.1 shows that the labor force participation rate of women, defined as the percentage of the female population aged fifteen or older who are employed, gradually fell from 1955 until the late 1970s and then began an upswing. This decline was a puzzle to labor economists

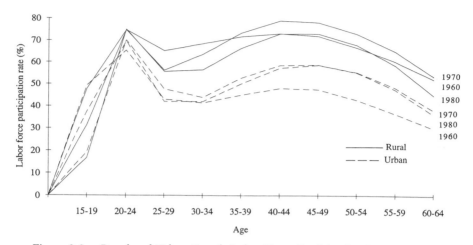

Figure 2.2. Rural and Urban Female Labor Force Participation Rates in Japan
SOURCE: Office of the Prime Minister, Japan, *Kokusei chōsa* (Population census), various years.

originally observing the phenomenon in the 1970s, for it runs counter to the experience of Western industrial nations. In those nations, the clear trend has been for women to enter the economy in greater numbers in the post–World War II period. But labor economists working with Japanese data soon came to realize that this points to a crucial aspect of the Japanese economy: the prevalence of informal employment for women, either piecework done at home or work in family-owned enterprises or agriculture (Hill 1983, 1984; Osawa 1988a; Yashiro 1981). The gradual decline in the employment of women reflected a decrease in this type of employment and a time lag before more women entered paid employment. Related to this, the decline resulted from a flow of women *out* of agriculture that was more rapid than the flow *into* the secondary and tertiary sectors. After 1975, the movement of women into these latter sectors finally outpaced the declining participation in agriculture.

WOMEN'S LIFE-CYCLE PATTERNS OF EMPLOYMENT

When Japan was primarily an agricultural economy women did not necessarily stop working when they got married, but rather divided their time between childrearing and agricultural labor or various household industries. Figure 2.2 shows the percentage of women working in each age group for rural and urban areas since 1960. In 1960,

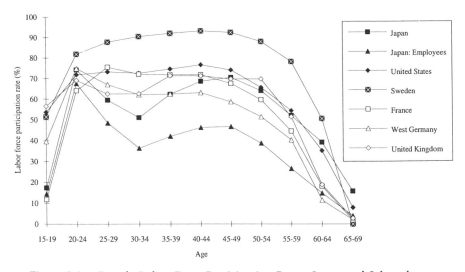

Figure 2.3.   Female Labor Force Participation Rates, Japan and Selected
Western Countries
SOURCE: International Labor Organization 1990.
NOTE: Figures for Japan, Sweden, and the United States are for 1989; for France and
West Germany, 1987. Data for the United Kingdom were only available for 1986, and
in ten-year age groups (25–34, 35–44, etc.).

there was a tendency for rural women to remain in the labor force
even after marriage and childbearing, compared to a large number of
urban women who worked prior to marriage, then left the labor force.
By 1980, the life-cycle timing of women's labor force participation had
changed in both rural and urban areas. The age distribution of wom-
en's labor force participation had assumed a stronger M-shaped form,
with large numbers of women temporarily leaving the labor force and
then returning again in their late thirties and early forties. Figure 2.3
demonstrates that Japan's M-shaped distribution of female labor force
participation by age remains conspicuous when compared to most
Western industrial countries. Sweden exhibits the highest and most
consistent rates of labor force participation across different age groups
of women. The U.S. pattern is similar to Sweden's in showing uniformity across the prime working ages. France and West Germany show
declining rates of participation among women in their late twenties.
Only Japan and the United Kingdom show a pronounced M-shaped
curve of labor force participation. But even the similarity between Japan and the United Kingdom is misleading. Figure 2.3 compares apples
to oranges in the sense that only 69 percent of the Japanese female

Distribution of 1987 Marriages by Age of Bride

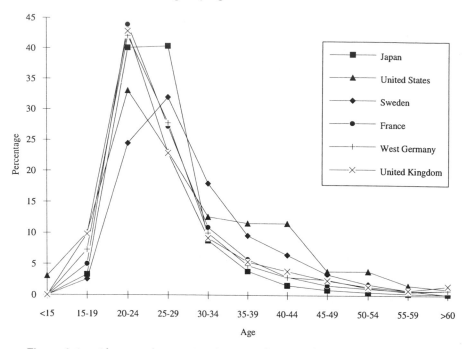

Figure 2.4. *Above and opposite:* Age Distribution of Marriages and Births, Japan and Selected Western Countries

SOURCE: United Nations 1988.

NOTE: U.S. figures are reported for 1986 and are for ages 35–39 and 40–44 together, and 45–49 and 50–54 together.

labor force are employees, compared to more than 85 percent of the female labor force in other countries. In the case of the United Kingdom, the figure is comparatively high, 93 percent. Thus a more accurate comparison is produced if we use a female labor force participation rate for Japan that is limited to employees. This is represented by the lower line in Figure 2.3.

The new comparison shows a dramatic result. Japanese women in their early twenties have a labor force participation rate as employees that is similar to that of women in other countries. But the drop in labor force participation in the late twenties and its resurgence by the late thirties follows the ebb and flow of Japanese women's family responsibilities. While the M-shaped pattern is maintained for both the total labor force participation rate and for the employee rate, the *level* of the employee rate is much lower once women reach their late twen-

Distribution of 1987 Live Births by Age of Mother

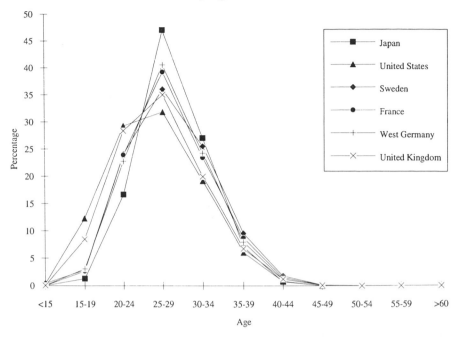

ties. Likewise, the smoother curve of labor force participation by age in most Western industrial countries indicates that fewer women are dropping out of the labor force completely upon marriage or child-bearing. Figures for the proportion of women who quit work upon marriage or the birth of their first child are not easily obtainable across countries. But one way to intuit how women's family responsibilities vary with age in a given society is to look at the age bunching of marriages and births. The first panel of Figure 2.4 shows the percentage of all marriages that occur within five-year age groups of women for the same sample of industrial countries as in Figure 2.3. The second panel shows the percentage of all births that occur within five-year age groups.[2] Japanese women's marriages are more concentrated in the twenties than marriages in other countries: 40 percent of all Japanese women who married in 1987 were between the ages of 20 and 24 and another 40 percent were between 25 and 29. While several other countries have a similar or slightly higher proportion of marriages in the

[2] Ideally it would be better to show the proportion of first marriages and first births because this would indicate the commencement of marriage and childrearing responsibilities. But the United Nations figures refer to all marriages and all births.

age group 20–24, no country except Japan shows an equivalent concentration in the adjacent age group (25–29) as well. The lower panel
demonstrates the concentration of Japanese births to mothers in the
25–29 and 30–34 age groups, compared to a more even distribution
beginning in the early twenties in other countries. These marriage and
childbearing patterns suggest the operation of strong norms in Japan
and are strikingly consistent with the marked drop in female labor
force participation for Japanese women in their late twenties.

While the M-shaped curve of female labor force participation is a
common historical pattern among Western industrial countries, Figure
2.2 shows that Japan's has become more pronounced over the past
twenty years, particularly in urban areas. This is consistent with the
sharp M-shaped pattern for employees (Fig. 2.3). It appears that few
Japanese women combine roles as wives and mothers with the role of
employee.

JAPAN AND THE UNITED STATES
AS CONTRASTING HISTORICAL CASES

Is Japan "lagging behind" countries such as the United States? In order
to judge this, contemporary Japan must be lined up against the recent
historical experience of the United States—that is, a time lag must be
built into our comparisons. Even once this is done, differences persist
between the two countries in the structure of women's employment
(employee versus various nonemployee statuses, such as those of family
enterprise workers and piece-rate workers); women's absorption into
clerical work; and the relationship between women's education and
labor force participation.

Figure 2.5 shows that, at least since 1950, Japanese women have
worked as family enterprise workers at a rate far exceeding the rate
for American women. (As noted in chapter 2, by 1980 about three-
quarters of this employment occurred in the nonagricultural, urban
sector of the Japanese economy, so the gap between the United States
and Japan cannot be explained by the greater size of the Japanese
agricultural sector.) In 1980 about 25 percent of Japanese women were
family enterprise workers, and even thirty years ago, only 6 percent of
American women worked in family businesses or on family farms. The
Japanese rate of female employment on a self-employed or piecework
basis has also consistently exceeded that in the United States. American
women overwhelmingly work as employees, and have done so through-

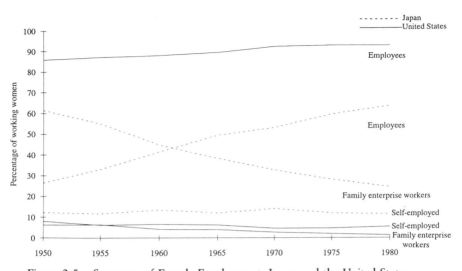

Figure 2.5.   Structure of Female Employment, Japan and the United States
SOURCE: U.S. Bureau of the Census, *Statistical Abstract of the United States*, various years; Office of the Prime Minister, Japan, *Kokusei chōsa* (Population census), various years.

out the time period shown in the graph (1950–80). In 1950 only 26 percent of Japanese working women were employees, and by 1980 the figure was 64 percent. Despite a dramatic increase, the 1980 Japanese rate remains 30 percentage points below the U.S. rate.

The continued strong presence of self-employment and family enterprise work is especially notable in urban areas of Japan, where these types of employment are declining at a slower pace than in rural areas. In 1960, over 50 percent of all self-employed and family enterprise workers were in agriculture, but that is no longer the case. Nearly two-thirds of family enterprise and piecework workers are now involved in manufacturing or service work. This is particularly the case for women. In a very important sense, Japanese women have not been fully absorbed into "modern" industrial and service-sector employment (wage labor). Nearly one-quarter of female workers outside agriculture in 1987 were either self-employed or employed in family enterprises, a figure that had declined by only 4 percent since 1975. Male self-employment, on the other hand, reached the same level in Japan in 1975 as it had in the United States in 1950. And the rate of Japanese male employment as family enterprise workers was negligible (3.7 percent) by 1980. Overall, a convergence in the structure of *male* employment in the two countries therefore appears to be occurring—albeit with

TABLE 2.2

PERCENTAGE FEMALE IN
DIFFERENT OCCUPATIONAL GROUPS,
UNITED STATES, 1920–1980

	1920	1940	1960	1980
Professional and technical work	48.2	45.4	36.2	44.3
Administrative and managerial	5.6	10.3	15.6	26.1
Clerical	38.6	41.0	67.8	80.1
Sales	5.7	8.8	39.8	45.3
Agriculture, forestry, mining	9.4	5.6	18.5	18.0
Upper manual	19.4	21.7	17.3	19.6
Lower manual	3.3	2.3	2.3	11.6

SOURCE: U.S. Bureau of the Census, *Statistical Abstract of the United States,* various years.

a time lag. But the same cannot be said for the structure of female employment.

There are also major differences between the historical transformation of women's occupational structure in Japan and the United States. The rapid growth of the clerical sector in the twentieth-century United States was a key factor in the increase in female labor force participation (Smith and Ward 1984). Table 2.2 shows that by 1920 nearly 40 percent of U.S. clerical workers were female, and this figure had doubled by 1980. In contrast, the female share in upper-level manual jobs (skilled blue-collar work, including manufacturing) remained quite steady throughout the twentieth century, hovering around 20 percent.

Japan presents a different picture (Table 2.3). Women's movement into the clerical sector occurred much later, with women occupying only about one-third of the clerical jobs in the economy in 1960 and about one-half such positions in 1980. In contrast, American women occupied 80 percent of these positions by 1980. Stated differently, men hold a much larger proportion of the low-level white-collar jobs in Japan than in the United States. At face value this may seem a dubious honor. But for the purposes of comparison over a long time period and across countries, we are relying here on highly aggregated occupational categories. Once the category of "clerical work" is disaggregated, it becomes clear that many of the positions categorized as low-level white-collar jobs in Japan are actually entry-level positions in

TABLE 2.3

PERCENTAGE FEMALE IN DIFFERENT
OCCUPATIONAL GROUPS, JAPAN, 1960–1988

	1960	1970	1980	1988
Professional and technical work	33.3	40.7	48.4	44.1
Administrative and managerial	2.5	3.8	5.1	7.3
Clerical	35.9	46.9	51.1	55.2
Sales	34.7	32.6	31.6	32.3
Agriculture, forestry, mining	38.6	33.8	25.0	25.0
Transportation and communication	5.3	10.1	6.1	4.8
Services	54.8	54.7	50.8	51.0
Skilled manufacturing and labor	26.9[a]	25.9	24.9	27.1
Unskilled labor		33.2	36.5	40.8

SOURCES: Office of the Prime Minister, Japan, *Kokusei chōsa* (Population census), various years; *Rōdōryoku chōsa* (Survey of the labor force), 1988.
[a]In 1960, skilled and unskilled labor were reported as one category.

well-defined career trajectories. The fact that Japanese women have not made greater inroads into white-collar jobs is therefore detrimental for their economic equality. As Robert Cole and Tominaga Ken'ichi put it:

> The tradition is strong in many Japanese organizations to treat young recruits as untrained and gradually lead them through "stages of difficulty." In practice this means many future managers and professionals are assigned to menial clerical jobs. Although this practice is present in other industrialized nations . . . its institutionalization in Japan leads to a significant number of male employees being classified as clerical in Japan who would be classified as managerial or professional in other nations.
>
> (Cole and Tominaga 1976: 74)

Close perusal of Tables 2.2 and 2.3 shows that one could make an argument for a general cultural "lag" in Japanese clerical work, because the change in the percentage female between 1960 and 1988 was roughly equivalent to the change in the United States between 1920 and 1950. But such an argument could not be extended at all to services and blue-collar work. The percentages female in Japanese services, skilled manufacturing, and unskilled occupations are all higher than in the U.S. upper and lower manual occupational groups. (An exact group-by-group comparison is difficult here because the gross historical categories used for blue-collar and service work in the two countries' censuses are not perfectly compatible.) In particular, the percentage female in unskilled or lower-level manual occupations in Japan is overwhelming compared to that observable at any time point in the United States, even the beginning of the twentieth century.

Thus, while the female share in clerical work in Japan did rise over 20 percentage points in the postwar period, the female share in blue-collar work has remained stable and high. This apparent stability in Japanese women's participation in manufacturing disguises a massive shift in the age distribution: whereas about one-half of female manufacturing workers were over age 30 in 1960, more than three-quarters were over age 30 in 1980. This change in age composition has not occurred to the same extent for Japanese men. These trends have been summarized by Osawa Machiko as follows:

> A unique characteristic of Japanese women workers relative to their U.S. counterparts is the higher proportion of married women employed in the manufacturing sector as part-time workers which, until recently, dominated the overall trend of women's labor force participation. In contrast, when the U.S. and other OECD nations experienced a rapid influx of married women into the labor force in the 1960's, those who dominated the trend were relatively well-educated clerical and professional workers.
>
> (Osawa 1987: 21)

On the one hand, the changes in the age structure of manufacturing and clerical employment for Japanese women might be seen as welcome shifts. After all, this means that younger women are going into white-collar employment at a greater rate than before, which should translate into higher prestige and earnings.

The question then becomes, is this indeed so?

We must answer in the negative. In fact, these changes in the occupational structure of women mask an underlying stability: Japanese working women of different ages are used to fill different slots in work organizations. What these slots—even the white-collar ones—have in common is that they are not career-track positions, and they are ill paid relative to the slots filled by men. (A comprehensive analysis of this must wait until chapter 5, where the starting jobs of men and women in the contemporary Japanese economy are compared; there it is demonstrated that the historical changes that have occurred do not mean that young women are now successfully entering career-track positions.)

A final historical difference between the experience of Japanese and American women in the labor market lies in the association between education and labor force participation. In the United States, higher levels of female educational attainment have been associated with greater labor force participation since at least 1940 (Smith and Ward 1985). Labor economists argue that between 1900 and 1940, the character of the labor market faced by American women was transformed in a way that reversed the hitherto negative association between employment and level of education. With continuing industrialization, the demand for clerical workers increased. As Table 2.2 demonstrated, women rapidly moved into these jobs. The demand for white- and pink-collar workers acted in combination with rising female education levels to bring more women into the labor force. These new women workers were almost all single, but World War II represents the great watershed in the history of American women's labor because married women began to enter the work force in much greater numbers than before. Once this trend was initiated, it represented an irrevocable break with the past. Women over age 35 were the first group to respond to the wartime and postwar demand for labor, followed by younger married women between the ages of 25 and 35 (McLaughlin et al. 1988). The association of women's education and participation in the economy became even stronger in the United States after 1970. Figure 2.6 shows that from that point on, there was an unprecedented increase in the labor force participation rates of all women aged 25–34, except for the least-educated. The strengthening association of higher education and employment is indicated by the steeper slope of the uppermost line in the graph (1983) compared to the other two lines (1940 and 1970). This trend held for women aged 35–44 as well. The greater likelihood of employment for highly educated women compared to the earlier part of the century can be accounted for by factors on both the "supply" and the "demand" side. As greater numbers of women go on to higher education, they acquire a "taste" for employment outside the home (Bowen and Finegan 1969; Spitze and Waite 1980). But their entrance into the labor force is also a response to the demand by employers for their labor. This demand stems from an increase in white-collar and service-sector occupations that had become "women's jobs" by the 1930s. Later, the effects of affirmative action and equal employment policies also reduced some of the barriers for women in previously male-dominated jobs such as managerial and legal work.

The positive association between female education and labor market participation in the United States since 1940 is a characteristic of in-

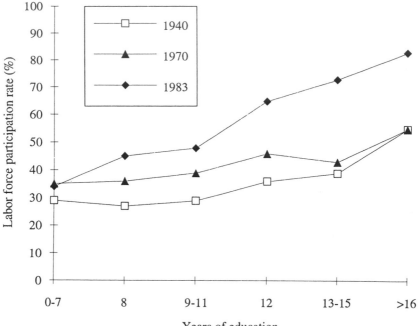

Figure 2.6.   Labor Force Participation of U.S. Women Aged 25–34, by Education
SOURCES: Adapted from McLaughlin et al. 1988: 111.

dustrial economies. The association tends to be weaker or even reversed in societies undergoing industrialization (Smith and Ward 1985). Has the Japanese situation been historically different from that in the United States? Here the limitations of data are somewhat frustrating. Even as late as 1971, Japanese labor force participation statistics by age and education were categorized into elementary/junior high, senior high, and junior college/university. These categories disguise important differences in the labor force behavior of different groups—for example, junior college and university graduates. Nevertheless, some conclusions can be drawn. Figure 2.7 shows that for Japanese women aged 25–34 in 1971, there was no linear relationship between education and employment: 45 percent of female elementary/junior high school graduates were in the labor force, compared to only 37 percent and 40 percent of senior high and junior college/university graduates. A comparison with Figure 2.6 shows that these patterns are almost the exact *reverse* of the case in the United States, whether in 1970 or in prior periods. In the 35–39 age group, there was a linear relationship

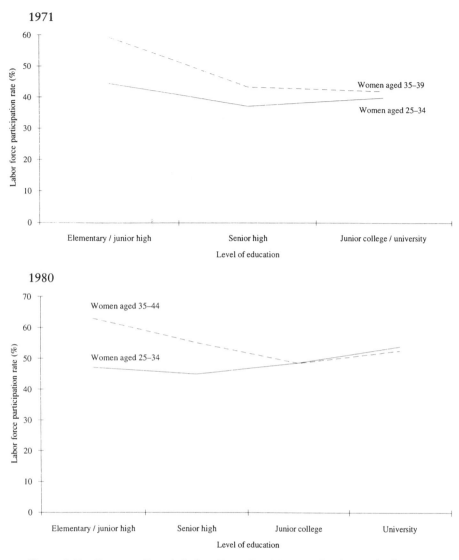

Figure 2.7.   Japanese Female Labor Force Participation, by Age and Education

SOURCE: Office of the Prime Minister, Japan, 1971, 1980.

NOTE: Labor force participation measures participation as employees (thereby excluding self-employed and family enterprise workers).

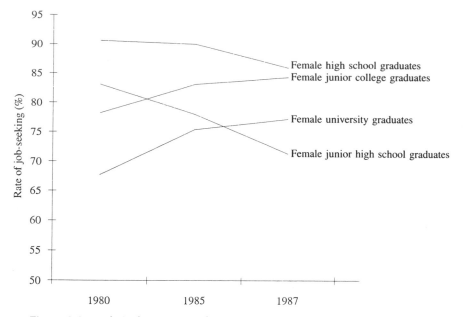

Figure 2.8.   Job-Seeking Rates of Japanese Women, by Education.
SOURCE: Ministry of Education, Japan, *Gakkō kihon chōsa* (Basic school statistics),
various years.

between education and employment in Japan, but it was in the opposite
direction from that in the United States: the *least-educated* women
were much more likely to be in the labor force than women with more
education. This is all the more striking because these figures are con-
fined to *employees*, the category in Japan most analogous to women's
work situation (as wage laborers) in the United States. Were we to look
at all women in the Japanese labor force, the figure for the least-
educated group would be even higher, because more women in this
group than in others are employed in family enterprises or piecework.

By 1980, higher-educated Japanese women aged 25–34 were more
apt to be in the labor force than less-educated women. University-
educated women had the highest rate (54 percent) of labor force participation, and women with a high school education had the lowest
rate. (Note from Figure 2.6 that in contrast over 80 percent of American female university graduates aged 25–34 were in the labor force
in 1980, and even in 1940, the figure was above 50 percent.) For Japanese women aged 35–44 in 1980, the relationship was more complex:
the least-educated women in Japan still had the highest employment

rate. But at the other end of the educational distribution, university-educated women were more apt to be in the labor force than junior college graduates.

Figure 2.8 shows the rate of job-seeking among Japanese women graduating from different educational levels in 1980, 1985, and 1987. Female junior high school graduates' rate of job-seeking declined between 1980 and 1987, mainly because increasing numbers of females were proceeding on to high school rather than immediately entering the job market; by 1987, this group thus had the lowest job-seeking rate. University graduates remain less likely than their high school or junior college counterparts to seek employment. About 85 percent of Japanese female high school and junior college graduates in 1987 sought employment, and only 77 percent of university graduates did so. But university graduates did show a sharper increase in this behavior between 1980 and 1987 than the other three educational groups.

What are the implications? In the United States, there has been a long-standing historical relationship between higher education and women's participation in the economy, a relationship that has strengthened since 1970. In Japan such a relationship was not in evidence in 1970. By 1980 it had begun to emerge, although not in a very distinct form.

Tanaka Kazuko (1987) and Osawa Machiko (1988b) use data from different cohorts of women in the Tokyo metropolitan area to show that the relationship between education and employment has recently begun to change. Thus it would be a mistake to regard the Japanese experience as totally different from that of the United States. But there seems to be a looser connection in Japan between the demand for white-collar labor, the increase in female education, and the increase in female labor force participation than is evident in the American historical record. "With the development of the high school [in the United States at the turn of the century], the character of women's schooling was altered, with the learning acquired presumably more useful in the labor market," suggest James Smith and Michael Ward (1985: S76). Claudia Goldin (1983) has argued even more strongly for the causal role of rising education levels in increasing American women's labor force participation over the twentieth century. And Pamela Barnhouse Walters (1988) has demonstrated that changes in the American occupational structure preceded increases in women's higher educational enrollments in the postwar period. She postulates an instrumental view of education, where women's higher education choices are a response to increased demand for white-collar workers in the economy.

The postwar period in Japan shows different patterns. In a replication of Walters's analysis, I found evidence that Japanese women's rates of advancement to high school and junior college have responded to greater demand for white-collar workers. There was much less evidence of a link between the need for white-collar workers in the economy and Japanese women's university advancement rates (Brinton and Lee 1991). This is consistent with the data presented above on employment rates and rates of job-seeking by educational level: women university graduates have not responded to the labor market as actively as their less-educated counterparts. This seems counterintuitive from a strict human capital viewpoint, where the value of education lies mainly in its economic returns in the labor market.

A final piece of evidence sets Japan apart in terms of women's human capital or educational acquisition. The emergent association between women's education and labor market participation in the United States and other Western industrial societies means that women's education has come to be used more and more in the labor market. One might therefore expect cultural disparities in parents' aspirations for sons' and daughters' education to level off with the process of industrialization. Comparative historical statistics on this are unavailable, but a contemporary comparison across several countries shows Japan's distinctiveness. Table 2.4 gives the percentage of mothers in Japan, South Korea, Sweden, the United States, the Philippines, West Germany, and England who aspired to university education for their sons and daughters in 1982. In no case except that of Japan does the gap between the proportions desiring university education for sons and for daughters exceed 7 percentage points. In Japan, the gap is 45 percentage points: 73 percent of mothers would like to see their sons receive a university education, as opposed to only 28 percent who hold this aspiration for daughters. (My own survey data, discussed in chapter 6, reproduce this result, so it cannot be regarded as an idiosyncrasy of this particular government survey.) South Korea and the Philippines are both much more similar than Japan to Western industrial nations. Not only do Japanese women use their education differently in the labor market than Western women, but Japanese mothers want considerably less education for their daughters than for their sons. Both the *use* of Japanese women's education or human capital in the labor market and parents' ideas about the importance of that human capital are different than in the industrial West.

TABLE 2.4

MOTHERS' ASPIRATIONS
FOR SONS AND DAUGHTERS:
A CROSS-NATIONAL COMPARISON

	Aspire to university education for sons (%)	Aspire to university education for daughters (%)
Japan	73.0	27.7
South Korea	88.3	81.2
Sweden	87.3	84.5
United States	68.9	65.8
Philippines	48.1	44.1
West Germany	31.1	30.8
England	19.6	14.3

SOURCES: Office of the Prime Minister, Japan, 1982a; Korea Survey (Gallup) Polls Ltd. 1987.
NOTE: This table shows respondents' answers to the question, "What level of education would you like your son [daughter] to receive?" With the exception of South Korea, the countries were not chosen by the author but are those included in a Japanese government survey. The respondents were a random sample of approximately 1,200 women, aged 20–59 years, in each country. The Gallup organization in Korea replicated the survey for a comparable sample of married Korean women in 1987.

In summary, it is not very useful to attempt to fit Japan into the mold of being a "follower" of historical patterns of gender stratification in the United States. American women's position in the economy was structured by historical and cultural processes, and Japanese women's position has been too. The causal factors that were present in the United States to bring married women into the labor force, and specifically into the clerical sector, have operated differently in Japan. The white-collar sector in Japan expanded at a later historical point, and it was already subject to permanent employment policies when expansion began—policies that had the effect of excluding women from career-track positions. In the next section I examine how processes in the Japanese and U.S. employment systems structure women's economic roles.

JAPANESE AND U.S. EMPLOYMENT SYSTEMS

PROCESSES OF EARNINGS DETERMINATION

The literature on Japanese work organizations is replete with assertions that work experience and workplace seniority have a greater impact on wages in Japan than in Western industrial nations. This aspect of the employment system disadvantages Japanese women compared to their Western counterparts. Women typically accumulate less work experience and seniority than men, even if they have equivalent education. This is because many women spend a large portion of their adult years exclusively in childrearing and household maintenance, whereas men do not. Of course, in a society where this is not the case, an emphasis on work experience and seniority would not necessarily work to the disadvantage of women. But neither the United States nor Japan is such a society (as discussed more fully in the next chapter).

In an examination of earnings profiles by age and experience for workers in Japan, the United States, Great Britain, France, and West Germany, Koike Kazuo (1983a) found that wages increase with age. The intercountry differences lie in the age at which wages peak and the degree to which blue- as well as white-collar workers benefit from wage increases across the life cycle. Wages peak for most countries' workers when they are in their early forties, but they do so at a later age in Japan.[3] Also, the patterns for blue- and white-collar workers resemble each other more closely in Japan than in other countries. Wages increase sharply over the life cycle as workers gain more and more experience, especially if they are in large firms.

While these comparisons are informative, they do not get precisely at the question of whether work experience and seniority count for more in Japan. The comparisons done by Koike cannot evaluate the contribution of a worker's experience and seniority above and beyond his or her other characteristics (e.g., education and marital status) or the nature of the work establishment (e.g., a large firm versus a small firm). Also, Koike's analyses were carried out for men only.

Further information is provided by studies that evaluate the relative importance of workers' characteristics for their wages in Japan and other countries. Early writers such as Abegglen (1958) saw Japanese methods of job assignment and compensation as a continuation of preindustrial employment practices. They predicted that these practices would eventually fall away as Japanese industrialization progressed and Japan came to resemble the West more and more. However, in their study of workers in manufacturing plants in Indianapolis and Atsugi, near Tokyo, Arne Kalleberg and James Lincoln conclude:

---

[3] Using a different data set, Shimada Haruo (1981) also suggested that Japanese wage profiles are steeper than American ones.

The results of our investigation provide scant support for claims of convergence in Japanese and Western employment systems and labor markets,
at least as far as earnings determination is concerned. The contrasts are
striking: American employees' earnings are heavily dependent on job/occu-
pational characteristics, authority position, and performance reviews and
job evaluations by the firm; these effects are small to nonexistent, even
negative, among the Japanese. The earnings of Japanese employees, on the
other hand, are more heavily conditioned by the life-cycle variables of dependents, age, and seniority.

(Kalleberg and Lincoln 1988: S148–49)

Two clusters of variables were found to be more important in determining managers' and workers' earnings in Japan than the United
States: (1) experience, and (2) life-cycle factors. Seniority falls into the
first category. Age does too, to the extent that it measures work experience. But age also taps the second dimension because it reflects the
individual's life-cycle stage. Kalleberg and Lincoln found significantly
steeper age-earnings profiles for male workers and managers in Japan
than in the United States, signaling a stronger connection between age
and earnings. The profiles were also steeper for Japanese than American women, but the difference was not statistically significant. There
was a significant sex difference in Japan: for male workers and managers, age was strongly tied to earnings, and for females this relationship was weaker. (It is interesting to note that Kalleberg and Lincoln
studied three groups in each country: male managers, male workers,
and female workers. Female managers and supervisors were excluded
from the study of wages because only about 5 percent of the female
sample in either country occupied such positions.)

The relationship of wages to tenure in a firm showed similar patterns. Tenure raised wages for U.S. male and female workers, Japanese
male managers, and Japanese male and female workers. The one group
for whom tenure with the firm did not affect wages was American
male managers. This is consistent with the common notion that to
attain a high position in U.S. management, some job-hopping among
employers may be beneficial. In contrast, promotion up through the
ranks internal to a firm is the main route to management in Japan. In
both countries, tenure with the firm had a stronger effect on raising
the wages of male workers than female workers.[4]

[4] When they looked at the actual trajectory of wages across the life cycle, Kalleberg
and Lincoln found that earnings rose with age and with seniority in the firm for male
and female American workers and for Japanese female workers, then declined again in
middle age. In contrast, the earnings of Japanese male workers and managers continued

Marital status was also more highly related to the earnings of Japanese male workers and managers than to those of American ones. Being married raises Japanese males' earnings more than it does those of American males (although the national difference was not statistically significant). Conversely, being married depresses the earnings of females in both countries. In a study of women's earnings in seven industrial countries, Patricia Roos (1985) found that Japan was the only country where women's occupational-wage rate (a measure of earnings that takes into account the difference between male and female jobs) was negatively affected by marriage. In other words, marriage constituted a greater liability for Japanese women in terms of earnings than for women in other countries.

These results offer consistent support for the assertion that Japanese firms place a higher value than American ones on age and length of service to the firm. Japanese firms also value a worker's responsibilities to his family (if in fact the worker is male), as measured by marital status. Other features associated with the operation of firm-internal labor markets were also found in Japan by Kalleberg and Lincoln. There was a relationship between the promotion expectations of male Japanese managers and workers and their earnings, and a relationship between on-the-job training and earnings for all groups in Japan, including male managers, male workers, and female workers. These relationships did not hold for American workers.

Evidence that work experience constitutes a particularly important input into wages in Japan comes from numerous other sources. Shinotsuka Eiko (1982) assesses how the factors accounting for the male-female wage gap differ in Japan and the United States, based on two decompositions of the wage gap—procedures that show the proportion of the wage gap that can be explained by various factors. The Japanese analysis she reported (carried out by Yashiro Naohiro in 1981) showed that 47 percent of the male-female wage gap can be explained by the difference between men's and women's years of work experience. This was by far the most important factor among those considered, including education and size of firm. This was also the most important factor in explaining the wage gap between American male and female workers, accounting for 39 percent of the gap. While the difference in male

---

to increase with tenure in the firm across the life cycle. This was similar to the pattern for American managers, except that earnings for the latter group increased at a sharper rate late in their careers.

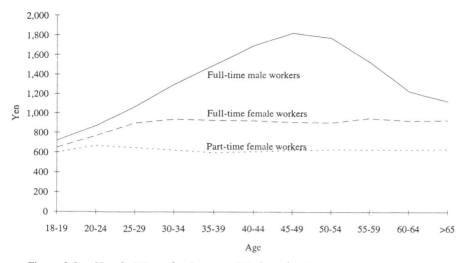

Figure 2.9. Hourly Wages for Japanese Workers, by Age
SOURCE: Japan Institute of Labor 1989.

and female work experience is a principal factor generating wage inequality in both countries, its greater importance in Japan may reflect either that men have more labor force experience relative to women in Japan than in the United States or that the contribution of experience to wages is simply greater in Japan (the point made by Kalleberg and Lincoln). In any case, Japanese women suffer a greater wage penalty than American women based on work experience.

Data from the Japan Institute of Labor go one step farther by documenting wage increases with age and length of experience for three groups of workers: full-time male workers, full-time female workers, and part-time female workers. (Wages for part-time male workers were not computed by the institute because so few Japanese men work part-time.) Figure 2.9 shows how steeply the wages of men working full-time rise with age.[5] A decline in wages sets in at around age 50, which

[5] Note that these wage figures are based on cross-sectional data—that is, data collected on a sample of workers of different ages at one point in time. Thus, age and cohort effects are confounded. For example, if older male workers, say above age 50, were much less educated than younger ones, that alone could explain the fact that their wages are lower. Alternatively, it could also be the case that age (or life-cycle stage) is dominating the wage curve, and that the effect of cohort is quite minimal. Cross-sectional data such as these are used extensively in labor economics because it is so difficult to obtain longitudinal data on a set of individuals. To the extent that we see the same patterns in multiple cross-sections (e.g., 1960, 1970, 1980), one is on stronger ground in asserting that a large part of what is being observed is indeed a life-cycle effect, independent of the particular historical cohorts involved.

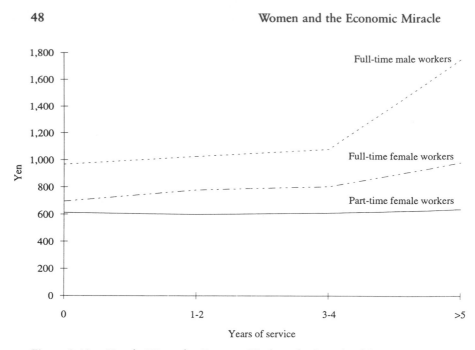

Figure 2.10. Hourly Wages for Japanese Workers, by Length of Service
SOURCE: Japan Institute of Labor 1989.

is also the phenomenon noted by Kalleberg and Lincoln for most
groups of workers. The wage curves for full- and part-time female
workers look very different. The wages of full-time female workers rise
until about age 30 and then remain basically flat. Wages for part-time
female workers are flatter still, across age. Starting wages for the three
groups of workers are not too different from one another—it is the
trajectory by age that differs dramatically.

The age-wage curves in Figure 2.9 do not control for experience,
but a second graph produced by the Japan Institute of Labor does.
Figure 2.10 demonstrates that the wages of female part-time workers
do not increase with experience, at least within the first five years of
work life. Wages of full-time female workers increase slightly during
the first 3–4 years and then more sharply after that. The wages of full-
time male workers start out higher than those of either of the other
two groups, increase at about the same rate as those of full-time female
workers for the first 3–4 years, and increase at a much more rapid
rate thereafter.

Finally, using comparable data for men aged 45–59 in the United
States and Japan, Shimada (1981) found that in both countries the
marginal effect on wages of work experience in a firm was considerably

greater than the effect of external experience (work experience spread across different firms). The magnitude of the difference between the two types of experience was higher for Japanese than for American males, and the Japanese workers who eventually earn the highest wages are those who are highly educated and who have spent their working life with one employer. Life-cycle earnings data substantiate the impression that Japanese workers exhibit a steeper wage profile than American workers. Differences in starting wage levels by education are large in the United States and very small in Japan. Thus, according to Shimada, education acts to stratify the American labor market by differentiating workers at the *start* of their careers. This is not so in Japan. These wage data are compatible with the theory that firm-specific training represents a contract between worker and employer: starting wages are low in exchange for the training costs borne by the employer (Becker 1964; Oi 1983). An employee's long tenure with the firm translates into a steep earnings curve across the life cycle. Likewise, the employer benefits by having workers whose skills are valuable to the firm.

Two major points emerge from these studies of wage determination. First, work experience is a more important determinant of wages in Japan than in the United States. This is particularly so if it is experience in the same firm. Second, life-cycle factors such as age and marital status are more important in determining wages in Japan than in the United States. Assuming that women are much more likely to have intermittent employment than men, both of these elements of the wage-setting process mitigate against equal wages for women.

Further evidence shows Japanese women's declining involvement with age in the large, seniority-based firms of the economy.

EMPLOYMENT BY SIZE OF FIRM

A much higher proportion of the Japanese labor force is concentrated in small firms than is the case in the United States. "Whereas the typical proportion of workers in U.S. manufacturing plants of less than 100 employees has hovered around 15% for much of this century, the comparable Japanese figure has been much closer to 50%," notes Mark Granovetter (1984: 330). In contrast, a higher proportion of the U.S. work force is in very large·firms of over 1,000 workers. Table 2.5 shows that nearly 40 percent of Japanese workers, compared to 26 percent of American workers, are in firms employing fewer than 30

TABLE 2.5

PERCENTAGE OF WORKERS
IN FIRMS OF DIFFERENT SIZES,
JAPAN AND THE UNITED STATES

	Size of firm					
	1–29	*30–99*	*100–499*	*500–999*	*1,000+*	*Total*
Distribution of male workers						
United States	24.2	14.5	13.5	4.8	43.0	100.0
Japan	36.1	16.9	17.3	5.2	24.4	100.0
Distribution of female workers						
United States	28.9	14.7	15.4	6.3	34.6	100.0
Japan	39.0	19.0	18.1	4.4	19.5	100.0
Distribution of all workers						
United States	26.3	14.6	14.3	5.5	39.3	100.0
Japan	37.0	17.5	17.5	5.0	23.0	100.0

SOURCES: U.S. Bureau of the Census 1979; Office of the Prime Minister, Japan, *Rōdōr-yoku chōsa* (Survey of the labor force), 1979.

people.[6] At the other extreme, nearly 40 percent of American workers are in very large firms, compared to only about half as many Japanese workers. In both countries, women are more concentrated than men in very small firms, and are less likely than men to be in very large firms. While it may appear from these figures that women's economic position relative to that of men is not very different for Japan and the United States, closer examination reveals how Japanese women's economic role changes with age.

The mean age of women workers is virtually the same across different-sized firms in the United States, declining only slightly in the largest

---

[6] This is especially notable because the figures I present here for Japan are for *employees* only, in order to make them the most compatible with the U.S. figures. If self-employed and family enterprise workers were included in the Japanese figures, an even higher proportion of the labor force would fall into the small-firm category. Note that the Japanese category for very small firms is slightly more inclusive (1–29 workers) than the U.S. category (1–25 workers). These figures are available yearly in Japan but were available for the United States only in the 1979 Current Population Survey. The fact that firm-size data are readily available in Japan but not in the United States in itself tells us something about the salience of firm size in Japan.

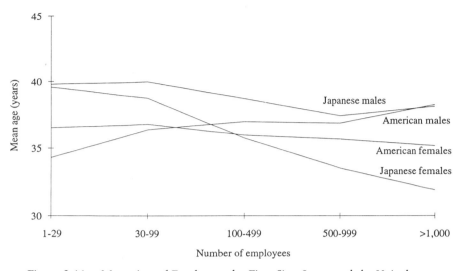

Figure 2.11. Mean Age of Employees, by Firm Size, Japan and the United States
SOURCE: U.S. Bureau of the Census 1979; Office of the Prime Minister, Japan, 1980, *Shūgyō kōzō kihon chōsa* (Basic survey of employment structure).

firms (Figure 2.11). American men show an opposite pattern: men in small firms are on average four years younger than men in the largest firms. The figures for Japan demonstrate a strikingly different picture. The mean age of men is lower in large firms than in small firms. Most dramatic of any group, though, are the patterns for Japanese women: their mean age in large firms is only 32 years, compared to 39 years in small firms. These figures suggest that large Japanese companies draw more heavily on the young female labor force than do large American companies. This is not as true for their use of Japanese men.

The movement of Japanese women out of large firms as they age—and the muting of this pattern for men—can be seen more clearly in Figure 2.12, which shows cohort data constructed from Japanese labor statistics. For each cohort born between 1936 and 1950, women were more apt to start out in large firms or in the government than to be there at later ages. Only for the most recent cohort, born between 1951 and 1955, has there been a change. There, women entered large firms in greater numbers than had earlier cohorts, although the pattern of dropping out was maintained. In contrast, men's participation in large firms fluctuates little as they age; if anything, such participation

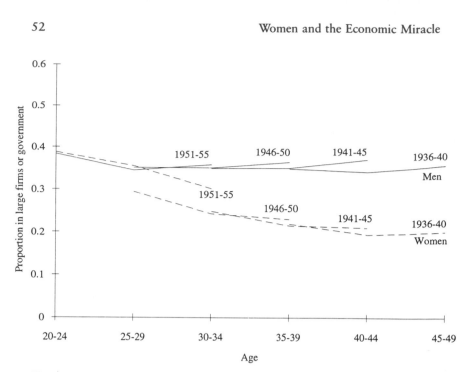

Figure 2.12.   Proportion of Japanese Male and Female Employees in Large
Firms or Government
SOURCE: Office of the Prime Minister, Japan, *Rōdōryoku chōsa* (Survey of the labor
force), various years.
NOTE: Years represent birth cohorts.

increases. And there has been little change across different cohorts of
Japanese men.

What does all of this mean? The fact that few middle-aged and
older Japanese women are in the largest firms of the economy does not
bode well for their earnings. Earnings are higher in larger firms and,
moreover, it is mainly as Japanese workers age that the benefits of
being in a large firm really become apparent. The relative absence of
middle-aged Japanese women in these firms means that few women
reap these benefits.

EMPLOYMENT STATUS

Not only do many Japanese women move out of large companies and
into smaller ones as they age, but their employment status changes
too. The likelihood that they will work in family enterprises or in self-
employment (usually piecework) increases. We have seen that Japanese
women are less likely to work as employees than women in other

TABLE 2.6

EMPLOYMENT STATUS OF WORKERS IN THE
AGRICULTURAL AND NONAGRICULTURAL
SECTORS, JAPAN AND THE UNITED STATES

	United States		Japan	
	Males	*Females*	*Males*	*Females*
Percentage of workers employed in agricultural sector	4.8	1.6	7.7	12.7
Distribution within agricultural sector				
Employees	41.9	41.3	8.1	3.3
Self-employed	54.3	28.2	75.4	21.0
Family enterprise workers	3.8	30.5	16.5	75.7
Percentage of workers employed in nonagricultural sector	95.2	98.4	92.3	87.3
Distribution within nonagricultural sector				
Employees	90.9	94.1	83.0	72.0
Self-employed	9.0	5.0	14.8	12.7
Family enterprise workers	0.1	0.9	2.2	15.3

SOURCES: U.S. Bureau of Labor Statistics 1980; Office of the Prime Minister, Japan, *Rōdōryoku chōsa* (Survey of the labor force), 1980.

countries. Table 2.6 shows in more detail the activities of working men and women in the United States and Japan in 1980. In the American agricultural sector, over 40 percent of both men and women were wage or salary earners. Nearly all of the remaining men were self-employed, whereas the women were equally divided between self-employed and family enterprise workers. In the Japanese agricultural sector, the trend is instead toward self-employment, at least for *men*. In almost direct proportion to the self-employed men are the women who work in family enterprises, mainly the farms of their husbands. These women are also the largest numerical group in agriculture in either country.

The higher concentration of Japanese women than Japanese men or American men or women in family enterprise work is also true in the nonagricultural sector. In that sector, where a much larger proportion of the labor force in both countries is located, Japanese women show the lowest rate (72 percent) of wage and salary employment of any group—and by far the highest rate of employment as family workers (15 percent). Japanese women in the nonagricultural sector work in

Proportion of Working Women Who Are Employees

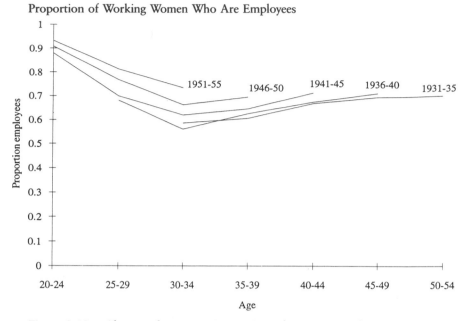

Figure 2.13. *Above and opposite:* Proportion of Japanese Working Women in Different Employment Statuses

SOURCE: Office of the Prime Minister, Japan, *Rōdōryoku chōsa* (Survey of the labor force), various years.

NOTE: Years represent birth cohorts.

family-based enterprises at a rate more than fifteen times that of American women and over seven times the rate of Japanese men. (So few American men occupy this position that the rate for them is not worth comparing.)

Just as the aggregate figures on women's participation in firms are produced by very distinct age patterns, so too are the aggregate figures on employment status. The first panel in Figure 2.13 shows that the proportion of the Japanese female labor force working as employees is highest at young ages (20–24) and declines until ages 30–34. Women move out of employee status with marriage and childbearing in the mid to late twenties. By age 35 or so, their youngest child has typically entered school and a higher number of women are employees again, although the figure never again reaches its earlier level of around 90 percent, found when the women were young. Thus the proportion of working women who are employees changes with age in an M-shaped pattern similar to the pattern for women in the economy as a whole.

Proportion of Working Women Who Are Family Enterprise Workers

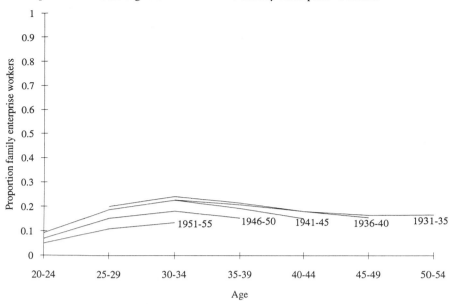

Proportion of Working Women Who Are Self-Employed

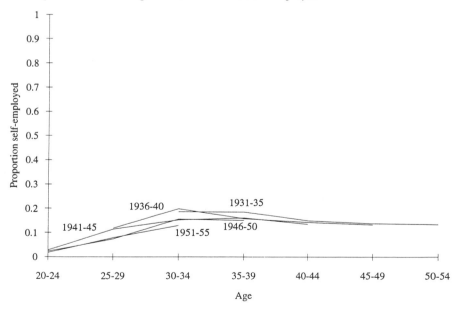

The proportion of employed women in each age group who work as employees has increased in each historical cohort. But the shape of the curve remains the same: large numbers of women move from employee to nonemployee status in their twenties. These data reflect the conflict between women's family responsibilities and the demands of paid labor on the one hand and direct employer discrimination as women reach marriageable age on the other (Japanese women's mean age at marriage is currently 25.8 years).

The movement of women out of the status of wage and salary earners is coupled with their move into family enterprises and, to a lesser extent, self-employment that is usually of a piecework nature. These phenomena are shown in the last two panels of Figure 2.13. Few women work in family enterprises at young ages, but in their late twenties and early thirties, when childrearing responsibilities are the heaviest, the proportions of women engaged in this type of work are higher.[7] Many women later abandon this status when their children are older.

Japanese men follow very different patterns over their life course. The proportion of working men who are employees has historically been at least 80 percent in every age group and cohort. This is shown in the top panel of Figure 2.14 (p. 58). Fewer than *1 percent* of men in any age group are workers in family enterprises. As the second panel shows, this activity is almost entirely restricted to young men. This contrasts sharply with the pattern of older women moving into this type of employment. The third panel shows that instead, the rate of *self-employment* goes up for older men.

In summary, most Japanese women start out as employees but many then either move out of the labor force or into family enterprise or piecework employment during the most demanding years of childrearing. By their early forties, about 70 percent of all working women are employees, compared to about 90 percent of young women. The cohort data on women's rates of employment as employees, family enterprise workers, and self-employed workers also show an increasing tendency over the postwar period for women to work as employees, with young women now as likely as young men to be in that status.

---

[7] Note that we cannot really tell from these figures whether the same women who started out as employees are the ones who are moving into unpaid positions in family businesses; it is more likely the case that many women who start out as employees simply leave the labor force altogether for a number of years. If women who started out as family enterprise workers are more likely to stay in the labor force than women who began as employees, this could produce the high proportions of working women who show up as family enterprise workers in the late twenties–early thirties age group.

But men's and women's work lives continue to play out very differently over the life course.

The increasing differentiation of men's and women's employment status as they age and the movement of women out of large firms with age are phenomena consistent with the Japanese wage-setting processes examined earlier. The comparisons between the United States and Japan demonstrate the force of the penalty paid by Japanese women in a seniority-based system. This can also be seen in the occupational structure.

OCCUPATIONAL STRUCTURE: SEX AND AGE SEGREGATION

Men and women in all economies are segregated into different occupations to some extent, a fact to which gender stratification researchers have paid a great deal of attention in recent years because women's jobs on average pay less than men's (England 1984; Treiman and Hartmann 1981).[8] This suggests that economies with greater occupational sex segregation may show greater wage disparity between men and women. But findings for Japan and the United States show that the story is not nearly so simple: the overall degree of occupational sex segregation in Japan and the United States is similar. In fact, the U.S. index of sex segregation (55.7) is slightly higher than the Japanese (47.9).[9] A straightforward interpretation of this is that 55.7 percent of

[8] This section is based heavily on work carried out with the research assistance of Hang-yue Ngo.

[9] The index of segregation (sometimes also called the index of dissimilarity) is calculated as: $S = \frac{1}{2} \Sigma |m_i - f_i|$, where $m_i = $ *the percentage of the male labor force employed in occupation i* and $f_i = $ *the percentage of the female labor force employed in occupation i*. Because the index is sensitive to the number of occupations that are used in the calculation, occupational categories in the Japanese and U.S. censuses had to be made compatible so that the index could be compared in a valid manner between the two countries. This procedure is necessary because comparing how the sexes are distributed among 120 occupations in one country and 230 occupations in another, for example, would be like comparing apples and oranges. It has been demonstrated that the finer the occupational distinctions, the higher the degree of sex segregation that tends to exist (Bielby and Baron 1984). Men and women generally work in different jobs, and some of this is obscured if we look only at an occupational category. The point can easily be seen if one thinks of the variety of jobs in medicine, where women have a much greater tendency than men to be nurses and men have a greater tendency to be surgeons. Lumping together medical jobs would obscure the high degree of sex segregation that exists in medicine as an occupation.

In the analysis presented here, we started with a list of 285 occupations in the Japanese census and 135 in the U.S. census. Occupational categories were collapsed where necessary, and were made compatible cross-nationally. This resulted in a collapsing of occupations into 89 categories. The indexes of segregation reported here are based on the occupational distribution of the labor force aged 20 and above.

American men or women would have to change occupations in order
for the sexes to be evenly distributed across the occupational structure.
In Japan, 47.9 percent of men or women would have to shift occupations for this to occur.

The higher rate of occupational sex segregation in the United States
is not what we would intuitively expect to find. Why isn't the index
higher in Japan, if gender stratification is in fact greater there? One
reason for the difference lies in the occupational structures of the two
countries. A larger part of the labor force in Japan is occupied in
agriculture and manufacturing, and both of these occupational groups
are more integrated in Japan than white-collar and professional occupations. An *employment-adjusted index of sex segregation* adjusts for
this, by measuring the degree of sex segregation in Japan that would exist
if the distribution of the total labor force across the occupational structure were the same as in the United States. After this adjustment is made,
the gap narrows: the adjusted Japanese figure is 54.7 compared to 55.7
for the United States. The new, higher figure for Japan results because

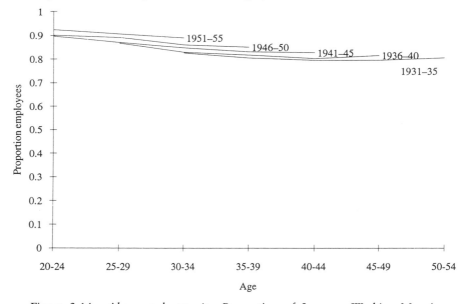

Proportion of Working Men Who Are Employees

Figure 2.14. *Above and opposite:* Proportion of Japanese Working Men in
Different Employment Statuses

SOURCE: Office of the Prime Minister, Japan, *Rōdōryoku chōsa* (Survey of the labor force),
various years.

NOTE: Years represent birth cohorts.

Proportion of Working Men Who Are Family Enterprise Workers

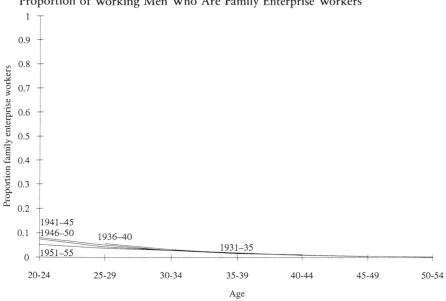

Proportion of Working Men Who Are Self-Employed

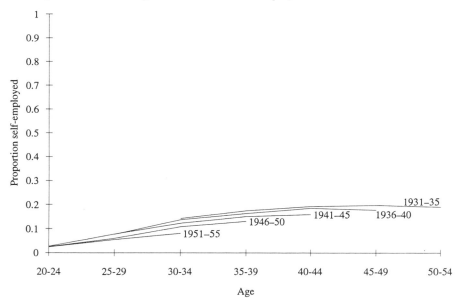

some of the apparent sex integration in the Japanese labor force is in fact produced by occupations such as agriculture that make up a larger part of the economy than in the United States. Once this size effect is removed, the level of sex segregation in Japan increases.

The American and Japanese figures are still closer than what we might expect. But just as the female labor force participation rate disguises the age patterns and types of work that women do, the overall index of sex segregation does not tell us which parts of the occupational structure are the most segregated and why. In fact, the reasons for slightly lower occupational sex segregation in Japan than in the United States are ironic: Japanese men and women are more evenly distributed in the low-status, lower-paying occupational groups. Conversely, sex segregation is greater in Japan than in the United States in the high-status, high-paying occupational groups. Table 2.7 shows the index of segregation for each of the eight main groups of occupations in each economy. The segregation index for each group is based on different numbers of occupations. For example, the administrative/ managerial category is an agglomeration of seven occupations, and the professional/technical category is comprised of twenty-four occupations. It is invalid to compare the index of segregation *across* occupational categories, because the numbers of occupations comprising a category differ. Instead, comparisons should be restricted to *between-country* comparisons of the same occupational category.

The index of sex segregation in Japanese administrative and managerial occupations is 34.0, compared to the American index of 16.2. The percentage female is also lower in Japan (14 percent) than in the United States (29 percent). Sex segregation is also more apparent in Japan in sales and service occupations, and in professional and technical occupations.

Only three occupational groups show less sex segregation in Japan than in the United States: agriculture, lower-level blue-collar work, and administrative support (low-level pink-collar and white-collar work— traditionally called clerical work). The first two of these groups have higher proportions female in Japan than in the United States. Administrative support is a special case. This set of occupations is much less feminized in Japan than in the United States: while over three-quarters of American administrative support workers are female, women make up only about half of this group in Japan.

TABLE 2.7

OCCUPATIONAL SEX SEGREGATION,
JAPAN AND THE UNITED STATES

Occupational category	Japan		United States	
	Index of sex segregation	*% female*	*Index of sex segregation*	*% female*
Executive, administrative, and managerial (7 occupations)	34.0	13.8	16.2	28.8
Professional and technical (24 occupations)	61.1	39.7	54.3	46.9
Administrative support (10 occupations)	19.5	53.0	31.9	77.1
Sales (5 occupations)	44.3	42.3	35.2	46.3
Service (11 occupations)	61.9	57.4	49.0	60.8
Upper blue-collar (precision production, craft, and repair) (15 occupations)	45.4	13.3	44.0	9.4
Lower blue-collar (operators and laborers) (14 occupations)	32.5	41.5	41.5	34.1
Farming, forestry, and fishing (3 occupations)	12.3	47.2	15.5	18.9
Total (89 occupations)	47.9	38.3	55.7	42.3

SOURCES: Calculations based on Office of the Prime Minister, Japan, *Kokusei chōsa* (Population census), 1980; U.S. Bureau of the Census 1984.

Table 2.8 shows the mean occupational prestige scores of Japanese and American men and women.[10] The mean prestige score for all workers is lower in Japan than in the United States (39.6 versus 42.5). But what we are mainly interested in is the extent of the sex difference in each country. In Japan, women have an average occupational prestige score that is 1.5 points lower than men's. The United States demonstrates the reverse: women have an average prestige score that is 1.3 points *higher* than men's. The American result replicates previous studies showing that

[10] The correlation between occupational prestige scores for the two countries is .90. This is based on the 67 occupations (out of 69) that had matching occupational titles in Japan and the United States and for which there was a Treiman prestige score (Treiman 1977).

TABLE 2.8

MEAN OCCUPATIONAL PRESTIGE,
JAPANESE AND U.S. WORKERS

	Japan	United States
Mean prestige score for all workers	39.6	42.5
Mean prestige score for male workers	40.2	42.0
Mean prestige score for female workers	38.7	43.3
Difference in mean prestige score between male and female workers	1.5	−1.3

SOURCE: Mary C. Brinton and Hang-yue Ngo, "Occupational Sex Segregation in Comparative Perspective" (working paper, 1991).

women's greater concentration in pink-collar and lower-level white-collar occupations leads to slightly higher overall prestige scores for women in the United States (England 1979). This is not the case in Japan.

Can these cross-national differences be attributed to differences in the processes governing occupational attainment in the two countries? Data on the age structures of occupations show that age is a more important factor in the Japanese occupational structure.[11] This is demonstrated in three ways.

First, while some occupations in Japan tend to be comprised of middle-aged or older workers and others tend to be held by young workers, such age distinctions are much more blurred in the United States (Table 2.9). In Japan, agricultural workers have the highest median age, 52 years. This is followed by managers, who average 49 years of age. In contrast, the "youngest" occupation is professional/technical, where the average worker is 35 years old. So the median age in the occupations with the oldest and youngest incumbents differs by 17 years. The United States has a very flat age distribution across occupational groups compared to Japan. Managers tend to be the oldest, with a median age of nearly 41 years. Administrative support, lower-level blue-collar, and farm workers are the youngest at 35 years.

[11] The age and sex compositions of occupational groups in Japan and the United States are explored in a log-linear analysis in Brinton and Ngo 1991. This analysis shows that there are stronger age-occupation and age-sex interactions in the Japanese occupational structure than in the American one. Substantively, this means that the age distribution of people varies more by occupation in Japan than in the United States. The age distribution of Japanese men within an occupation is also more distinct from the age distribution of women than is the case in the United States.

TABLE 2.9
MEDIAN AGE OF WORKERS IN
DIFFERENT OCCUPATIONAL GROUPS

	Median age					
	Japan			United States		
Occupational group	Total	Males	Females	Total	Males	Females
Executive, administrative, and managerial	49.1	48.6	52.4	40.7	41.7	37.8
Professional and technical	35.1	37.6	32.0	36.1	37.3	34.7
Administrative support	35.3	38.0	32.9	35.4	36.9	35.0
Sales	36.6	33.8	41.2	39.0	39.7	38.2
Service	40.0	35.9	42.3	38.0	37.3	38.4
Upper blue-collar (precision production, craft, and repair)	39.2	38.6	43.4	37.7	37.6	38.3
Lower blue-collar (operators and laborers)	40.8	39.6	42.2	35.4	34.1	38.3
Farming, forestry, and fishing	52.2	53.0	51.4	35.3	34.9	36.9
Total	40.5	40.3	40.9	37.3	37.9	36.6

SOURCES: Calculations based on Office of the Prime Minister, Japan, *Kokusei chōsa* (Population census), 1980; U.S. Bureau of the Census 1984.

The second major difference in occupational age patterns in the two countries is in the age gap between men and women in the same occupational group. This gap is also larger in Japan than in the United States. (This cannot be traced to a greater *overall* age difference between male and female workers in the Japanese labor force: the median age of male workers is 40.3 years, and of females, 40.9.) There is never a difference of more than 4.2 years in the ages of men and women in an occupational group in the United States, and generally the difference is even smaller. In Japan, every occupational group exhibits an age gap between men and women, ranging from 1.6 years in agriculture (where women are younger than men) to 7.4 years in sales (where women are older).

Third, the age structure of the same occupation often differs between the two countries. The median age of both males and females in managerial occupations is much higher in Japan than in the United

States. This reflects the seniority and experience requirements of Japanese managerial jobs.

What do these differences mean? The age structure of an occupation may reflect the growth or decline of that occupation, changes in technology that necessitate hiring new young workers, or the processes of promotion that operate in the occupation (Kaufman and Spilerman 1982). Agriculture is a good example of how the decline of an occupation can affect the age structure of people in that occupation. In Japan, the agricultural sector has continued to shrink in size in recent years, whereas the decline of the U.S. agricultural sector was more or less complete at an earlier point in time. So it is not surprising that Japanese workers in agriculture tend to be older: few young people are moving into this shrinking sector. But a comparison of occupational growth and decline patterns in the two countries between 1970 and 1980 reveals few other differences.[12] Instead of occupational growth or decline being responsible for the patterns here, it is likely that the age patterns reflect fundamental differences in the recruitment and promotion processes of occupations in Japan and the United States. The age and sex patterns in managerial, blue-collar, and administrative support occupations illustrate how the Japanese processes disadvantage women.

Managers versus Blue-Collar Workers   Table 2.10 shows the ages of people in each country who are in the high-prestige group of managers and administrators and the low-prestige group of unskilled blue-collar workers. In Japan, male managers are heavily concentrated in the older groups: over 60 percent are 45 years old or over. Male managers tend to be much younger in the United States. In fact, nearly 20 percent are under age 30 (compared to 3 percent in Japan!). The age trends for Japanese male managers are mirrored by women. In the United States, female managers are even younger than male managers, a trend that probably represents the recent increase in female MBAs.

Table 2.11 shows the index of sex segregation by age group. In Japan, the index for managers increases sharply with age, from a low of 20 in the 20–24 year age group to a high of 38 in the 55–59 year

---

[12] This comparison is hard to carry out because the detailed occupational codes changed in the United States between the 1970 and 1980 censuses. However, after making occupational categories as consistent as possible between the two years and looking at the occupational growth patterns, I found little difference between Japan and the United States.

TABLE 2.10
AGE DISTRIBUTION OF WORKERS, JAPAN AND THE UNITED STATES: MANAGERS AND UNSKILLED BLUE-COLLAR WORKERS (1980)

Age group	Managers and administrators (%)		Unskilled blue-collar workers (%)	
	Japan	United States	Japan	United States
20–24				
Men	.4	6.9	9.9	22.1
Women	.7	12.5	6.4	16.2
25–29				
Men	2.5	12.1	12.7	17.2
Women	2.1	16.1	7.9	13.9
30–34				
Men	7.8	14.7	15.1	13.2
Women	5.8	15.1	12.8	12.7
35–44				
Men	27.5	24.4	26.8	18.4
Women	20.2	22.3	32.1	21.8
45–54				
Men	32.4	21.5	20.6	15.4
Women	28.6	18.7	25.9	19.3
55–59				
Men	11.3	9.5	6.4	7.1
Women	13.5	7.8	7.2	8.7
60–64				
Men	7.5	6.2	4.0	4.5
Women	10.9	4.6	4.3	5.2
65 +				
Men	10.6	4.7	4.5	2.1
Women	18.2	2.9	3.4	2.2
Total				
Men	100.0	100.0	100.0	100.0
Women	100.0	100.0	100.0	100.0
Median age				
Men	48.6	41.7	39.6	34.1
Women	52.4	37.8	42.2	38.3
Interquartile age range				
Men	16.7	20.8	19.3	21.8
Women	18.8	20.9	16.9	22.2
Index of sex segregation	34.0	16.2	32.5	41.5

SOURCES: Calculations based on Office of the Prime Minister, Japan, *Kokusei chōsa* (Population census), 1980; U.S. Bureau of the Census 1984.

TABLE 2.11

INDEX OF SEX SEGREGATION BY AGE,
JAPAN AND THE UNITED STATES: MANAGERS
AND UNSKILLED BLUE-COLLAR WORKERS
(1980)

Age group	Managers and administrators		Unskilled blue-collar workers	
	Japan	United States	Japan	United States
20–24	20.1	14.3	41.8	36.6
25–29	22.1	15.9	40.6	39.2
30–34	25.9	14.8	40.4	39.6
35–44	33.2	16.4	35.9	41.3
45–54	35.4	16.2	33.6	43.6
55–59	37.8	16.7	33.6	44.5
60–64	33.2	16.4	41.0	53.2
65+	29.1	16.2	25.3	48.4
Index of sex segregation (across age groups)	34.0	16.2	32.5	41.5
Percentage male in the occupation	87.2	72.2	58.5	65.9

SOURCES: Calculations based on Office of the Prime Minister, Japan, *Kokusei chōsa*
(Population census), 1980; U.S. Bureau of the Census 1984.

age group.[13] (Similar patterns are also found in the 1970 census.) In
older age groups of Japanese managers, the tendency toward sex-
segregated work roles is even higher than in young groups. But the
United States shows only a slight increase in sex segregation with age.

These results demonstrate well the different operation of labor markets in managerial occupations in the two countries. The *nenkō joretsu*
(seniority-based) system in Japan results in a concentration of prime-
age workers in managerial occupations, and sex segregation increases
with age. The *nenkō joretsu* system creates a very poor "fit" between

[13] In the age groups above 55–59, the index of sex segregation declines among Japanese managers. This may be because some older women become de jure business owners
or managers upon the deaths of their husbands. Also, many Japanese companies have a
retirement age of 55 or 60, which forces male managers to seek alternative employment.
Both of these trends would narrow the index of managerial sex segregation in the age
60 and above categories in Japan.

Japanese women's life-cycle patterns and managerial occupations. In the United States, managers are younger, show a greater age range, and the balance of men and women does not change very much with age, findings consistent with the lesser importance assigned to seniority there.[14]

Blue-collar occupations offer another sharp U.S.–Japan contrast. Male unskilled blue-collar workers are quite young in both countries, and female workers are slightly older (Table 2.10). In Japan, sex segregation *declines* with age, showing that Japanese women become more integrated into a variety of unskilled occupations as they age (Table 2.11). In contrast, sex segregation increases with age in the United States.

Administrative Support Workers   Finally, the administrative support, or lower-level white- and pink-collar, occupations deserve discussion because they are tied to recruitment and promotion practices that also affect managerial occupations. As discussed previously, administrative support occupations in the United States are held mainly by women and much less commonly by men (Figure 2.15). They are also highly sex-segregated. For example, secretaries tend to be women and clerical workers involved in stock and inventory operations tend to be men. Japan is different. The proportion of women in administrative support occupations is lower than in the United States, but the index of sex segregation is also lower. This makes it *appear* that Japanese women and men in this occupational group are competing to a greater extent in the same jobs. But the ages of Japanese male and female administrative support workers suggest otherwise. Nearly 50 percent of young (aged 20–24) Japanese women are in these occupations—a figure even higher than for American women (Fig. 2.15). This figure drops precipitously at older ages, so that by age 45–54, only 17 percent of all employed Japanese women work in such occupations. In contrast, American women participate at fairly even rates in all age groups. Japanese men's participation in these occupations shows a slow decline with age, in contrast to the extremely sharp decline for Japanese women.

[14] This is true despite the fact that statistically speaking the younger age of American managers should act to make the age variation narrower than in Japan. The interquartile age range, a measure of the spread in the age distribution, is 21.0 years for managers in the United States and 17.1 in Japan (Brinton and Ngo 1991).

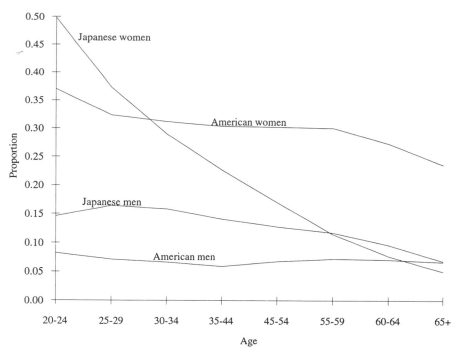

Figure 2.15.   Proportion of the Labor Force in Administrative Support
Occupations, Japan and the United States

SOURCE: U.S. Bureau of the Census 1984; Office of the Prime Minister, Japan,
Kokusei chōsa (Population census), 1980.

Where do young female clerical workers eventually go? Certainly
not into managerial occupations—even by age 45–54, fewer than 4
percent of employed women are managers or administrators (Fig.
2.16).[15] Nor are they moving into professional and technical occupations; the proportion of older employed women in such positions is
also low. Instead, the age pattern for lower-level white-collar work
reflects the "slot" that Japanese companies have for young women. For
older women, another "slot" exists: low-level manufacturing jobs and
jobs in sales.[16]

[15] In contrast, with age, American women show a more even probability of being in
managerial occupations. American men do too. Japanese men show a very deviant pattern: the likelihood of being a manager or administrator rises very sharply with age for
this group alone. This again constitutes a graphic depiction of seniority-based promotion
systems.
[16] Cross-sectional data, of course, only reflect the current age structure of occupations
rather than the movement of a given set of individuals as they age. In the absence of
high-quality survey data on large numbers of individuals for the two countries, we

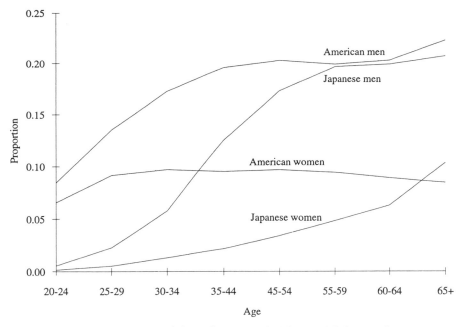

Figure 2.16.   Proportion of the Labor Force in Managerial Occupations,
Japan and the United States
SOURCE: U.S. Bureau of the Census 1984; Office of the Prime Minister, Japan,
Kokusei chōsa (Population census), 1980.

CONCLUSION

Women's direct role in the Japanese economy is not easily predicted
by the historical experience of the United States. Japanese women have
continued to participate in the family enterprise and self-employment
sectors of the economy at higher levels than American women, and
their absorption into clerical work has been slower. The association
between education and women's labor force participation has also
been stronger in the United States.

This chapter has focused on differences between Japanese and
American employment practices as a central explanation for these na-

---

cannot totally separate out the cohort effect—the unique experiences of a group of
people born at a particular time—and the age effect, which is the effect of aging on
certain events (such as being in a particular occupation). The strategy used here is to
look at other cross-sectional data where possible (e.g., for 1970), and compare the
observed patterns with 1980. If the patterns are very similar, one is on surer footing in
claiming that what is being observed is indeed a function of age rather than of a particular cohort (Brinton 1989). I have also constructed data for cohorts where possible, in
order to follow groups of people through time.

tional variations. Japanese practices place a higher value on work experience and organizational seniority, thereby disadvantaging women relative to men as they age. Labor economists may be drawn to a second explanation: perhaps the difference between Japanese men's and women's economic roles, especially when older, is attributable to a difference in their stock of human capital. Japanese men and women are clearly delineated by educational level. The gap between the educational attainments of males and females has narrowed in recent years, but in 1990, over twice as many males (33.4 percent) went on to four-year universities as females (15.2 percent) (Ministry of Education, Japan, 1990). Men's greater acquisition of human capital was especially the case for older cohorts. Can this be responsible for the sexes' divergence in work patterns? For example, Osawa (1985) argues that the cohorts of Japanese women educated before World War II have not been able to take advantage of the recently expanding clerical sector because their educational levels are low. This is a reason why clerical work has not become "feminized" in Japan to the extent that it has in other industrial countries.

Although some credence should be given to a cohort explanation, I have taken pains in this chapter to use data available on men's and women's movements across the life cycle among different-sized firms and employment statuses. Younger cohorts are repeating the same basic patterns of older cohorts. Furthermore, the slow pace at which an association is emerging between education and labor force participation for women renders insufficient an explanation based solely on educational differences between the sexes. Later chapters will document the discrimination against highly educated Japanese women during the postwar period, especially university-educated women.

THREE

Human Capital Development Systems

A comparative theory of gender stratification needs to start with the question of how social institutions differ between societies. Current gender stratification theories are not well suited to answer this question. At one end of the spectrum are the broad-brushed theories of Marxist-feminists (concentrated in anthropology, history, political science, and sociology). These perspectives focus on the role of the "big structures" of patriarchy and capitalism in producing gender stratification. In doing so, they run the risk of being overly deterministic. A reading of these theories makes it easy to see why gender stratification is pervasive but hard to determine why it *varies* among capitalist societies. At the other end of the spectrum are scholars in sociology and economics who put forth theories of gender differences in wages and occupations in the U.S. economy. These theories have little to say about why gender stratification patterns might differ between two "modern" capitalist societies, for they take the structures of capitalism as given and look at how individuals behave within these structures. Status-attainment theory (in sociology) and human capital theory (originating in economics) both put forth a highly individualistic model. Status and wages are predicted from the family backgrounds of men and women and from the individual's own constellation of education, training, marriage, and fertility choices. These theories illuminate individual factors that lead to outcomes in the labor market, but do not offer an explanation for why the male-female gap is greater in some industrial societies than others. As Margaret Mooney Marini puts it, the problem with research that concentrates only on the micro-level is that "it permits analysis of only the unfolding of individual action within a given social structure—that is, within a given system of gender differentiation and stratification. It does not tell us how that system of gender stratification came into being or what is likely to produce change in it" (Marini 1988: 389).

The key to a comparative theory of gender stratification lies in finding a way to link macro- and micro-level theories by locating individual action in the context of social structure.[1] A comprehensive theory must analyze how the *structure of labor markets*, the *structure of education*, and the *structure of the family* reproduce different economic roles for men and women. The structure of these three institutions, the interactions among them, and the norms that direct individual action within these institutions constitute the building blocks for such a theory.

How best, then, to proceed? While one could review the diverse theories of gender stratification and offer a critique of their inability to account for national differences, this is a rather tedious exercise, with no clear outcome. Instead, this chapter first considers those parts of existing theories that are useful, especially in reference to the Japanese case. The chapter then demonstrates how a theory of human capital development systems elucidates the differences between Japan and the United States.

MARXIST-FEMINIST THEORIES

An eclectic literature in anthropology, sociology, political science, and economics deals with the origins of subordinate female status and the effect of economic—particularly capitalist—development on patterns of gender stratification. Much of this work is Marxist-feminist, the most macro-level genre of explanation for gender stratification. The principal contribution of this body of theory is that it makes explicit the link between women's position in the family and the economy, and the feedback effects between these two arenas.

Many cross-cultural analyses of women's position in society begin with an exegesis of Engels's description of the decline of female status

---

[1] At its best, this is what labor market theory (whose practitioners are sometimes called the "new structuralists" or the "new institutionalists" in the field of social stratification) has tried to do. The attempt involves examining structures in the labor market, looking at how different individuals end up in different structures (such as internal labor markets), and analyzing the implications for individual economic outcomes.

with the emergence of capitalism and class society in *The Origin of the Family, Private Property, and the State*. Engels argued that the historical shift from communally owned property to a system of private property dominated by males transformed women from public members of society to private producers limited to the confines of separate family households. Why was women's work privatized and devalued while men's work was kept within the public sphere and valued? Engels's formulation revolves around the fact that the ability to accumulate private property through "productive" labor and to pass property on to heirs made women's reproductive role at once critical and undervalued. Women could produce heirs, but they were not themselves instrumental in directly producing and augmenting the family's private property. A revisionist view of Engels does not regard private property as the linchpin that consolidates women's subordinate status, but emphasizes instead the greater mobility of men that resulted from their lack of responsibility for bearing, nursing, and rearing children. Men's mobility made them more available as public labor under the employ of the ruling classes (Sacks 1974). This use of male labor was then legitimated, and male labor came to be regarded and rewarded as superior to female labor, even when females occasionally did enter the public sphere.

Other theories subsequent to Engels's have placed even greater emphasis on women's original relegation to the domestic sphere based on the biological dictate that they alone are mothers. Such theories have argued that this development did not need to await the emergence of a strong private property system and capitalism. Quite simply, "women become absorbed primarily in domestic activities because of their role as mothers" (Rosaldo 1974: 24). According to this theory, females are viewed by society as moving easily into their adult roles because their primary role (motherhood) is so clearly an ascriptive one. On the other hand, males must *achieve* their adult roles and collect visible material signs of their competence. This leads to males' creation of a complex and hierarchical division of labor, in which they compete against one another.

Related theories attribute an even greater role to the purposive collective action of men to oppress women, or, in short, to patriarchy: "a set of social relations which has a material base and in which there are hierarchical relations between men, and solidarity among them, which enable them to control women" (Hartmann 1976: 138). These theories see patriarchy as an early arrival, prior to capitalism, through which men learned direct techniques of hierarchy and control. These techniques were extended with the development of capitalism, and kept women's labor power concentrated in the home and undervalued. The domestic division of labor weakens women's position in the labor market, forcing them back into the home, and so on in a cyclical process (Hartmann 1976). Theories in this genre attribute a strong role to the conspiratorial motives of men and their ability to act collectively.

Although Marxist-feminist theories (see also Beechey 1978; Kuhn 1978; Walby 1986) differ from one another in the degree to which they attribute gender stratification to conspiratorial, divide-and-conquer strategies on the part of men, they have a number of points in common. These are: (1) an emphasis on the division of productive labor into private and public spheres, with women dominating the former and men the latter; (2) the relegation of women to the private sphere in large part because of biological factors (childbearing and nursing); and (3) the recognition that temporary changes in the sexual division of labor in the public sphere will not likely be sustained unless corresponding changes take place in the domestic sphere.

The most important contribution of Marxist-feminist theories is the emphasis on the mutually supportive relationship between gender stratification in the paid work force and a strong sexual division of labor within the family.[2] A second contribution of the theories is that

---

[2] Economic and sociological studies of the household division of labor have consistently demonstrated that women contribute significantly more time and energy to household tasks than men do, regardless of their participation in the paid labor force (Vanek 1974; Walker and Woods 1976; Berk and Berk 1979). This conclusion holds whether household labor is measured in terms of time inputs or discrete tasks. Similar results have been found in a number of countries besides the United States.

Other evidence also speaks to the issue of the interaction between household and market production and its effects on women's labor force behavior. Women are more likely than men to consider work hours and location as important factors in accepting a job (Niemi 1974; Hill 1978). Their usual status as the secondary wage earner in marriage and their additional home responsibilities are no doubt crucial determinants of these attitudes. Although job quit rates are higher for women than for men (Landes 1977), this must be balanced against the fact that women are more likely to quit their jobs in order to exit from the labor force altogether, whereas men have higher rates of actual job-switching than women (Barnes and Jones 1974).

It is extremely difficult to disentangle the causal chain between home responsibilities and labor force behaviors, although the work of Reuben Gronau (1988) suggests that women would not be as intermittently employed were employer behaviors and low wages not such strong discouraging factors. Some studies have also shown that percentage increases in earnings reduce job quitting by women to a much greater extent than for men (Barnes and Jones 1974), indicating that women's job commitment may be highly elastic and could be positively altered by changes in the demand side of the labor market.

they implicitly suggest reasons why men as both employers and employees would discriminate against women. The movement of women into positions of higher authority in the work force may not only threaten women's performance of domestic labor, from which men benefit, but may also threaten men's own achieved status in society as the principal support of their families.

Despite these insights, problems arise when one tries to use Marxist-feminist theories to explain why gender stratification patterns differ among industrial economies. How do different forms of capitalism affect gender stratification in the economy? Capitalism is not a monolithic structure, but instead varies across national settings on a number of dimensions. First, capitalist economies differ in the value attached to certain worker characteristics. If part of the story behind greater gender stratification in Japan is the existence of firms that reward a worker's continuous participation in the labor force, seniority in the firm, and responsibilities as household head, then focusing on the emergence and continuation of such firms is more important than focusing on the emergence and continuation of capitalism alone. A theory that will explain gender stratification differences in the Japanese and U.S. economies needs to deal with the differences in labor market structures—structures that are economically rational within the confines of their own capitalist systems—and the implications for women.

Second, Marxist-feminist theories do not explain why some occupations are "female" in the United States and "male" in Japan, and why other occupations have low rates of female participation in the United States and high rates of female participation in Japan. These theories argue that women's place in the labor market is an extension of their place in the home. But as Ruth Milkman has convincingly demonstrated, definitions of women's work shifted even *within industries* during World War II in the United States. A reduction in the supply of male workers forced a reevaluation of the jobs considered appropriate for women (Milkman 1987). In a like way, low-level white-collar jobs largely became "women's work" in the United States, but not in Japan. And young Japanese women tend to be involved in clerical work in Japan, whereas older women are more likely to be unskilled manufacturing workers. If clerical work is based on a gen-

---

In any case, discussions of job turnover must incorporate the division of familial responsibilities between men and women as well as employer behaviors.

dered definition, why would this skewed age distribution of female clerical workers occur? Considering women's duties in the workplace as a natural extension of work in the home does not predict which jobs in an economy will be female. Nor does it predict why some jobs will be female in one economy and male in another.

Finally, the motives of men as patriarchs and as capitalists do not always coincide. Marxist-feminist theories do not predict either when men's gender interests will predominate over their class interests or when men will be able to organize efficiently to promote their gender interests. Samuel Cohn argues persuasively that patriarchy may be a "secondary utility" after profit maximization for some employers (1985). Milkman argues in her historical study of the U.S. electrical and auto industries that in fact patriarchal interests overrode those of profit maximization. Both scholars point out that Marxist-feminist theories do not predict when one motive will predominate over the other. This also becomes a problem when we turn to comparative issues: would such theories predict that Japanese men are more or less likely than American men to act on their gender as opposed to their class interests? On what basis would a cross-cultural prediction be made?

In sum, theories of gender stratification that give full scope to patriarchy and capitalism do not say enough about how different forms of capitalism and labor market structures affect women's status vis-à-vis men.

HUMAN CAPITAL DEVELOPMENT

Whereas Marxist-feminist theories can be criticized as being too macro-level and deterministic in their predictions, human capital theory errs in the opposite direction. Human capital theory has been the dominant approach used by American labor economists to explain why men and women have different earnings and tend to be clustered in different occupations. Human capital theorists propose that people are forward-looking and invest in their education and skills (human capital) for the purpose of maximizing long-run productivity (Becker 1964; Mincer 1974). Although some of the returns to investment in human capital may be psychic, and thus nonmonetary, economists have concentrated their empirical studies on monetary returns because they are the easiest to measure (Lloyd and Niemi 1979). Mark Blaug provides a concise statement of the perspective of human capital theorists:

The concept of human capital, or "hard core" of the human capital research program, is the idea that people spend on themselves in diverse ways, not for the sake of present enjoyments, but for the sake of future pecuniary and nonpecuniary returns. . . . All these phenomena—health, education, job search, information retrieval, migration, and in-service training—may be viewed as investment rather than consumption, whether undertaken by individuals on their own behalf or undertaken by society on behalf of its members. What knits these phenomena together is not the question of who undertakes what, but rather the fact that the decision-maker, whoever he is, looks forward to the future for the justification of his present actions.

(Blaug 1976: 829)

It is eminently reasonable to postulate that people invest in their education and skills with an anticipated future goal in mind. But human capital theory restricts the focus to two actors: the individual as a reflexive actor, and the employer who makes decisions about which employees to invest in. Within the human capital paradigm, occupational-choice theory argues that women make educational decisions based on their anticipated work plans—intermittent or continuous. According to this logic, women who plan to intersperse work in the labor market with household and childrearing activities will invest in skills that will not depreciate during periods spent out of the labor market (Polachek 1975, 1979, 1981, 1985). Recent empirical studies in sociology have cast doubt on the idea that women plan their education and work careers in this way (England 1984, England et al. 1988). But leaving aside the issue of whether the logic operates well in the United States or not, this theory assumes that individuals have control over the early investments made in their education. The theory does not take into account that this varies empirically among societies. In educational systems such as Japan's, the individual gets on a particular educational track at a younger age than in the United States, and switching tracks at a later stage is quite problematic. Because of this, Japanese parents arguably have greater control over their children's education (what economists term *general human capital*) than in cultural settings that allow new educational decisions to be made at later points, when the individual is not under parental control. This underscores the importance of parents' ideas about gender and about the appropriateness of different types of human capital and skill attainment by their sons and daughters.

In short, human capital theory obscures important cultural variation when it views the individual as an autonomous decision maker vis-à-vis human capital decisions. This conception of how educational decisions are made derives partly from the development of the theory within one social context, the United States, with inadequate investigation into whether the assumptions of the theory are valid in other contexts. By holding social structure (in this case, the flexibility or inflexibility of the educational system) constant, we also hold constant the constraints and opportunities implied by that structure.

We need a theory of gender stratification that has general principles and that postulates the linkages between economy and society that Marxist-feminist theories and human capital theory have ignored. Arguing for a more cultural and social-institutional approach to gender stratification in the economy means that we need to analyze how social institutions structure the development and evaluation of individuals' human capital. Four issues are critical:

1. Who in society is primarily responsible for human capital development?
2. What are the motives of these individuals?
3. On what basis are they making their decisions?
4. What resources do they have to carry out their decisions?

An analysis of these issues in Japan and the United States shows why gender stratification and women's dual role as direct and indirect producers are more pronounced in the Japanese economy.[3]

THE STRUCTURE OF A HUMAN CAPITAL DEVELOPMENT SYSTEM

I define a system of human capital development as consisting of two dimensions. The first is the social-institutional context or configuration within which human capital development and evaluation occurs. This refers to the structure of the educational system and the labor market, including the mechanisms by which work organizations recruit workers from school. This part of the human capital development system therefore has to do principally with the processes of labor demand.

[3] Some of the material in this chapter has also appeared in "The Social-Institutional Bases of Gender Stratification: Japan as an Illustrative Case," *American Journal of Sociology* 94, no. 2 (1988): 300–334, and "Christmas Cakes and Wedding Cakes: The Social Organization of Japanese Women's Life Course," in *Japanese Social Organization*, ed. Takie Sugiyama Lebra (University of Hawaii Press, 1992).

The second dimension is the structure of exchanges that occur within families, especially between parents and children. This part of the human capital development system encompasses the processes by which young people are socialized into society and trained for adult roles—labor supply processes.

THE EDUCATIONAL SYSTEM AND THE LABOR MARKET: U.S. AND JAPANESE CONTRASTS

The structures of the educational system and the labor market play a major role in gender stratification processes. Together they determine the *diffused* or *condensed* character of human capital investment decisions across the life cycle. A society such as the United States is characterized by diffused timing of human capital development decisions. Individuals show a fair amount of variation in their life-cycle patterns of human capital development. Some individuals leave school and enter the workplace, later returning to school for a period of years and subsequently reentering the workplace. Others finish school and start working for one employer, with whom they remain for their adult working lives. The United States is characterized by: (1) few age restrictions in educational institutions, and (2) a vigorous labor market with higher rates of interorganizational mobility for workers of most ages than in Japan. The educational system and work organizations accommodate people with different ideas about how to sequence their time in educational, family, and work activities across their lives.[4] This institutional flexibility is especially valuable to women, who more than men tend to be heavily involved in family commitments and to alternate their energies among education, family, and labor force activities throughout the life cycle.

Japan represents a different situation because its human capital development system leads to the *condensed* timing of decisions: there are a few key points in the life cycle of all individuals when human capital development decisions are critical. The timing of these points varies very little among individuals. Severe economic disadvantages accrue to people who do not succeed in the series of structured "contests" (Turner 1960) on different rungs of the educational ladder. In the Japanese-style system, individual failure or indecisiveness cannot be compensat-

---

[4] This is not to deny that there may be important economic consequences of the path one chooses. Both the opportunity and the willingness to pursue a "typical" life schedule may also be related to one's social class, ethnicity, or other characteristics.

ed for by further human capital investment later in the life cycle. A highly educated Japanese woman in her early forties, interviewed in Tokyo during fieldwork in 1984, spoke of the regularity with which Japanese move through life stages such as education, marriage, and work: "It is like a life plan that [we Japanese] have." The significance of this statement can be appreciated if one imagines how unlikely it would be for an American spontaneously to offer to sum up the "life plan" of all Americans. The concept of set timing of life stages was not shocking to Japanese with whom I discussed it. As one person put it, "To be Japanese is to follow the patterns society prescribes." The concept of life stages is also quite apparent in Japanese advertising. For instance, a newspaper ad for a bank queried: "Where are you in life right now?" Underneath were five succeeding swirls, each encircling in sequence, one by one, the following: *kekkon* (marriage), *shussan* (birth), *jūtaku* (owning a house), *kyōiku* (education), and *rōgo* (old age).

Japan is characterized by: (1) school-level tracking in the educational system, meaning that parents and children must select schools from the high school level onward, (2) sharp age-grading in the educational system (one is supposed to finish school by a certain age, and schools at all levels have upper and lower age barriers to admission), and (3) a pattern of firm-internal labor markets, where workers are hired into an organization when young and promoted through a combination of seniority and merit principles. The consequence of this configuration of education and labor markets is that decisions about preparation for work roles are condensed into the early part of a person's life. This places women at a disadvantage, for reasons we shall see shortly.

THE STRUCTURE OF THE JAPANESE EDUCATIONAL SYSTEM: SPONSORED CONTESTS

School-Level Tracking   Although education in Japan is compulsory only through the junior high school level, nearly 95 percent of Japanese youth currently proceed on to high school (Ministry of Education, Japan, 1988). Moreover, the great majority graduate.[5] The postwar educational system was modeled on the U.S. system, with elementary

---

[5] Rohlen (1983) reported 1977 dropout rates of 5.5 percent for public vocational high schools and 0.4 percent for public academic high schools.

school comprising six years and junior and senior high school each comprising three years. While the Japanese and U.S. systems resemble each other in outward form, however, there are fundamental differences between them.

An important aspect of an individual's successful participation in the Japanese educational system is passage of the standardized examinations to successive levels of education. The first entrance examination or "contest" is for high school. Japanese school districts contain several high schools, generally of varying academic quality, and students must pass an entrance examination in order to be admitted to a particular school. Getting into the best academic high school in the area is a very important step for getting into a top university three years later. While within-school tracking is virtually unheard of, the constellation of schools within a district can be thought of as a system of tracks, with each school representing a track. Entering a "good" high school prepares one to be able to succeed in the next contest, which is either the examination for a "good" company or the examination for a "good" university and then the job market.

Age-Grading   U.S. schools have few built-in age barriers. Children who are behind in school may be kept back for a year; others who are very quick learners may skip a grade. An individual can conceivably continue to invest in his or her human capital through formal education even after becoming an adult (Hogan and Mochizuki 1985). For instance, men and women can return to university after spending several years in the workplace or raising children. At that point, they may enroll in special training courses or an M.B.A., J.D., or other professional degree program. In contrast, Japanese education is strongly age-graded. If a person goes to university, it is expected that four years and no more will be spent there. At this point, most people leave the institution, never again to be full-time students. Table 3.1 shows that the proportion of the Japanese population in school halves between ages 22 and 23, then halves again between 23 and 24, and by age 25–29, fewer than 1 percent of Japanese are in school. (These low figures are all the more surprising given the existence of *rōnin*—literally, "masterless samurai"—who fail a university entrance examination the first time and choose to sit out for one or more years in order to study for and then retake the entrance examination, which is given only once a year.) The proportion of Americans in school declines at a much more

TABLE 3.1

PERCENTAGE OF THE POPULATION IN
SCHOOL, BY AGE, UNITED STATES AND
JAPAN

Age	United States	Japan	
		School only	*School + work*
18	62.3	66.3	69.4
19	42.3	42.6	47.2
20	34.3	33.2	37.6
21	30.6	25.2	28.9
22	23.9	17.5	20.1
23	18.3	8.0	9.4
24	15.6	3.5	4.3
25–29	10.3	.8	1.0
30–34	7.1	.1	.2
35–39	4.8	.05	.06
40–44	3.7	.02	.03
45–54	2.2	.02	.02

SOURCES: U.S. Bureau of the Census 1984; Office of the Prime Minister, Japan, *Kokusei chōsa* (Population census), 1980.

uniform rate over a wider age span, so that it is not until age 40–44 that the proportion is as low as it is in Japanese schools at age 24.

The Relation between Education and the Labor Market   There are fewer opportunities in Japan than in the United States for higher education beyond university (i.e., graduate and professional school).[6] The vast majority of Japanese enter the labor market immediately after they finish their general education, whether it be junior high school, high school, junior college, or university. A school bestows upon the individual a credential that signals successful passage of the school-specific entrance examination. This provides a ticket into an *organizational setting* (the workplace) and the set of human relations in that organization. In the American case, the job itself rather than the or-

[6] The proportion of the Japanese post-high school student population in specialized post-secondary schools other than universities is .20, about half the United States figure of .37 (United Nations 1982b).

ganizational setting typically acts as the prime motivation for the individual. The U.S. educational system is more attuned than the Japanese to providing job-preparation skills. From an early point in children's education, some energy is focused in American schools on the task of discovering talents and creative abilities and helping them to blossom. This was most clearly seen in the move during the 1960s in the United States toward innovative schools, and the publication of books such as Sheldon Leonard's *Education and Ecstasy* (1968).

The relationship between what one learns in school and whether one succeeds in the job market was demonstrated in a survey of employed men and women in their late twenties in Japan, Britain, and the United States. Nearly 80 percent of Americans reported that their education in school had helped shape their careers. This contrasted with a figure of only 50 percent for the Japanese. Young British men and women were closer to the Japanese in their responses; only 55 percent said that they perceived a connection between the content of schooling and their jobs (National Institute of Employment and Vocational Research, Japan, 1988). Preparing young people to fit into an organizational setting involves a good deal of psychological investment on the part of educators and parents. As one high school teacher commented: "In the Japanese educational system, rather than drawing out ability, we try to put children into a framework. We make every effort to fit children into society." The structure of the Japanese educational system necessitates that parents make crucial decisions and investments early in the child's life. That is, the structure of the educational system affects the timing of human capital decisions in such a way as to magnify the importance of *parents as social actors* responsible for the human capital development of young males and females. A popular term for the process of studying for the entrance exam is *nininsankyaku* ("three-legged race"): a young person's successful performance in the entrance examination is tied to his or her parents' psychological and financial help. Early adolescent decision-making vis-à-vis education is described in the following way by Thomas Rohlen:

> Many important virtues . . . are tied together at a formative period and are motivated largely by a rather selfish individual desire to get ahead (or as many put it, "to not fall behind"). Whether the desire is the parents' or the child's is never that clear, and this too seems characteristically Japanese. This desire is hardly individualistic in the sense of stemming from individual choice or the uniqueness of personality.
>
> (Rohlen 1983: 109)

Given the importance of placement in a particular organizational setting upon school graduation, we might expect to find mechanisms for matching students to jobs to be more institutionalized in Japan than in the United States, and this is in fact the case. School placement offices play a central role in helping Japanese students find jobs. Schools benefit by placing their good students with reputable firms, because the resulting prestige in the community allows a school to attract strong applicants for its entrance examinations, and this good reputation attracts recruiters from local companies year after year (Rosenbaum and Kariya 1989).

In addition to school-level tracking, strong age grading, and the importance of education for the labor market, two other aspects of the Japanese educational system are important in condensing the timing of crucial educational decisions into an early period in people's lives. These are: (1) the existence of schools and tutorial services designed to help children pass school entrance examinations; and (2) the early choices young people must make about major field of study.

"Extra-School" Schools and Tutorial Services   Increasing privatization of educational expenses in postwar Japan has occurred in two ways: with the proliferation of private schools and with the mushrooming of a dense network of "extra-school" schools. The latter category includes *juku* (exam preparation or remedial schools, catering to younger as well as older children), *yobikō* (schools to prepare high school students to take university entrance exams), and *katei kyōshi* (private tutoring). Criticisms of extra-school schooling have become widespread in Japan. For instance, the wildly popular film *Kazoku geimu* (1984) is a black comedy that parodies the bullying attitude of a third-rate university student toward the anxious parents who have hired him to tutor their son. The film represents a thinly veiled self-mockery of Japanese willingness to pay for extra help in getting their children, especially sons, through "examination hell" (*juken jigoku*).

Despite widespread domestic criticism of schools that supplement compulsory schooling, Japanese parents continue to pay to send their children to such schools in an attempt to ensure success in the entrance exams of prestigious high schools and universities (Rohlen 1980). Household expenditures on extra-school schooling have shown a four-fold increase in recent years, from about 5 percent of the total household expenditures on education in 1965 to nearly 20 percent in 1982 (Office of the Prime Minister, Japan, 1983). One study reported that for the period 1955–73, the elasticity of total educational expenditures to income was higher than that of any other consumption expenditure, including consumer goods. On average, for every 10 percent increase in income, educational expenditures increased by 17.5 percent (Yamamura and Hanley 1975). The proportion of young Japanese adolescents in their third year of junior high school who attend *juku* rose 10 percent between 1976 and 1985, from 37 to 47 percent. In cities of over 100,000, the rate was over 50 percent by 1985 (Ministry of Education, Japan, 1985). Over one-third of the successful applicants in 1980 to Tokyo University, the most prestigious of all educational institutions in Japan, had taken the entrance examination for the second time. This means that they sat out for at least one year as *rōnin* (Rohlen 1983). Almost all *rōnin* are males and are supported financially by their families as they study an additional year for university entrance examinations.

Tutoring services analogous to *juku* are rare in the United States, and the rate of attendance at private "preparatory" schools prior to university entrance is also relatively low. Consequently, compared to Japanese parents, American parents are responsible for less direct economic contribution to their children's education. Even after university entrance, tuition and other fees in the United States are in many cases partially or fully covered by scholarship funds or by the student's own part-time work. Such funding is much rarer in Japan, where parents generally continue to finance their children's entire education.[7]

Choice of University Major   A final factor that makes the crucial educational decision-making period earlier in a child's life in Japan than in the United States is the flexibility most American universities grant the individual in terms of choosing a major. It is customary to require the declaration of a major only when the student has "tried out" a number of courses over a one- or two-year period *after* entering university. This gives considerable leeway as well as responsibility to the individual to decide how to invest in his or her own human capital. The United States probably represents an extreme among industrial societies in allowing the individual to delay making educational decisions. In Japan, by contrast, application to a specific *gakubu* (department) is typically made when taking the entrance examination to a university.

[7] *Asahi Shinbun* recently reported that 80 percent of high schools have rules against students working part-time.

In summary, the structure of the Japanese educational system means that the individual must emerge as a winner in a series of what can be termed *sponsored contests*. The probability that this will occur is increasingly linked in parents' minds to *their* sponsorship of children through investment in private education. Likewise, schools are important sponsors in matching the individual with a company.

Who benefits and who loses in such a system? Employers' preferences for certain types of workers have historically been a principal driving force behind Japanese educational contests, and this continues to be the case. Japanese employers look for employees who will remain with the firm (thus making on-the-job training a profitable investment) and who will also function well together in work groups. Once strong social norms in relation to marriage and childbearing are brought into the picture I have sketched, it is easy to see why employers tend to exclude women from the "good" starting jobs: the assumption is that women are temporary employees. This means that parents and educators have much to gain by putting more effort into sponsoring young men rather than young women through the series of highly competitive educational contests described above.[8] The Japanese employment system picks up where parents and educators leave off, providing what might be called *sponsored mobility* up career ladders for a subset of promising young men.

THE STRUCTURE OF THE JAPANESE EMPLOYMENT SYSTEM: SPONSORED MOBILITY IN INTERNAL LABOR MARKETS

The phenomena of low interfirm mobility, seniority-based wage and promotion systems, and firm-specific training in Japan combine to make an individual's first job crucial in terms of getting onto a successful career track (Brinton 1989).[9] Although the external labor mar-

---

[8] The degree to which sponsorship, as opposed to individual ability and achievement, accounts for success in the Japanese educational system is hotly debated among both Japanese and American scholars. See, e.g., the contrasting views of Cummings (1980), Rohlen (1983), and Seiyama and Noguchi (1984). This relates directly to the issue of whether rates of intergenerational occupational mobility are lower in Japan than in other industrial countries. In fact, comparative studies of social mobility do not depict Japan as an outlier (Tominaga 1979; Grusky and Hauser 1984). However, there is no a priori theoretical reason why high rates of intergenerational mobility and a high degree of gender stratification cannot exist side by side within the same economy. This can be seen most clearly if we understand intergenerational mobility to be related to processes of inheritance/disinheritance between *generations*, whereas gender stratification processes originate in allocation patterns among *siblings* within the same family.

[9] The origins of the permanent employment system have engendered lively debate among Japan specialists and are discussed in the next chapter. The currently prevailing

ket has become more active in recent years, studies of interfirm mobility consistently show that Japanese employees change employers less often than American employees. This is particularly the case once men reach their late twenties and beyond (Cole 1979; Hashimoto and Raisian 1985). (Research on interfirm mobility in Japan has uniformly been based on the behavior of men.) Low mobility is related to the recruitment policies of firms. About 49 percent of Japanese firms carried out some recruitment at the mid-career level in 1985; stated differently, 51 percent restricted *all* of their recruiting that year to new graduates. This varies little across firms of different sizes (Ministry of Labor, Japan, 1985a).

Low interfirm mobility is linked to employers' investments in on-the-job training and job rotation for potentially valuable employees. As shown in chapter 2, these investments in workers' specific human capital (Becker 1964; Oi 1983) translate into the development of a career within the firm because work experience contributes more to earnings if the worker has been employed continuously in one firm rather than several firms (Shimada 1981). On-the-job training has represented the dominant mode of skill formation in Japanese industry in the post–World War I period (Koike 1983a). Japanese managers and foremen have considerable discretionary power in allocating work responsibilities and making decisions about who will be trained. Koike observed from fieldwork in Japanese factories:

> When the operation of the system is observed in more detail, it is recognized that in practice the system is less egalitarian than it first appears. A young recruit who joins a work group following formal training is usually backed up by the sub-foreman for a period of time—say, several months. Even after that, he is instructed and attended by a senior worker who occupies the next position in the rotation sequence.
>
> (Koike 1983a: 43)

Koike concludes that "the foreman in Japanese labor markets is much more involved than his Western counterpart in a worker's ca-

---

view is that the system's development can be traced to a combination of labor supply conditions, employers' conscious reinterpretation of elements of the traditional cultural heritage, and the state's support of employer associations to this end. Cooperation between employers and the state was particularly critical in the period between World War I and World War II, when embryonic industrial labor unions were seen as a potentially serious cause of political turmoil (Crawcour 1978; Fruin 1978). I do not deal with the role of the state in human capital development except in terms of two points: (1) the contemporary endorsement of internal labor markets, and (2) the absence of strong social welfare provisions, meaning that parents are implicitly encouraged to invest in the "quality" of their children for reasons of security in old age.

reer" (1983a: 46). Japanese employers are therefore critically important in the human capital development process. As the slogan of one
automobile parts manufacturer goes: "We focus on making people,
before products" (*Mono o tsukuru mae ni, hito o tsukuru*).

This model of human capital development in the workplace has
been accepted to a large degree as the ideal pattern for the past three
decades in Japan. Popular as well as government ideology has supported the notion that long-term participation in a work organization, on-
the-job training, and seniority systems are privileges. Interfirm mobility, in the words of a government publication in the early 1970s, is "a
response to defective human relations" and is more characteristic of
the individualistic industrial West than of industrial Japan (Office of
the Prime Minister, Japan, 1973: 27). Firms with internal labor markets have been popular choices of graduates from the top universities.
A 1982 survey reported that 62 percent of male university students
hoped to be employed in a large firm (*daikigyō*) in the future (Nihon
Recruit Center 1983a). This represented an increase of 11 percent since
the mid 1970s. As Paul Noguchi notes, university graduates "seek out
the *hanagata* ('star') and *ninki* ('popular') employers" (1983: 76). Surveys of high school students have also shown that white-collar jobs in
large firms are the most sought-after jobs (Rosenbaum and Kariya
1989). This is true for both males and females, although chapter 5 will
show how different these jobs actually are for the two sexes.

Small- and medium-sized firms practice human capital development
practices that are strikingly similar to those of large firms. In a survey
of 5,200 companies, the Ministry of Labor (1981) reported that 97
percent of companies employing over 1,000 workers and 80 percent
of firms with 100–299 employees carried out educational training.
Similar proportions used job rotation practices. Forty-five percent of
the smallest firms (30–99 employees) practiced mid-career recruitment,
compared to 54 percent of the largest firms.

These strategies of employer investment in workers have strong implications for gender stratification. Fewer than 30 percent of companies who recruited university graduates in the early 1980s recruited
women, and 83 percent of all companies had "positions in which
women are not placed." In addition, among companies that carried
out periodic job rotation, half did not offer any women such experience. Among companies that carried out educational training, about
40 percent reported that they "give training to women but the content
differs from the training given to men," and over 20 percent reported

that they did not give training to women (Ministry of Labor, Japan, 1981).

Nearly half of all employers in the mid 1980s stated that there were no promotional possibilities for women, and more than one-third of these based this on the expectation that women would leave the workplace (Ministry of Labor, Japan, 1985a). This represents the notion of "statistical discrimination," where an individual with certain ascriptive characteristics (e.g., being female) is judged on the basis of the *average* attitudes and behaviors of his or her group rather than on the basis of personal attributes (Arrow 1973; Phelps 1972). The future prospects of the individual Japanese woman have generally been judged by the modal behavior of all women: quitting upon marriage or childbirth.[10] Japanese women's direct role in the economy as suppliers of inexpensive labor is thus closely related to an educational system and employment system that put strong decision-making power in the hands of parents and employers. Processes in the Japanese family itself are also critical to gender stratification.

THE STRUCTURE OF INTRAFAMILIAL EXCHANGES

The second dimension of a human capital development system, affecting labor supply, is the pattern of intergenerational exchange in families. These exchanges in the Japanese family encourage intensive psychological investment in sons' rather than daughters' education. This has two outcomes for women, one obvious and one less obvious. First of all, many fewer young Japanese women than men receive a university education. Second, mothers' role in the human capital development of their children, especially that of sons, is highly respected. Women receive social credit for their performance of this indirect role in the economy: their role in nurturing males.

[10] The Japanese tax system also encourages married women to work part-time, if at all. A spouse's earnings below 1,000,000 yen (about $6,200) per year are tax-exempt. This creates an incentive for wives to earn only up to this amount. The law is not sex-specific, so a couple could legally choose to designate the husband as the spouse for tax purposes, and he could limit his earnings. But given the wage disparity between men and women, this would not be a logical choice for it would nearly always be the case that the husband could earn more than the wife. Japanese employers are also very sensitive to the fact that the family-related expenses of a male increase as he gets older, as expenditures for children's education and for other necessities accumulate. This makes it rational to tie men's wages to seniority. In contrast, American workers are more likely to be paid as individuals irrespective of family responsibilities (Kalleberg and Lincoln 1988).

Sons' and Daughters' Education   Japanese parents' role as sponsors of their children's early human capital development is accentuated not only by the structure of the educational system and the articulation between that system and the workplace, but by the strength of Japanese intergenerational ties across the life cycle. These ties are expressed in both the financial and the emotional spheres, for many parents anticipate help in both areas in old age. A retirement age of fifty-five or at most sixty in the majority of companies exists alongside levels of government support to the aged that are the lowest among industrial nations. Parents therefore have strong incentives to invest in at least one child in an effort to ensure their financial security in old age. The intergenerational bond across the life cycle is further reinforced by factors such as high housing costs and inadequate childcare facilities, making extended family residence a desirable option for many families (Morgan and Hirosima 1983). Despite the increasing trend toward "nuclearization" of the family, the proportion of extended family households in Japan remains high for an industrialized nation (21 percent in 1980).

Japanese parents' lifelong expectations of sons and daughters have traditionally been quite different. Under the Japanese family system, not only was men's economic role important but parents expected to live with a son and/or rely on him financially in old age. Survey data in chapter 6 show that when parents with at least one child of each sex are asked if they hope to live with any of their children in old age, nearly 40 percent state that they hope to live with a son, fewer than 10 percent hope to live with a daughter, and the remaining parents anticipate not living with any of their children. Nearly three-quarters of all parents report that they hope to receive financial help from a son in old age and only 6 percent have this expectation vis-à-vis a daughter. This is balanced by greater expectations of emotional help from daughters (44 percent) than sons (31 percent) in old age.

Opinion polls show that Japanese parents have firm ideas about sex roles. Parents prefer to socialize their sons to be "masculine" (*otoko rashii*) and their daughters to be "feminine" (*onna rashii*) rather than raising children in a more gender-neutral way. Attitude surveys also demonstrate the continued prevalence of son preference and the importance placed on both a son's general economic role and his specific role in the succession of the household. When asked, "If you were only able to have one child during your lifetime, would you want a son or a daughter?" in a public opinion survey (Office of the Prime Minister,

Japan, 1979), 44 percent of a national random sample of Japanese adults replied that they would want a son, and only 26 percent that they would want a daughter. The remaining 31 percent indicated that either would be acceptable or answered, "Don't know." Among those who replied that they wanted a son, over one-third gave as their primary reason, "He would become a successor," and another one-third said, "I would be able to rely on him." On the other hand, nearly half of the people who wanted a girl cited a clear emotional reason: "She would be someone to talk to." An additional 30 percent said they wanted a daughter because she would be "gentle." This demonstrates a division of labor in parents' minds between sons and daughters: sons are valued largely for their economic role and for their role in continuing the household, and daughters are valued more in terms of an affective or emotional role.

Sex segregation in Japanese parents' expectations of their children's future roles is undoubtedly based in part on "traditional" values. But these expectations seem to be reinforced by the labor market as well. Surveys in the 1980s showed a widespread perception among the Japanese public that sex discrimination in employment is commonplace. In a national poll of a random sample of 3,000 adults conducted by the *Yomiuri* newspaper in April 1984, four-fifths of those surveyed believed that women were treated "disadvantageously" in hiring decisions, and slightly more felt that this extended to decisions regarding job rotation and promotion. Moreover, there is also evidence of popular perceptions of the low marginal utility of higher education for women entering the job market (Nihon Recruit Center 1984).

Incentives to rely on the younger generation for economic and emotional support combine with the perception of strong sex discrimination in the workplace to mean that Japanese parents are "acting rationally" if they use their financial and psychological resources to further the education of sons rather than that of daughters. The son who graduates from a good school has a greater chance of financial success than the daughter who does. This continues to have practical significance for parents into their old age.

Women's Indirect Economic Role: Nurturers of Males   Research on the Japanese family has emphasized the emotional predominance of the parent-child tie over the tie between spouses (Blood 1967; Vogel 1967; Coleman 1983). This is particularly the case for mothers and

TABLE 3.2

YOUNG JAPANESE WOMEN'S PREFERENCES
IN RESPONSIBILITY FOR CHILDREARING

	University graduates (%)	Junior college graduates (%)
Wish to raise children entirely on my own	88.5	96.8
Wish to carry out the important parts of childrearing on my own, and willing to entrust minor parts to another person	10.4	3.1
Whoever raises the child, it is acceptable	1.1	0.1
Total	100.0	100.0
N = 1,935		

SOURCE: Nihon Recruit Center 1984.

sons. The comments of an upper middle-class Tokyo mother in her late
thirties portray the importance mothers attach to their responsibilities:

> When a person is evaluated for some purpose, such as a job, the attitude
> is, "What kind of background do they come from?" They are entering an
> organization, so the company wants to know their organizational type of
> background—the kind of group they are coming out of. As mothers, we
> put aside our own desires for a number of years because we want to give
> our children the best kind of background that we can to prepare them.

This mother is putting herself squarely in the role of investing in
her children. Within the family, she is the high-status, knowledgeable
person (just as in the business enterprise, the employer or manager
plays such a role vis-à-vis young employees.) Japanese mothers' strong
sex segregation in educational aspirations for children was discussed in
chapter 2: mothers are three times more likely to express university
aspirations for a son than for a daughter.

Most Japanese mothers expect to invest much time and care in the
rearing of their children. Babysitting as a social institution—the temporary turning over of one's children to a near-stranger—has never
been a popular alternative. Table 3.2 demonstrates that an overwhelming percentage of young women want to raise their children entirely
on their own. Female university graduates are somewhat more willing
to entrust the care of their child on a part-time basis to another person,
but even so, only about 10 percent hold this attitude. Live-in, or part-

TABLE 3.3

HOUSEHOLD DIVISION OF LABOR:
RESPONSIBILITY FOR CLEANING

Country	Person responsible (%)					
	Wife	Husband	Children	Family as a whole	Other people	No answer
Japan	92.1	0.4	0.5	4.7	2.3	—
West Germany	86.9	0.8	0.3	8.2	3.3	0.5
England	85.0	1.6	0.6	9.0	1.4	2.5
United States	74.4	3.3	0.6	20.3	1.2	0.2
Sweden	74.3	3.3	0.7	20.7	0.7	0.3
Philippines	73.5	1.0	7.1	10.0	8.3	0.1

SOURCE: Office of the Prime Minister, Japan, 1982a.

time live-in, mothers or mothers-in-law are a boon to some working women, but frequently complicate family politics.

Casual observers often suggest that one of the principal ingredients of the Japanese economic miracle is that women assume virtually all the emotional and caretaking responsibilities for the family and leave men free to devote long hours to company life. Cross-cultural statistics demonstrate how sharply the sexual division of labor is defined in Japanese households as compared to the households of several other nations. As an example, Table 3.3 shows the distribution of responsibility among household members for cleaning tasks. (Cleaning is chosen here as a representative household task for illustrative purposes; the distribution of responsibility for cooking, washing, shopping, and cleanup after meals is very similar to the distribution for cleaning.) In Japan, over 90 percent of wives indicate that they are the ones responsible for carrying out the work. For this and other tasks surveyed, Japan consistently shows the highest percentage for wives' responsibility and almost always the lowest proportion for husbands'. In the United States and Sweden, on the other hand, more households have a distribution of domestic labor among family members. Along with the responsibility for household work also comes responsibility for decision-making—over the purchase of consumer goods, the household budget, savings and investment, and a range of other areas. Table 3.4 shows the answers to the question, "Who holds the final decision-making power over the management of the household budget?" Very

TABLE 3.4

HOUSEHOLD DIVISION OF LABOR:
MANAGEMENT OF HOUSEHOLD BUDGET

	Person responsible (%)					
Country	Wife	Husband	Both spouses	Family as a whole	Other people	No answer
Japan	79.4	5.2	11.8	1.2	1.8	0.6
West Germany	11.5	15.4	70.4	2.1	0.0	0.6
England	32.6	32.7	33.6	0.1	0.0	1.0
United States	36.5	14.6	45.5	2.3	0.1	1.0
Sweden	22.1	15.1	59.7	2.5	0.0	0.5
Philippines	84.1	3.4	11.5	0.1	0.2	0.7

SOURCE: Office of the Prime Minister, Japan, 1982a.

high proportions of women in Japan and the Philippines report this role relative to women in the other countries surveyed. A traditional saying reflects the degree to which Japanese women cherish their control in the household: "The best husband is healthy and absent."

Consistent with the highly sex-segregated division of household labor, Japanese women are more likely than women in other countries to feel that men are privileged within the household—this even though women make most of the household decisions. Fully 67 percent of Japanese wives hold this attitude, compared to 48 percent of American wives and similar or lower percentages of wives in the Philippines, Sweden, West Germany, and England (Table 3.5).

The comments of middle-aged men and women are striking in their humorous and light-hearted depiction of women's role as nurturers of males. A favorite expression I heard from more than one mid-career male white-collar worker describing his wife and children was "I have two children and one housekeeper." Likewise, women have their own modes of expression, such as the tongue-in-cheek comment of a married woman with two sons, "These days I am busy taking care of my three boys" (husband and two sons). Not coincidentally, the largest association of women in Japan remains the Shufuren, or association of housewives, offering testimony to the idea that an adult woman is first a housewife and perhaps secondarily a wage-earner.

TABLE 3.5

WOMEN'S OPINION AS TO
WHETHER MEN AND WOMEN HAVE
EQUAL POSITIONS IN THE HOME

	Opinion (%)			
Country	Men are favored	Men and women have an equal position	Women are favored	No answer
Japan	66.8	27.1	4.1	1.9
West Germany	40.3	47.1	10.8	1.8
England	48.5	42.5	7.5	1.5
United States	47.6	39.9	8.8	3.8
Sweden	31.2	62.8	2.5	3.5
Philippines	30.1	59.1	10.3	0.5

SOURCE: Office of the Prime Minister, Japan, 1982a.

A skilled blue-collar worker summarized work and family in his world as follows:

> We're lucky because we can give up almost everything for our work if we have to, and our family still holds together. If Americans behaved this way, I think the U.S. divorce rate would be much higher than it already is. In Japan, it is the contentment and well-being of the family as a *unit*, as a whole, that is important, not the contentment of individual family members. I can *understand* the American way, because after all we only have one life to live. But still, this is not the Japanese way of thinking.

He added a clear statement about the balance of power:

> My friend here and I, if we behave within certain limits outside our houses, we are welcomed by our wives when we go home. If we transgress those limits, our wives get mad at us [loud laughter]. We are all afraid of our wives.

These comments could be dismissed as the silly remarks of a worker with an attentive Western audience of one (me), except that the content of the conversation was repeated over and over again by other middle-aged people in different contexts and social settings. While women have been left out of the permanent employment process in postwar Japan and have not been invested in as valued employees, they have been positive actors (or actresses?) in the human capital development of husbands and sons. As the above quotations show, any account of male employment would be lopsided without an account of women as the emotional support of husbands. Conversely, any account of female employment would be lopsided if it focused only on women's shadow in the Japanese corporate world and did not consider women's role as investors in the human capital of household members.

The structure of the educational system and labor markets on the one hand and intrafamilial exchange on the other constitutes a system of human capital development that maintains gender stratification in the Japanese economy and a dual direct and indirect role for women. But social structure does not account for everything. Norms also influence the human capital development process. For example, if norms for women to marry at a certain age and to quit work soon afterward were not so strong, a statistical discrimination rule would make less sense to employers. Likewise, norms supporting the investment of much time and effort on the part of older, high-status people in the human capital development of younger people provide legitimacy to employers' investment in young employees and mothers' investment in sons. The remainder of this chapter considers the complementary role played by these two sets of norms—plus a third one that could be called the "norm of statistical discrimination"—vis-à-vis the institutional structure of Japan's human capital development system.

THE NORMATIVE ENVIRONMENT IN JAPAN

NORMS FOR MARRIAGE
AND OTHER LIFE TRANSITIONS

Talking to Japanese women approaching the *kekkon tekireiki* (or appropriate marriage age) is like listening to a clock tick. Evidence of this is the analogy comparing young women to Christmas cakes (sold every year around Christmastime in Japan). A popular Japanese riddle asks, "What resembles a Christmas cake?" The correct reply is: "A young woman." Why? "Because they are popular and sell like hot cakes up until 25, and after that you have a lot of trouble getting rid of them."

This is not just a stray riddle. Rather, it represents the common perception in Japanese society of when a woman should get married. According to a father in his forties, "In Japan, a woman should get married by the time she's 25. If she reaches 29 or 30 and she's still

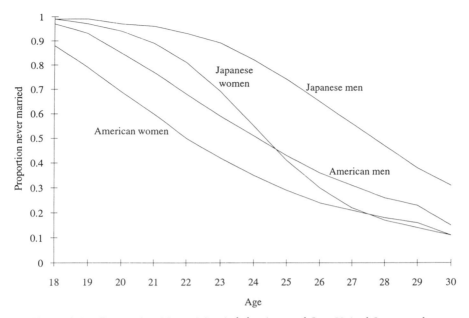

Figure 3.1.   Proportion Never Married, by Age and Sex, United States and Japan

SOURCE: U.S. Bureau of the Census 1984; Office of the Prime Minister, Japan, *Kokusei chōsa* (Population census), 1980.

single, well, it's almost hopeless." As a woman in her sixties, a retired government bureaucrat, commented, "Men don't want the *urenokori* [leftovers that didn't get sold]."

Not only is there a strong normative consensus on age at marriage, but the statistically low variance in behavior is striking. Chapter 2 put Japan in the context of Western industrial nations. Figure 3.1 compares the proportion of women who remain unmarried in Japan and the United States on a year-by-year basis and also includes data for men. The majority of Japanese women marry "on schedule" between the ages of 23 and 27. (Recent articles in Japanese newspapers suggest that the marriage age may be rising for women, but it is not clear whether or not this is being accompanied by an increase in the variance in age at marriage.) While about 95 percent of Japanese women are single at age 20 (compared to about 70 percent of American women), fewer than 25 percent are still unmarried at age 27. An equivalent proportion of American women remain unmarried at this age, but marriages up until that point have been spread out over a much broader age range.

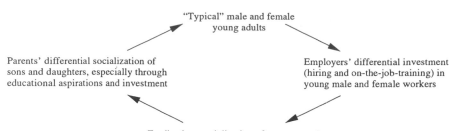

Figure 3.2.   Intergenerational Transmission of Sex-Role Stereotypes in Japan

Both American and Japanese men also show quite a bit of variation in age at marriage, and on average Japanese men are the last to marry.[11]

The dilemma facing Japanese women is that they encounter strong pressures to marry "on time," but, if they succumb to these, they are written off by employers, who consider them poor risks for investment in human capital via on-the-job training. As long as Japanese women continue to exhibit low variation in their age at marriage, employers can effectively minimize their losses by using a statistical discrimination rule, judging the timing of marriage and the subsequent quitting behavior by the sex of the job applicant. In this fashion, marriage norms and employer behaviors have fed back on each other in a vicious cycle. Kenneth Arrow terms this type of feedback process a "perceptual equilibrium" (1973, 1976). He argues that it is possible for the labor market to reach an equilibrium where employers assign women to jobs that involve little on-the-job training and few career prospects. By structuring some jobs in this way and expecting incumbents (women) to exhibit high turnover rates, employers actually encourage women to quit—to behave in the manner for which they have been labeled. In effect, the negative expectation comes to be built into the job. This notion also appears in the sociological literature on secondary labor markets, or labor markets whose jobs have relatively low wages and unstable working conditions (Doeringer and Piore 1971). Figure 3.2 shows the types of feedback processes that reinforce "expected" behaviors for Japanese men and women.

[11] Marini has argued that measurement of social norms necessitates the following: "(1) information on the acceptability of a behavior within the population of interest and (2) information on the strength of sanctions brought to bear when behavior is unacceptable" (1984: 240). I argue that much lower variance in the timing of a behavior such as marriage in one culture compared to another culture is also a way of demonstrating the existence of strong norms.

The strong pressure on Japanese women to get married and to have children on schedule is also felt by their superiors, who share in the responsibility for smooth, timely life transitions. One professor discussed with me the expectation on the part of parents that he, as a *sensei* (teacher), would assist in the delicate operation of finding marriage partners for his former female students. A few of these women were in their late twenties and still single. As their former mentor, the professor felt a responsibility to help introduce them into the next *ba*, or organizational setting, of their lives: marriage. He confided to me wearily that one anxious mother had a habit of calling him on the phone periodically and asking delicately, "Do you have any good news?"

This is one example of how the movement of a person from one group or organizational setting to another (e.g., from education to marriage, or education to work) is orchestrated partly by former mentors and others in a superordinate status, reflecting the strong norms of hierarchy in Japanese personal relations. Many Japanese have a sense that these life passages are not solely conducted for their own private benefit. An older woman who had worked most of her life said: "When you get married, you do it for the people around you. Of course you make sure the person is okay, but you have to take into account the person's background and so forth—even if the person is a good person himself it isn't good to marry him if his family isn't good. You have to take his background into account. . . . This used to be the way, and there are still a lot of people who behave that way." Similarly, when I asked one friend, a middle-level manager on his way up the promotional ladder in a major Japanese corporation, his opinion of why people seemed to be so marriage-oriented, his reply was: "It's what society and the people around you expect—it's the dominant *kachikan* [value orientation]. Gradually you feel you have to conform to it. It's expected." He continued on to say that among the hundreds of male white-collar employees he knew in his corporation, he did not know one case of divorce. His explanation? "It would hurt their job chances."

NORMS GOVERNING HUMAN RELATIONS

In 1970 Nakane Chie published what has since become a classic, if not totally accepted, description of Japanese social relations in her book *Japanese Society*. Nakane describes two types of social relations: hor-

izontally and vertically structured ones. A horizontal structure of relations involves more interactions among people who are status equals,
while a vertical structure involves a predominance of interactions
among people who are unequal in status (thus making the relation
"vertical"). Nakane views most social relations in Japan as being quin-
tessentially of the vertical type.

A less familiar, but quite complementary, view of Japanese human
relations was put forth in the late 1970s in *Bunmei to shite no ie shakai*
(*Ie* Society as a Pattern of Civilization), a massive treatise by Murakami Yasusuke, Kumon Shumpei, and Satō Seizaburō, three prominent
Japanese social scientists.[12] In their view, the *ie* (generally translated
into English as "household" but used by Murakami et al. as a broader
analytical construct) is the most common organizational form in contemporary Japanese society, economy, and politics. One of the most
significant organizational features of the *ie* is functional hierarchy,
which "aims at collectively fulfilling some function by assigning a specific part of this function to each individual stratum within the hierarchy" (Murakami 1984: 309). This principle of hierarchical role
differentiation involves an intense web of interpersonal relations and
repeated exchanges among people of different statuses within the same
organization.

I argue that in a society where vertical social ties and long-term
exchange relations predominate, human capital investment will be
more other-oriented (and less self-oriented) than in a society with a
preponderance of horizontal relationships. There is a great amount of
"social capital" (Coleman 1988) in an other-oriented system. Social
capital refers to the extent of obligations in relationships and the level
of trust that exists, trust that guarantees that obligations will be fulfilled and that both partners in the exchange will benefit. Long-term,
repeated interactions constitute the micro-level processes through
which human capital development is encouraged within the larger context of a social institution such as a family or a work organization. A
society like the United States, where horizontal ties are more prevalent,
will have a self-oriented system of human capital development. That
is, people will be "on their own" to a greater extent in investing in
their education and skills.

[12] *Bunmei to shite no ie shakai* received several awards in Japan, including the Odaka
Prize in 1981 for the best book in sociology. The authors' principal arguments are
summarized in English by Murakami Yasusuke in "*Ie* Society as a Pattern of Civilization," *Journal of Japanese Studies* 10, no. 2 (1984): 281–363.

These culturally patterned norms of interaction between people have important implications for the maintenance of gender stratification: other-orientation in human capital development has a conservatizing effect—in other words, the effect of maintaining continuity in existing social patterns. This can be seen in the contexts of both firm and family in Japan.

Norms for Hierarchical Relations within the Firm   Norms for human relations within the work organization constitute an important element of the Japanese employment system. A frequently cited Organization for Economic Cooperation and Development publication in 1977 concluded that the uniqueness of Japanese industrial relations lay not in its allegedly distinct institutions such as lifetime employment, seniority wages, and enterprise unionism but in a "fourth pillar"—the "social norms within the enterprise" (quoted in Shimada 1983: 4). These norms include an image of the enterprise as a community, a web of vertical relationships and reciprocal obligations, and a consensus-style decision-making system.

Japanese employers are important investors in other people's human capital through on-the-job training, but *senpai*, or older members of the work organization, also guide the individual (because my concern in this book is with how men and women fare differently in employment in urban settings, I focus here on the typical interpersonal relations within large work organizations; these relations would vary somewhat in other types of organizations). Men participate more than women in *senpai-kōhai* (senior-junior) relationships for a number of reasons. One is that the age-grading among male employees is stronger. The hiring process in Japanese firms accentuates the importance of the age cohort. Hiring occurs on a ritualized schedule, with job-hunting in the autumn (officially, students who will graduate the following spring cannot accept a job offer for that time until October 1) and the commencement of new jobs in April, the month after school graduation. These seasons are preceded by a summer during which many students seriously consider which company they would like to enter and a frenetic early autumn when published handbooks listing major Japanese firms flood university campuses. The fresh school graduate enters a company in the same month with a cohort of people. This phenomenon is taken for granted. In fact, many young Japanese with whom I talked could not picture how the timing of the U.S. recruiting system— or the lack thereof—could possibly result in an orderly labor market.

The efficient matching of individuals and firms is one clear outcome of these hiring practices (Rosenbaum and Kariya 1989). A second outcome varies for men and women: men have a much stronger sense of being in an entering cohort or group. Young men have no doubts about the fact that they are embarking on a lifetime of work. Many will remain with the same company for the duration of their working lives. In fact, a 1984 survey by the private research organization Recruit reported that the majority of young men who enter large companies feel they are competing, not with people who entered other companies in the same year, but with members of their age cohort in that company (Nihon Recruit Center 1985). Competition and camaraderie go hand in hand. In their study of employees in Japanese and U.S. manufacturing plants, Karyn Loscocco and Arne Kalleberg (1988) report that young Japanese men are more concerned than older men with getting along with their co-workers. This was not the case for U.S. manufacturing workers. The authors hypothesize that this reflects the hierarchical age structure of Japanese work groups, where Japanese men may feel considerable pressure to please their superiors.[13]

Japanese men start a lengthy new chapter in their lives when they enter the working world and a particular work organization. They are part of what Jean Lipman-Blumen (1976) calls a "homosocial" world—a world where social ties among members of the same sex will be very strong. A man in his mid thirties made the following statement to me about the salience of the workplace for Japanese men: "If a man loses his job or otherwise fails in his work life, his social life crumbles—they are that intimately related. If you correctly understand that, I think you can begin to see the pressures under which Japanese men work. And understanding that helps you to understand the position of Japanese women too."

In contrast to the great psychological salience of work for Japanese men, which is wrapped up partially with continuity in one work organization and membership in an age cohort, women are likely to experience intermittent employment in the course of their lives. Their consistent reference group will not be the other female members of the

[13] Loscocco and Kalleberg also report that tenure in the company is positively related to work commitment on the part of Japanese, but not American, men. Of course, causality could operate in both directions here. Those Japanese men who have a greater commitment to work may have a higher probability of being selected into career-track positions. Likewise, men in career-track positions may develop a greater work commitment because of the wage increases and promotions associated with their jobs.

cohort entering a company upon school graduation. I interviewed the
first woman in Japan ever to become a *buchō* (department chief) in a
corporation, who had this to say:

> Since everyone enters the company in April, when a few women start
> quitting later on, the work attitude of the others weakens. Likewise, the
> men who start out as a cohort are closely knit. . . . When I started out, if
> one didn't have a boyfriend in the company, it was very hard to get much
> of the valuable, casual type of information about the work or job [laughter].
> Now things have changed and it's not so much that way, but a lot of the
> *tsukiai* [socializing and discussion] still takes place outside of formal
> "working" hours. This makes it difficult for women.

In a similar vein, a white-collar worker in his late twenties expressed
the frank worry that "there are no *senpai* [older colleagues or men-
tors], no models for young female employees, and we [men in my age
group] don't feel like we can do a very good job [in that respect]."
Even when women express seriousness about their career intentions,
their senior colleagues are ill-equipped to train them. In reference to
the civil service, generally touted as the most gender-blind occupational sphere in Japanese society, Lebra states: "Being a risky investment
as a career employee, a woman needs a special 'guarantor' responsible
for whatever will happen to her" (1981: 299). In an other-oriented
system of human capital development, the scarcity of higher-status others or "guarantors" willing to socialize and train female workers per-
petuates gender stratification in the labor force. This scarcity is
likewise reinforced by the predictability with which Japanese women
marry at particular ages. At this point, they take on their primary
commitment, reflected in the fact that marriage is sometimes jokingly
referred to as women's "lifetime employment" (*eikyū shūshoku*).

The widespread custom among white-collar workers of socializing
after work also reinforces ties among males. The practice is upheld
mainly through a feeling that socializing or engaging in *tsukiai* (loosely
translated as informal social functions) with one's workmates helps
people to understand each other better and to carry out joint tasks at
the workplace more efficiently (Atsumi 1979; Rohlen 1975). The per-
vasiveness of after-hours drinking was reflected in comments by a *tanshin funin* (worker dispatched to a different part of the country). In
recent years, *tanshin funin* have become common. When transferred by
the company to another office for one or two years, most male workers
do not move their families. The costs of finding new housing and the

fear of adversely affecting children's education (and subsequent examination success) mitigate against a family move. A *tanshin funin* spoke frankly to me about the adjustments in his family life while he was away, adjustments that sound comical but bittersweet:

> [My wife and I] decided from the beginning that I would telephone home on Wednesday evening at a certain time to talk to the children—we were the most worried about the communication between me and the children. Often I was out drinking at the appointed hour, so I called from wherever I was. My children could hear the background music. I remember them saying to me, "Daddy, you are always listening to music, aren't you?"

More accurately, the children could have asked, "Daddy, you are always spending time with your co-workers, aren't you?" This is a question few Japanese children would have occasion to ask their mothers.

Norms for Hierarchical Relations in the Family   A tendency toward other-oriented investment is also strong in Japanese families. Most Japanese move straight from their family's home into marriage, with perhaps a stint in a boardinghouse while at university or in a company dormitory between these two stages. For the majority of people, there is no period of living on one's own. In contrast, for many young people in the United States, such a period is a very important formative time— a time when one adjusts to the idea of adult responsibilities. For Japanese, adulthood comes in tandem with the assumption of the familial responsibilities of husband or wife, and, soon thereafter, parent. Being an adult *means* being a spouse and parent. In this sense, one's status is very much tied to one's place in a group; a group that will be permanent, a group to which one has a commitment.

There are several reasons why many Japanese in their twenties continue living with their parents. Two of the main ones are the pressure from companies and the extreme financial difficulties of being on one's own, especially in Tokyo with its high housing costs. Many large companies have traditionally refused to hire young unmarried women living in apartments of their own, viewing them as less than virtuous. As one middle-aged woman commented to me: "Many companies won't hire a young woman who lives alone because they think that there is something wrong with her. And if some kind of trouble occurs, the manager is responsible for her and has to look into it. So in order to avoid such problems, they don't hire women who live alone to begin with." In contrast to the United States, where many young highly educated women defer marriage and have a period of time in which to experience financial and psychological independence, adulthood for the vast majority of Japanese women means transferring from being a daughter to being a wife—one's status or place is defined in relation to others (Lebra 1984).

This self-definition in relation to others or to the group holds for men as well. The developmental sequence for young men could be more accurately capsulized in a son-employee-husband sequence, with work status as an inevitable component of the transition to adulthood. The sense of being a son or a daughter remains stronger among Japanese than among Americans across the life cycle. People have a certain sense of what they should be doing with their lives vis-à-vis parental expectations rather than vis-à-vis self-expectations. A subtle yet profound difference in the roots of identity in Japan and the United States is summed up in the stark statement of a Japanese graduate student in educational psychology who commented, "When I read [Erik] Erikson's work, I couldn't understand it. We don't need a self-identity."

The links between parents and children—the threads of obligation, expectation, communication, sometimes resentment—were portrayed in many comments made to me by men and women in their twenties who were facing the difficult decisions of young adulthood. The following juxtaposition gives the views of three generations on parent-child relations in the Japanese family.

An unmarried 28-year-old *kaishain* (company employee) who had graduated from a private, internationally oriented Japanese university, said:

> I just wouldn't feel right if I looked at my parents several years from now and saw them living by themselves. It's not that I would feel guilty, exactly, but that I would think it was sad and lonely for them. . . . In Japan, a big reason people have children is so that they will have company and have someone to look after them [*mendō o miru*] when they get older. I feel that way too about having children. If that kind of parent-child relationship doesn't exist in the United States, I wonder why people have children. . . . I also want to have children so that my parents can have grandchildren to play with and enjoy.

Nowhere in our conversation did the possibility of *not* having children arise. Another man, who was in his early forties, said:

> I think Japanese look at children differently than you do in the West. We consider our children as direct extensions of ourselves, as almost indistinguishable from ourselves. Can you understand what I mean? It seems to

me that in the West you try to teach your children to be independent and autonomous. It's not quite the same in Japan. I think we rely on each other more.

And a man in the next generation, in his late sixties, commented to me: "The individual Japanese leads a historical existence, whereas Americans live more in the present. The connections between ancestors, parents, and children are closer for Japanese than for Americans."

These norms for maintaining close connections between older and younger people mean that socialization processes and intergenerational exchanges and investments continue over a long period of time; the individual is cradled, yet constrained, by a certain degree of security and predictability. A pervasive norm of statistical discrimination in Japan adds to this.

The Norm of Statistical Discrimination   In Japanese education and employment, people are treated as if they fit the "average." And in fact there is little variance around the mean in many social behaviors. During the public debate in 1984 over a proposed Equal Employment Opportunity Law in Japan many employers protested that they would be forced to hire women who did not have a strong commitment to work and who would leave the company after a few years to get married. The issue of whether some women did *not* represent the statistical average, or would prefer not to, rarely arose in public discussion. Rather than criticizing the unfairness of treating all women as if they fit the mean, a comment one would expect to hear in the United States, discussion went round repetitively about whether women, as members of a particular social category, *should* work or not. This tendency to regard people in terms of their membership in a social category pervades Japanese social institutions. Women are supposed to be a certain way because they are women, men because they are men. In the educational system, children are treated equally—no one can either skip or be held back a year, and tracking by ability *within* schools is heavily resisted. By law, one must be eighteen to enter university. In short, Japanese society has a highly refined system of both age and gender grading, working against people who do not fit the norms of behavior for their age and sex. Quite revealing was the comment made by a foreman during a factory tour I took in 1985 with a group of students and a (female) professor from a junior college: "Where is the man? I mean, where is the *sensei* [teacher]?"

This treatment of the individual according to the "average" manifests itself visually in many curious ways in Japan. In banks and other customer-oriented workplaces, women often wear uniforms and men do not. In the Tokyo bank where I did business, the person who handled routine bill-paying was a man. Despite his low status in the organization, he did not wear a uniform. He was surrounded, though, by young female tellers who invariably *were* in uniforms of a bright, whimsical print. Also, men carry business cards giving their name and status within the organization. Women typically do not, presumably because their status in the organization does not merit such individuation. The sheer predictability of the distribution of these social indicators across the sexes is often breathtaking.

The Recruit company, which publishes magazines targeted for job-hunters, joined with a number of employers in the late 1980s in opposing the Japanese Ministry of Labor's plans to ban job advertisements that specify the sex of the applicant (Saso 1990). Traditionally, many classified job advertisements in Japanese newspapers have specified not only the sex but the age range for applicants. Despite objections by bar associations and women's groups, the Ministry of Labor decided to permit employers to continue to advertise "women's jobs" as such. Once again, the social designation of the "average"—what is considered appropriate for members of one sex and not the other—has been asserted. The system of grading by age and gender is reinforced by the fact that Japanese society is dominated by norms of hierarchical association and other-oriented investment. The investment in a younger person's human capital means that if the younger person succeeds (e.g., in marriage or in the labor market), the investor gets returns. The returns may be in the form of social prestige, in a society where one is judged almost as much by the quality of the people closest to one as by personal accomplishments. Or it may be in the form of increased labor productivity (accruing from employee to employer) or old-age support (accruing from children to parents).

This chapter has shown how Japan's system of human capital development shapes distinct roles for men and women, roles that come to be viewed as "rational" and legitimate. Intersecting and supporting the two parts of the human capital development system—the articulation between the educational system and the workplace, and the structured exchanges within families—are norms regarding marriage timing, human relations, and statistical discrimination (non-deviance). The picture sketched here should not, however, be interpreted as a monolithic, forever-static system, but rather as a system in equilibrium. Change could come from a number of directions, and this will be the subject of the last chapter. The task of the next three chapters is to explore the historical development of the institutions that structure gender roles, and to investigate their implications for individual lives more deeply.

FOUR

The Evolution of a Gendered Employment System

Many foreign observers, and most of all foreign business-
men, look at Japan as a kind of "paradise." Perhaps
no factor is more readily responsible for this assessment
than the labor situation.

Ohkawa Kazushi and Henry Rosovsky,
Japanese Economic Growth *(1973: 118)*

Japanese companies do not promote women.

Rodney C. Clark,
The Japanese Company *(1979: 118)*

These two statements represent divergent evaluations of Japanese labor relations in the postwar period. On the one hand, the Japanese employment and industrial relations system has reaped a rich litany of praise from Western observers. Some of this praise has focused on efficiency and productivity, and some on the equalities generated among workers (but not, notably, between men and women). Observers have noted a number of indications of efficiency in Japanese labor relations: low turnover and absenteeism rates, low rates of strike activity, and careful matching of workers to jobs. Japanese manufacturing industries show an average monthly separation rate, a measure of employee turnover, that has consistently been about half that in U.S. manufacturing throughout the postwar period (Koshiro 1983c).[1] Rates of absenteeism are also extremely low in Japan—around 1 or 2 percent when absences owing to paid vacations and leaves are eliminated. The

---

[1] The separation rate is calculated as the ratio of the decrease in the number of employees during a given month to the number of employees at the end of the prior month. The decrease in number of employees includes those who were dismissed, discharged, or transferred to other plants in the same company; those who were not paid during the month because of labor disputes or suspensions; and those who retired (Koshiro 1983c).

109

Japanese government actually took steps in the 1980s to encourage workers to take their *paid* vacations (Japan Economic Institute 1990). A further indicator of efficiency is reflected in the youth labor market, which in the United States exhibits a high level of turnover as young workers and employers attempt to make mutually beneficial matches. The total youth turnover rate (including voluntary and involuntary job separations) in Japan is about one-third that of the United States; involuntary job separations alone (being fired or laid off) are even less frequent in Japan (Rosenbaum and Kariya 1989).[2]

Discussions of high Japanese productivity have also permeated the recent popular and academic literature on Japan, centering especially on quality-control circles (Cole 1979; Koshiro 1983c) and the rapid adoption of automation without deleterious effects on either the demand for labor or on workers' satisfaction. The earnings of Japanese male employees in manufacturing increase with the level of plant automation; the earnings of their counterparts in the United States decrease (Kalleberg and Lincoln 1988).[3]

The Gini coefficient of income inequality, a commonly used measure, is low in Japan relative to other industrial countries. The wages and working conditions of male Japanese blue- and white-collar workers who work in firms of the same size are also similar. With firm size controlled for, the wages of Japanese male employees in different occupations bear a greater resemblance to each other than in the United States (Kalleberg and Lincoln 1988). Further, the age-wage profile of Japanese *blue-collar workers* in large firms (the rate of increase in wages as the worker ages) resembles that for *white-collar workers* in countries such as France and Germany. And Japanese fringe benefits, at least for workers in firms with thirty or more employees, vary little by occupation (Koike 1983a).

This collection of observations should not be taken lightly. Clearly, there are many laudable aspects in the postwar development of the Japanese employment system and industrial relations. But one crucial

---

[2] Observers also have claimed for many years that Japan demonstrates more *harmonious* labor relations than other industrial countries. This claim appears to be somewhat more tenuous. Far fewer workdays are lost owing to work stoppages in Japan than in the United States, Canada, Italy, and Britain, but more are lost than in France, West Germany, and Sweden. The average duration of Japanese strikes is low for an industrial country but by no means the lowest (Shirai 1983). Measures of worker satisfaction also leave unresolved the issue of whether workers in Japan are markedly more content with their jobs and working conditions than workers in other countries.
[3] These findings do not hold for female workers.

element is left out in this picture, an element addressed by the second of the two quotations with which this chapter opened: Where do women fit in? How does the structure of employment and industrial relations, praised for efficiency, productivity, and equality, affect women's position in the economy? I argued in chapter 3 that the Japanese system of human capital development works against equal positions for men and women in the labor force. It is the task of this chapter to examine how that system came into being.

THE CONSCIOUS EVOLUTION
OF THE JAPANESE EMPLOYMENT SYSTEM

The Japanese employment system exhibits what could be called a "conscious evolution." Early research on the system emphasized continuities from Japan's preindustrial past, the tone for this view being set by James Abegglen's classic study, *The Japanese Factory* (1958). Abegglen was the first Western observer to report to the American scholarly community many of the now-familiar characteristics of the prototypical Japanese factory: long-term employment, wages based heavily on length of service, extensive on-the-job training, and what he perceived to be a strong sense of commitment and shared community between employers and workers. These he viewed as carryovers from preindustrial labor relations, where workers and employers participated in a shared community and in a structured system of hierarchical, paternalistic relations.

Subsequent to Abegglen's ground-breaking work, further research into the nature of employment in nineteenth- and early twentieth-century Japan revealed that long-term employment in industry was rare. The Japanese employment system represents neither a natural continuation of agricultural labor policies nor an innovation that occurred in the industries, such as textiles, that initiated Japan's industrialization. Although wage-labor did exist in textiles, it was short-term employment. Outside of textiles, most industrial labor operated on a putting-out system in the nineteenth century. Agricultural labor in the Tokugawa period (1600–1868) often involved long-term hierarchical relations on what could be termed a Japanese-style patron-client (*oyabun-kobun*) model. But by the mid nineteenth century, these relations had been largely replaced by daily or seasonal wage labor.

Instead of representing a natural evolutionary process, the permanent employment system was a conscious response by management and workers to specific structural conditions in heavy industry in the period between the two world wars. This is quite different from a view that argues for the natural continuity of cultural traditions. Tradition and ideology played a role in the development of the system, to be sure, but this role is best seen as constructed by the important social actors of the historical moment. An early article by Robert Cole expressed this point in the following way:

> It is necessary to examine the role of ideology in legitimating a new practice such as permanent employment. At the very least, it can be maintained that the adoption of permanent employment in the World War I period was supported by and cloaked in traditional values of familism, unity of the social group, and emphasis on place (membership in the firm) rather than the specific qualities of individuals. That is, this new practice was cloaked in the rhetoric of traditional values—the importance of the corporate group—to insure its acceptance.... Under permanent employment, company officials applied the remolded traditional symbols to relate the employee to the firm.
>
> (Cole 1971b: 51–52)

Japanese permanent employment is, to use Eric Hobsbawm's terms, an "invented tradition," a set of practices that represent an "attempt to establish continuity with a suitable historic past" (Hobsbawm 1983: 1).

What forces shaped the development of the permanent employment system and why were women excluded from it? To answer these questions, it is necessary to examine the nature of Japan's industrialization process and labor supply conditions from the late nineteenth century on.

EARLY INDUSTRIALIZATION: TEXTILES

The textile industry played a critical role in early Japanese industrialization, beginning in the last quarter of the nineteenth century. In the decade 1874–85, the textile industry was responsible for 26 percent of Japanese manufacturing output. By the last decade of the Taishō period, 1917–26, this figure had risen to 36 percent. Not only did textiles dominate pre–World War II industrialization in Japan to a greater extent than in Western countries, but by international standards the Japanese textile industry was very heavily female. In 1930, fully 81 percent of Japanese cotton textile workers were female, a decline of only 2 percentage points from 1909. In contrast, women made up about 60 percent of the cotton textile labor force in the United Kingdom throughout the nineteenth century, and figures for the United States and France show that women's participation there was closer to 50 percent and was steadily declining by the turn of the century (Saxonhouse 1976).

The great majority of Japanese women textile workers were young women of rural origin. Rural poverty and a labor surplus in agriculture at the turn of the twentieth century gave impulse to this in rural areas—many parents signed labor contracts of several years' duration for their daughters to work in factories, and wages were remitted back to the family. Women were housed in dormitory conditions that are remote indeed from our modern conception of "the firm as family" and benevolent welfare capitalism. Indeed, in contrast to the positive incentive structure of seniority wages and extensive fringe benefits that would eventually develop for male blue-collar and white-collar workers, the incentive structure for female textile workers seems to have been largely based on negative sanctioning for absenteeism, tardiness, drowsiness on the job, or other offenses (Tsurumi 1990). Diaries and songs of the early factory women reveal that the ideal was to work one's term and return home to marry and resume village life. Instead, many young women were worked to the bone and died of tuberculosis or other diseases (Hosoi 1925; Tsurumi 1990). A survey of twenty-eight of Japan's forty-seven prefectures in 1910 showed that only about 40 percent of the temporary female textile workers eventually returned to their homes, and of that group about 16 percent had a serious disease such as tuberculosis (Ishihara 1914, as cited by Hazama 1976). Returning home was difficult partly because women with factory experience were often looked down upon in their home villages and had difficulty finding a good marriage partner. Women who stayed in the cities generally either married another factory worker or, owing to the lack of other alternatives, entered prostitution (Hazama 1976).

Permanent employment policies did not develop in the textile industry. Throughout its dominance into the 1930s as the main engine of Japan's industrialization, the industry was plagued by high turnover. As Gary Saxonhouse has written: "What is probably most unusual about this industry in the Japanese context is the composition of its labor force. In a nation which has made lifetime employment its ideal if not its practice, the cotton textile industry throughout its fifty-year journey to world dominance relied almost entirely on a labor force of women whose average (mean) entrant lived in a company dormitory and stayed at work no more than two years" (Saxonhouse 1976: 98). Although male competition for textile factory jobs did occur in a number of other countries, this did not happen in Japan. Young, female short-term labor remained the rule.

To investigate why turnover remained so high in the textile industry, Saxonhouse carried out a creative counterfactual analysis. He showed that an increase in workers' length of service, had employers been able to achieve it, would have increased productivity in the industry. But in the pre–World War II period, employers did not pay textile workers high enough wages to keep them from moving to another factory or back to rural areas; beginning workers generally earned less than agricultural workers of the same sex, age, and experience level. Saxonhouse's explanation is that employers were unwilling to pay the costs of training (by offering higher starting wages) because of the technical uniformity across cotton-spinning mills. The uniformity in machines and the intensive flow of technical information among firms rendered any training offered by the employer *general training* rather than training specific to that firm. Thus a worker, equipped with initial training, could quit the company in search of higher wages and the employer would suffer the loss incurred by the expense of having trained a worker, only to lose her subsequently.

Although not pointed out by Saxonhouse, this constituted a vicious cycle for employers and female employees. If wages were low and working conditions harsh, turnover was apt to be high. Likewise, if the threat of turnover was high, the employer's incentive to offer higher wages and better working conditions was low—especially if, as in Saxonhouse's argument, technology mitigated against offering training that would bind the worker to the firm.

In short, permanent employment policies failed to develop in the part of the industrial economy where women labored prior to World War II. Nor were such policies relevant in agriculture, where the remainder of the female labor force was located.

Asserting that the system of lifetime employment either did not exist or was quite rare in early industrialization is not the same as saying that there was no ideology to support such a system. Here, the debate becomes muddier. At various points, scholars such as Cole (1971b) and Dore (1973) have suggested that ceteris paribus (i.e., if it is economically practicable), there may be a Japanese cultural preference for welfare corporatism. (See Fruin 1978 for an excellent capsule review of the nuances in the debate over the origins and continuation of the lifetime employment system.) But the majority of scholars agree that the system existed only in pockets of industry in the prewar period and only came into its own with post–World War II economic growth.

The above discussion should serve to demonstrate that the Japanese employment system was *not* a natural outgrowth of either preindustrial or early industrial employment relations. Instead, it is a *designed system*. Although compatible with cultural values stressing hierarchical human relations and a conception of community, it did not flow naturally and irrevocably from such values. What conditions, then, were necessary for long-term employment relationships, on-the-job training, seniority-based compensation, and welfare corporatism to become economically rational policy choices for Japanese employers?

LABOR SUPPLY AND DEMAND IN PREWAR JAPAN

In the early phases of Japanese industrialization, unskilled rural labor was plentiful. The early mining and textile industries had a highly elastic supply of labor from which to draw. But the supply of *skilled* workers was substantially different. Although basic literacy levels were high, fewer than 5 percent of the population received more than the compulsory six-year education (Cole and Tominaga 1976). Workers with either vocational education or higher education were thus scarce. Poaching of skilled workers became a serious problem by the 1890s, even among government factories in the munitions industry (Crawcour 1978). Early attempts on the part of employers to draft and enforce regulations to prevent labor from moving from firm to firm in search of higher wages and better working conditions were sometimes successful, sometimes not. Recruiting agents were common in the textile industry because of the need to search out and recruit labor from rural areas. Infringements were common: some recruiters pledged that a girl would work for multiple factories and then collected agent fees from all of them (Tsurumi 1990).[4]

---

[4] Such abrogations of the agreement between recruiters and employers demonstrate the classic problem of agency to which American economists and political scientists have devoted so much attention in recent years (Moe 1984). Curiously, the problem has rarely if ever been discussed in the literature of Japanese studies in terms of agency and monitoring costs. This is but one demonstration among many of the unfortunate divergencies between the area studies literature, replete with empirical examples, and the theoretical social science literature.

In the 1890s, the way many skilled laborers entered factories was through the auspices of *oyakata*, master artisans, who in the pre-Meiji (pre-1868) era had passed on craft privileges to their apprentices (Jacoby 1979). Employers in the early factories depended by necessity on the *oyakata* in finding skilled laborers. But such laborers often moved among *oyakata* in order to increase their wages. Thus employers' reliance on *oyakata* as intermediaries was not a very satisfactory solution to the skilled labor shortage. In response, employers in some industries attempted to form cooperative associations, vowing not to hire applicants who did not have discharge papers from their previous employer detailing the length of their employment and the wage rate (Crawcour 1978). It has been argued persuasively by Sydney Crawcour and others, however, that given the coordination among employers this necessitated, a two-pronged approach to labor mobility was critical: not only would employers attempt to cooperate with one another in controlling the inflation of wages and the demands of skilled workers, but incentives would be offered to skilled workers to remain with the firm. In other words, the labor pool, already segregated between skilled and unskilled labor, could be further segregated between those skilled workers who were willing to be hired at low starting wages, with the promise of job security and increases in wages over time, and those who preferred to job-hop. The employers' preference was to enlarge the former category and cause the latter to shrink.

Whereas textile workers were available in large supply from rural households, skilled workers in machine-related trades were scarcer (Clark 1979). In the early factories in the machinery, shipbuilding, and rolling-stock industries, a typical apprenticeship was intended to last three to five years. In practice, many workers left one factory midway through their apprenticeship to seek employment as skilled workers in another factory. Traineeships in metal or glass factories were somewhat longer, on the order of five to six years. Yokoyama Gennosuke reported that in the late 1890s, the trainees in such factories were highly mobile: only about one-third finished out their terms (Yokoyama 1898, cited in Gordon 1985). At the Ishikawajima Shipyard and the Shibaura Engineering Works, two of the oldest and largest privately owned factories in Tokyo at the beginning of the twentieth century, more than 80 percent of the workers had been at their current job for five years or less (Gordon 1985).

The shortage of skilled labor and the inability of employers to retain workers they had trained became more acute by the 1920s as the metal, machinery, and chemical industries adopted more advanced technologies in order to compete in international markets.[5] As Hazama Hiroshi writes:

> The managers of large enterprises during this period had two major goals: to train and retain superior skilled workers and to deal with the labor movement, that is, to retain on a long-term basis capable workers whose ideologies were moderate. Those considered most suitable were children from middle-level farm households, or a level close to it, with no occupational experience. In terms of capability, graduates of middle schools (that is, those with more than compulsory education) with good scholastic records were preferred. As large factories began to hire with emphasis on quality rather than quantity, they began to select their own workers rather than recruit them publicly or hire them through *oyakata* [labor bosses].
>
> (Hazama 1976: 35)

Some employers in heavy industry in the first few decades of the twentieth century had hired *oyakata* and their apprentices into the company as a group. This had been an uneasy solution to the labor shortage, given laborers' mixed allegiances to the *oyakata* and to the firm, and the extremely questionable allegiance of the *oyakata* to the firm. Over time, employers reduced their dependence on *oyakata* by effectively coopting them through offers of varied incentives, such as predetermined salaries and titles. More significant, by the 1920s, many large factories instituted a policy of hiring workers directly into the company in April, when graduates started new jobs after the end of the school year in the winter. "The result was a hiring system in which a minority of inexperienced young boys regularly entered a firm each year as a favored group expected to become future workshop leaders and career employees, while managers drew the majority of factory laborers from a pool of mobile, often unemployed adult wage earners," concludes Andrew Gordon (1985: 126).

---

[5] Some scholars have argued that employers' adoption of seniority-based wage payment schemes and promotion policies was a response to the need to retain workers who had received firm-specific training. It is not altogether clear whether this is a good explanation in the context of the early twentieth century. As Sanford Jacoby points out, "it is not at all certain that machinery or technology was becoming more enterprise-specific at the time of the formation of internal labor markets in Japan (or even in the U.S., for that matter)" (Jacoby 1979: 189). Data on the specificity of factory technologies are very hard to come by. Yet this is what would be required in order to test the hypothesis that it was the development of firm-specific technologies and training that led employers to institute policies to reduce labor turnover. Whether or not this is indeed part of the explanation, a major reason for employers' efforts was their desire to wrest the control of labor supply from *oyakata* and to foster skilled workers' dependence and allegiance to the firm.

WOMEN WORKERS AND THE DECLINING IMPORTANCE OF THE TEXTILE INDUSTRY

Workers in the newly developing heavy industries were almost all male. Women made up 62 percent of the manufacturing sector in 1909, the date of the first factory census in Japan. But of these women, fully 84 percent were in the textile industry. Whereas men constituted only about a third of the manufacturing labor force at that time, they were much more evenly spread across the textile, machinery, chemical, food and beverage, and other industries. By 1940, the situation had changed dramatically. The textile industry had constituted over half of all manufacturing employment in 1909, but it represented only one-quarter of such employment in 1940. In contrast, the initially small metal and machinery industry and chemical and ceramic industries had risen to a position of prominence: about 60 percent of manufacturing workers in 1940 worked in these industries. Most such workers were males (Cole and Tominaga 1976). Indeed, the number of male manufacturing workers increased by a factor of 1.7 in the decade between 1928 and 1937 alone, whereas the number of women increased only by a factor of 1.2 (Office of the Prime Minister, Japan, 1938).

While it is tempting to ask where female workers went if they did not go into the textile industry, this question is prompted by a contemporary Western conception of female employment. It is important to remember that the majority of female textile workers were young, single rural women who were working as part of the family economy. They were neither autonomous wage earners supporting themselves nor were they typically the heads of households. Single women were by no means starting careers, and if employment opportunities were not expanding as rapidly in the textile industry as before, these women were likely to be employed on the farms that their brothers and other male relatives were leaving in ever-larger numbers. Women were not absorbed into any other wage-employment sector besides textiles. True, the proportion of women among white-collar employees doubled in the 1930s. But the numbers were low: women made up only 6.5 percent of white-collar employees in 1930 and 15 percent in 1940. Thereafter this rate crept slowly upward. Moreover, neither manufacturing nor clerical work was at all common among *married* women prior to World War II; even by 1950, fewer than 10 percent of all married women worked as paid employees in the economy. Thus it is apparent that women were simply not present in that part of Japanese industry

where permanent employment policies were taking shape in the pre–
World War II period. As the development of the textile industry and
heavy industry increasingly diverged, a dualistic structure emerged in
the heavy industries of the Japanese economy.

THE DEVELOPMENT OF DUALISM IN THE ECONOMY

Although the size of the average factory remained fairly small in the
pre–World War II period, heavy industries showed a steep increase in
the proportion of labor employed in factories of over 500 people. By
1928, nearly 60 percent of labor in the machinery industry was concentrated in such factories, compared to 40 percent in the spinning
industry (Hazama 1976). Major changes between the time of the first
census of factories in 1909 and the end of the prewar period led to a
demarcation of industries from one another. Yasuba Yasukichi (1976)
has classified industries as dualistic or homogeneous, according to the
size of the wage differential between establishments of different sizes.
Dualistic industries show more wage variation, and homogeneous industries demonstrate a flatter distribution of wages. By the 1930s, a
dualistic structure had developed in most heavy industries such as iron
and steel, bricks and tiles, primary metals, cement and cement products, ceramics, and printing. Workers were concentrated mainly either
in very large firms or in firms of under ten workers; many of the
smallest firms operated on a subcontractual basis under large ones.
The dualistic industries, like spinning and other textile industries in the
earlier period, were undergoing rapid technical changes as a result of
the adoption of foreign technology. The wage structure in these new
dualistic industries of the 1930s was marked by wages in large establishments that were higher than the average for large enterprises in the
economy overall. The lighter industries that had gradually developed a
more homogeneous wage structure paid lower-than-average wages in
the large firms and wages in small firms that were equivalent to those
in small enterprises in other industries (Yasuba 1976).

Women's virtual absence in heavy industry meant that they were not
among the workers who benefited from the wage structure developing
in large firms there. Nor did they benefit from the more homogeneous
structure of wages by firm size in the textile industry, for wages overall
were lower than in heavy industry. In the earlier part of the century,
many of the dualistic industries in Japan had been textile-related,
whereas the heavy and chemical industries had shown little wage

variation by establishment size. But dualism in the textile industry had not benefited women, for in contrast to the dualism that later developed in the heavy industries, dualism did not raise the wages in large textile factories above the economywide average for large establishments.

The benefits eventually reaped by the male monopoly in skilled labor in heavy industry are reflected in the historical trend in the male-female wage differential. In 1882, women's mean average wages in the economy had been 59 percent of men's. By 1938, this figure had dropped to 34 percent (Hazama 1976). Whereas the male-female wage gap narrowed among agricultural workers between 1900 and 1940, the gap in manufacturing grew ever wider (Taira 1970). This was an outcome of the long-term employment and seniority wage policies that employers in heavy industries offered their most valuable employees, all of whom were male.

Still, it would be a mistake to conclude that permanent employment policies with seniority-based wage systems and on-the-job training were extended to a very broad segment of the population in the pre–World War II period. Even restricting the discussion to male employees, the vast majority were not permanently employed. Permanent employment remained a prerogative of large firms. Throughout the early decades of the twentieth century, nearly 40 percent of Japanese manufacturing employees worked in establishments with fewer than 50 workers, and an additional 10 percent or so worked in enterprises of 50–100 workers (Granovetter 1984). High rates of self-employment and family enterprise employment obtained for both men and women. Even as late as 1950, fewer than one-half of all Japanese men and fewer than one-quarter of women were paid employees. Nearly 40 percent of men were self-employed, and the majority of women workers were in family enterprises, either agricultural or small manufacturing or sales establishments. Thus, only a small minority of men worked under seniority-based wage systems, while the majority worked under less permanent employment conditions, in their own small businesses, or on their farms. Women were mainly outside the system of wage employment altogether. Those who did receive wages were young, single women who were working only temporarily before attaining the desired goal of marriage.[6]

---

[6] The explanation given above for the evolution of Japanese incentive schemes, based more on the strategic reactions of employers to the labor market than on cultural proclivities for long-term, harmonious relations, finds support in the American labor economics litera-

THE POSTWAR PERIOD AND THE STABILIZATION
OF LONG-TERM EMPLOYMENT

The shortage of skilled labor as well as the threat of unionization had prompted some employers in the pre–World War II period to institute firm-specific training and a wage determination process that rewarded seniority in the firm. But during and after the war, the constellation of social actors arguing for seniority-based employment policies shifted. In his work on labor-management relations in heavy industry, Gordon claims that the government emerged during the 1930s as a principal actor in the worker-management relationship. In the late 1930s, the state issued a series of regulations on wages and company welfare policies:

> A continuous flow of books, pamphlets, and official statements encouraged managers to design wages to meet the livelihood or life-cycle needs of workers: wages should rise with age, the best single proxy for need; income should meet minimum livelihood needs and should therefore be stable, ideally distributed in the form of a monthly salary; incentive pay, subject to fluctuation and rate-cutting, should be reduced or eliminated; family allowances should be provided. In theory, such wage reform would encourage long-term employment as well. If this combination of regulation and exhortation spread the seniority wage system to much of Japanese industry, seniority wages and permanent employment can be explained in part as products of Japan's war experience.
>
> (Gordon 1985: 262–63)

The war thus saw a gradual shift to monthly wage systems, the policy of giving raises to workers at regular intervals (usually twice a year), and the institution of the family wage. As Japan entered the postwar period, workers took up the call for these policies and for a heavy seniority component in wages as well. In the aftermath of the

---

ture. One strand of research has argued that under certain conditions, employers and workers enter into implicit contracts where the spot wage diverges from the spot value of the marginal product. In other words, contrary to the assumptions of neoclassical theory, wages and productivity may not correspond at any one point in time. Instead, the worker and employer implicitly agree on an arrangement whereby the worker receives a wage lower than the value of marginal productivity at the beginning of his career, whereas by the end of his career, he is receiving a wage that is higher than marginal product value (Lazear 1979). Further characteristics of such contracts should be mandatory retirement (so that the employer will not continue to pay high wages indefinitely), pensions, and long job tenure. This is an accurate description of the system whose early development I have traced in prewar Japan.

war, stable employment was viewed by *workers* as a highly desirable goal. Japanese wage rates had fallen much more markedly than wages in the United States, Germany, or Britain during the war, as had the real value of consumer spending (Gordon 1985).

The American Occupation authorities encouraged the formation of workers' associations, considering them to be an important mechanism for building democratic values in a Japan recovering from the throes of what had virtually been a military dictatorship. Union membership exploded by 1946, but the basis of membership was the business enterprise rather than craft or industry. There was no strong prewar craft or trade union tradition to serve as an organizational model; the ebb and flow of union activity in the prewar period had been based at the factory level (Gordon 1985). Furthermore, employers in the early postwar period were anxious to exert as much control over union activities as possible, and they sometimes orchestrated preemptive attempts at organization by forming discussion groups between workers and management. (For discussions of Japanese trade unionism, see Garon 1987; Gordon 1985; Koshiro 1983a, 1983b; Naito 1983.)

With the economy devastated and large numbers of men returning home from the country's former colonies, Japan faced a labor surplus in the years immediately following the war. These conditions structured workers' priorities: simply retaining a job was of more pressing importance than negotiating for higher wages. Thus, as Rodney Clark writes, " 'Lifetime employment,' which before the war had been the expedient of management, was now the conscious objective of labour unions" (1979: 46).

The growth of enterprise unions also brought the kernels of the permanent employment system to fruition, because wage-related bargaining was conducted with an emphasis on age. Electric power workers set a precedent in 1946 by negotiating an agreement whereby wages were based not only on workers' skill and experience but on age and number of dependents as well (Clark 1979). A "living wage" ("family wage" in Western parlance), boosting up extremely low postwar wages for individuals with heavy family responsibilities, was instituted in many other industries and gained legitimacy (Taira 1970). Even in the late 1930s, advocates of livelihood wages had used rhetoric that glorified such a system: a dichotomy was drawn between the "Japanese-style" wage system, based on family needs, and a "Western-style" system that was selfish and individualistic by virtue of being based on skill (Gordon 1985).

IMPLICATIONS OF POSTWAR POLICIES FOR WOMEN

The organization of labor into enterprise unions in the postwar period and the demands voiced by labor vis-à-vis employers had strong implications for the role that women would play in the labor force once they began to enter it in greater numbers. Because so few women, especially married women, had been in the wage-earning sector of the economy let alone in the large enterprises in industries where lifetime employment policies were formulated, the eventual policies provided an ill fit to women's lives. Enterprise-based unions meant that full-time, long-term employees had the greatest stake and the greatest voice in union activities. Such employees were men. Agreements negotiated between unions and employers, such as the family wage, worked to the advantage of this subset of workers and to the disadvantage of temporary, part-time, or other categories of workers in the firm. In this way, permanent membership in the firm, which from the early days of Japanese industrialization had been a male-only pattern (and then only for a minority of males), became a basis for employment policies in large firms. The advantages such policies wrought for permanent, long-term employees further reinforced the disadvantages for women. It was of little interest to unions to arrive at policies that accommodated the intermittent employment patterns typical of married women coordinating family and wage-earning activities.

Hiring young workers with a view to long-term employment had been the practice of a few large firms in the 1920s. By the 1960s and 1970s, the pattern had spread, and over one-third of each year's new recruits in the manufacturing sector nationwide started employment in March or April, at the end of the school year. The advantages to a worker of being hired into a career-track position (an internal labor market) in a large firm are familiar from chapter 3: (1) the wage and promotion structure of large Japanese firms; (2) low interfirm mobility rates; and (3) the prevalence of on-the-job training in large firms.

INTERNAL LABOR MARKETS IN LARGE FIRMS

WAGE AND PROMOTION STRUCTURE

The wage structure of Japanese firms incorporates both length-of-service and merit principles, but length of service continues to predominate to a larger degree than in Western nations. Over time, promotion to managerial levels in large Japanese firms also came to occur almost entirely from within the organization. Shirai Taishiro (1983) uses data from the Keizai Dōyūkai, a leading association of managers, to support the following claim:

> An overwhelming majority of Japanese managers have advanced to their present positions from the ranks of general employees through the system of internal promotion, or "promotion from within" the particular company. Rather than being a postwar innovation, this system of regular career paths for all employees was well established among large Japanese corporations, both public and private, before World War II. The companies hire groups of new university or college graduates and, as they climb the managerial ladder, they accumulate experience in various jobs, not confined to any specialized field, through job rotation at regular intervals. Finally, those who survive this extensive training and screening are promoted to top management positions.
>
> (Shirai 1983: 373)

Of the 134 firms that responded to the survey conducted by the Keizai Dōyūkai, all had at least some directors who had been promoted from the ranks of employees. And 91 percent of full-time directors in the firms had been promoted from within their own companies.

Not only do the principles of length of service and promotion from within a company make entry into an internal labor market an advantage to the worker, low interfirm mobility rates and the accompanying ideology also magnify the importance of one's first job.

LOW INTERFIRM MOBILITY

Koike (1983a) reports a sharp drop in job separation rates after age 25 in Japan. After some initial job-switching, workers quickly settle into their jobs. The most stable workers are those aged 30–50 in large firms, who exhibit a separation rate of only 4 to 7 percent per year. Separation rates by age are generally not available for the West, but Japan has a higher percentage than the United States of workers with length of service of all durations between one and twelve years. In his comparison of workers in Detroit and Yokohama, Cole (1979) reports that for each cohort entering the labor force since 1940, about 2.5 times as many Japanese workers had remained with their original employer as had American workers. Although current popular reports suggest an increasing rate of job-changing in Japan, recent data on interfirm mobility confirm that the great majority of male workers are still recruited directly out of school, and that interfirm mobility rates remain lower in Japan than in the United States (Hashimoto and Rai-sian 1985). Rates of interfirm mobility are lowest for Japanese male employees who start in large firms. A middle-aged male worker in a major Japanese bank described to me via an analogy the prospect of leaving stable employment in a large firm and switching jobs: "Being in a large company is like bathing in warm water—it's not very chal-lenging, but on the other hand, it's cold when you get out."

ON-THE-JOB TRAINING

Entrance into an internal labor market in a large firm also entails the benefit of on-the-job training. A survey by Koike of over 400 Japanese firms showed that about two-thirds had a work force that had been trained almost entirely within the firm. Externally trained workers were defined as those with three or more years experience in their present occupation but in a different company. Such workers were rare, even though the survey included firms ranging in size from 30 to 300 employees and therefore excluded very large firms, where internal training is most prevalent. "The answer to the question about which type of workers the managements prefer—those trained internally or externally—is that, overwhelmingly, they prefer to train their workers themselves," Koike concluded (1983b: 97)

Merton Peck and Tamura Shūji (1976) found that Japanese firms invested more heavily in the training of their engineers than U.S. and British firms. Rohlen's ethnography of a Japanese bank remains one of the best descriptive accounts of training in the workplace (1974). In the bank he studied, young men recruited directly from school spent three months at the bank's training institute before their first assign-ment. Rohlen writes:

> Recent graduates entering the bank, therefore, seldom have any training in banking procedures or general business skills. In fact, it has been public policy to leave much technical and business training to the nation's com-panies, and because they have their own particular educational require-ments and perspectives, companies seldom cooperate in joint educational ventures. Each characteristically invests heavily in its own program. The low male turnover rate makes this a sound investment. Large outlays and maximum return are two characteristics of training in large Japanese companies.
>
> (Rohlen 1974: 192–93)

Job rotation was also a key feature of employment in the bank Rohlen studied: "Men are called upon to perform many varied tasks and to assume increasing degrees of responsibility and leadership. Whether they eventually occupy high positions or not, their career leads through many kinds of work. They are expected to show flexibility, and they must be ready to learn new skills. Contrary to the classical theory of bureaucracy, individual specialization is not pronounced" (1974: 193).

Rohlen found high rates of lateral and vertical mobility in the work organization. Cole (1979) argues that Japanese employees expect to experience high intrafirm mobility with seniority in a firm. In his comparison of Detroit and Yokohama auto workers, Japanese workers were much more likely to say that intrafirm mobility was something that just happened rather than something they actively had to seek out (Cole 1979). Higher education was related to the greater frequency of intrafirm job changing, and the volume of such job changes was greatest in the largest firms (1,000 or more employees).

Data collected by the Labor Ministry provide a summary view of the extent of on-the-job training in Japanese firms. Table 4.1 shows the proportion of firms in each industry and firm-size category who use job rotation (called *haichi tenkan* in Japanese). Overall, nearly 60 percent of firms do so. There is considerable variation in the extent of the practice by industry. In the finance and insurance industries and in utilities, over 80 percent of firms practice job rotation, whereas it is much less common in transportation and communication, as well as mining. Japanese manufacturing industries fall in the middle of the industrial distribution in terms of the prevalence of job rotation.

Job rotation familiarizes individuals with a range of departments and tasks in the firm. Because the practice is considered an investment in human capital, it is likely that the most promising workers are chosen for this type of training. We might expect highly educated workers—those with high initial human capital when they enter the firm—to be more likely to receive this training. Firms that can afford to hire university graduates may practice job rotation more than other firms. Although the Labor Ministry data pose problems in terms of being highly aggregated, one rough way to check this hypothesis is to see whether the industries and firm-size categories where job rotation is commonplace are also ones where university graduates are hired.

The second column in Table 4.1 shows the proportion of firms in each industry and firm size category in 1986 who recruited university graduates directly out of school. The same basic hierarchy of industries exists here as in job rotation practices. In particular, it is striking that

TABLE 4.1

JOB ROTATION AND HIRING
PRACTICES IN JAPANESE FIRMS

	Percentage of firms that use job rotation	Percentage of firms that hire university graduates
By industry		
Finance and insurance	89.6	74.9
Utilities	85.7	38.4
Wholesale and retail sales	74.8	44.0
Services	69.4	25.4
Real estate	68.9	27.0
Manufacturing	62.8	22.7
Mining	48.7	9.5
Transportation and communication	42.6	9.9
Construction	34.3	15.8
By firm size (no. of employees)		
5,000+	97.7	94.0
1,000–4,999	97.8	87.4
300–999	91.9	69.3
100–299	76.0	38.2
30–99	48.7	14.5
Total	58.8	25.0

SOURCE: Ministry of Labor, Japan, 1987b.

many more firms in the finance and insurance industries than in others recruit university graduates. Rohlen's observations about the bank he studied thus seem to be representative of this industry. It is also apparent from the Labor Ministry figures that large firms—especially those employing over 1,000 workers—are much more likely to hire university graduates than small firms; 94 percent of firms with more than 5,000 workers make employment offers to university graduates, whereas only 15 percent of firms with 99 or fewer workers do so.

In sum, large firms are more apt to hire university graduates, promote from within the firm, and pay higher wages to their long-term employees than other firms.

The above discussion has shown that over the course of industrial development in Japan, a consensus developed among managers about the attributes and behaviors of workers that would be rewarded. These decisions about valued attributes and behaviors were based on the particular features of Japan's industrialization process: a shortage of skilled labor and a surplus of unskilled labor; rapid technological change necessitating training in the workplace; and the absence of a strong craft union tradition that would serve to organize workers across rather than within firms. Employers in large firms developed work structures that would allow them to offer incentives (at the lowest cost to the firm) to the workers they most needed.

This historical analysis is consistent with the discussion in chapter 3 of the worker characteristics most highly related to wages in Japan. The history of labor-management relations in Japan has shaped the wage-determination process in a fundamental way. Workers who are willing and able to work for large firms and can convince employers that they will remain with the firm over a long period are rewarded by secure jobs and predictable increases in wages with length of service. Seniority-based compensation therefore stratifies the labor force into those who are able to take advantage of this and those who are not.[7] Likewise, the practice of rotating valuable employees among different positions in the firm so that they can gain comprehensive knowledge of the firm's production or sales operations means that job content (occupation) is not one of the most important bases on which the work force is stratified. Admission into a large firm and access to firm-specific training do, however, stratify the labor force. As Gordon states: "Clearly, the Japanese factory is home to a labor relationship distinct from that found in North America and Western Europe. . . . It is built upon the premise of secure jobs and livelihood wages, *for full members only.* The wage is determined by attributes which inhere to membership in the firm, such as seniority, rank, and merit evaluations, with some attention to independent and objective attributes of the individual, such as age and family size" (1985: 410–11).

The implications for female workers seem clear. If women are expected to devote a portion of their time as adults solely to raising children, the seniority and training systems of large Japanese companies are fundamentally incompatible with women's lives. Women can-

---

[7] Burawoy (1983) also argues for the importance of examining the role of context in wage-setting practices.

not be hired at a later point in the life cycle after they have received some type of additional training to supplement their early education, because such non—company specific training is perceived as more or less worthless. Nor are companies willing to train women who reenter the labor force after childrearing, just as they would be unwilling to train mid-career male entrants to the firm. Coming into a firm in one's mid thirties or forties means starting over at the bottom of the wage scale. Female high school graduates reentering the labor market in 1987 at age 30–34 or 35–39 had lower starting wages than either male junior high school or high school graduates who were only 18–19 years old (Ministry of Labor, Japan, 1987a). This is what has happened in the postwar period as more and more married women have reentered the labor force after quitting during the early childrearing years.

The very traits and behaviors that Japanese employers have chosen to value, largely out of economic exigency, have virtually excluded women *by definition* from the "good" jobs in the economy.

POSTWAR ECONOMIC DUALISM: IMPLICATIONS FOR WOMEN

"One wonders seriously whether . . . it might have been more fruitful to examine Japan's 'modern' century of development not only in terms of commonly shared successes and failures, but also in terms of the relative successes it produced for some and the relative failures it held for others. Certainly it did not hold the same meaning for everyone," observe Ross Mouer and Sugimoto Yoshio (1986: 30–31). Along with the emergence of large firms and seniority-based wage policies came two types of "dualism" in the Japanese economy.[8] The first is one that

---

[8] Many observers have asserted that both the Japanese and the U.S. economies demonstrate a high degree of dualism (Clark 1979; Edwards 1979; Yasuba 1976). In the late 1970s and early 1980s, a large number of attempts were made in the American sociological and economic literature to divide the U.S. economy into segments or sectors; "economic dualism" became the intellectual rage, especially among Marxist-oriented scholars and those who perceived that the human capital and status attainment traditions in American social science had neglected important issues of political economy. Although the dimensions of economic segmentation continue to be a source of debate, most empirical work in the United States has focused on the differences between product markets. This has led to various conceptualizations of industrial segmentation. One practical reason why this line of research probably developed in the manner it did is that data on the characteristics of workers and the level of wages by size of firm are not regularly collected in the United States. Data on a worker's industry are more easily obtainable.

Discussions of the structure of the Japanese economy also typically begin with the observation that the economy is dualistic. But in contrast to the *industrial* focus of the literature on the U.S. economy, discussions of the dual economy in Japan have paid a great

was discussed earlier in the context of the development of light and heavy industry. In each industry a dualistic structure of large and small firms developed, with higher wages being paid in the large firms. This dualism did not benefit women in large firms because the large textile firms paid less than the average for firms in other industries. The people who did benefit were the men in large firms in heavy industry, where wages outstripped those in every other sector of the economy. The other type of dualism has only been implied by the discussion so far: the division *within* large companies between the permanently employed "haves" and the temporarily employed "have nots." Both forms of dualism have exercised a profound effect on the nature of women's working lives in the postwar period. Women were left out of the process of economic growth in a way that men were not. The repercussions of the permanent employment system for women are best understood by looking at the post-1950s functioning of the system as the economy has cycled in and out of high growth periods.

THE ERA OF HIGH ECONOMIC GROWTH

High economic growth and the establishment of new firms and factories after 1955 occurred at a time when the Japanese male labor force was on average quite young. In 1961, nearly one-half of Japanese manufacturing workers were under age 24, compared to 15 percent in the United States (Rohlen 1979). Large Japanese companies could make good on the promise of successive promotions and pay increases for significant numbers of young men. "To express the matter differently, internal labor markets constituted the major arena within which individual socioeconomic achievement has been played out for large numbers of employees in the postwar period," Robert Cole observes (1979: 41). Whereas only a small fraction of the male labor force was covered by permanent employment policies in the prewar period, the figure for the 1960s onward has been put at about one-third.[9]

---

deal of attention to the contrast between the small- and large-firm sectors of the economy (Broadbridge 1966; Nakamura 1981). Much less attention has been devoted to possible industrial divisions. There are probably two reasons for this. When industrial classifications have been used in empirical work on Japan, such as to predict wages or promotion trajectories, these classifications have not performed well (Brinton 1989; Kalleberg and Lincoln 1988; Kawashima and Tachibanaki 1986). In contrast, many studies have documented that data on the characteristics of workers and the level of earnings by size of firm demonstrate that small Japanese firms are indeed distinctive from larger ones—notably, wages are lower, they increase more slowly with age than in large firms, and fringe benefits and general working conditions are not as beneficial.

[9] Efforts at measuring the proportion of employees who are covered by the permanent employment system are hampered by the fact that permanent employment is an implicit

Not all men in large firms or the government bureaucracy are in seniority-based internal labor markets, but these men are certainly the *most* likely of any group to be "permanently employed." The proportion of men in firms of 500 or more employees or in government has remained quite stable since 1965. At any given point during the past 25 years, between 37 and 43 percent of all male employees (a lower proportion if we use the male *labor force* as the denominator, for this includes self-employed men in very small firms) have been in these employment situations.

The continued growth and stability of the *nenkō joretsu* system (seniority-based promotion and wage increases) was contingent on two factors: high economic growth and a youthful labor force. These were both historically temporary conditions. Economic expansion in the late 1950s and 1960s moved the Japanese economy from a condition of labor surplus to one of labor shortage. By 1968, the ratio of job vacancies to applications rose to over 1.00, a condition that continued until 1975 (Kurosaka 1989). Jobs were plentiful, but applicants were not. By the mid 1970s, economic growth and the supply of young, inexpensive labor were both on the wane. Japan entered its worst postwar economic recession with the worldwide oil shock in 1973. Meanwhile, the country had rapidly moved from having one of the most youthful labor force structures in the industrial world to one of the oldest. This was the inevitable result of the low birth rate from the late 1950s on, coupled with substantial increases in life expectancy.

As successive cohorts of men reached middle-management status by the mid 1970s, large Japanese firms faced a demographic problem: the wage bill was becoming larger and larger with the bulge in the high-wage group of workers in their mid forties. These men had been raised with the expectation that their wages would continue to increase over time, and that they would not only be immune to layoffs but would receive successive promotions. Under these conditions, permanent employment and stable labor-management relations in large firms might have been seriously threatened. Yet slack did exist, and it was utilized. In fact, "employment adjustment" measures were more widespread among large firms than among smaller ones. The latter had little fat

---

contract between employer and employee. No explicit contractual agreement exists, either for the employer not to dismiss the employee or for the employee not to quit and seek employment elsewhere.

to trim, having faced a labor shortage for years. Large firms had virtually guaranteed lifetime employment to the young male workers hired during the halcyon days of rapid economic growth. In the post–oil shock recession of the mid to late 1970s, "large-scale manufacturing enterprises effected the highest rate of employment adjustment during the course of economic slowdown. This means that large enterprises, while offering high wage increases to their workers who are protected under the lifetime employment system, waited for natural attrition, enlisted voluntary early retirements, and prevented the entry of new workers from the external labor market by not hiring new recruits. It was the small-scale, labor-intensive sector that absorbed large quantities of excess labor thus created" (Mizuno 1988: 72).

Labor force "slack" lay in three groups of workers: older men, young women, and part-time workers. Notably, given the fact that nearly all part-time workers in Japan are female, two of the three groups were women. Older men were vulnerable because the mandatory retirement age of 55 or 60 had gotten out of line with Japanese life expectancy, and many Japanese men had several more potentially productive working years ahead of them after they retired. The majority of Japanese male workers preferred to continue working after retirement, owing partly to low pensions and partly to the psychological benefits of a productive life-style. This became more difficult during the economic downturns of the 1970s, as more and more companies of all sizes adopted mandatory retirement systems. In 1973, 100 percent of firms of 1,000 or more workers had in place a mandatory retirement system, as did 94 percent and 58 percent respectively of medium (100–999) and small (30–99) firms. By 1984 the figures for medium-sized and small firms in particular had increased substantially. Nevertheless, small and medium-sized firms absorbed the bulk of retirees from larger firms. Of workers who retired in the early 1980s but continued employment in some form, 30 percent faced a wage reduction of 20–39 percent and fully 20 percent experienced at least a 40 percent reduction in wages (Sakuma 1988).

Although older male workers suffered, the full brunt of "employment adjustment" was borne by women. Part-time workers were laid off in large numbers in 1974 and 1975, and young full-time women workers were encouraged by many firms to leave earlier than they "normally" would have (at marriage or birth of the first child). Consequently, the female employment rate went down during the first few years of the recession. In manufacturing, female employment declined by 11 percent in 1974–75, whereas male employment declined by only 3 percent. In contrast, the decline in manufacturing employment in West Germany and the United States during the same period affected men and women equally (Rohlen 1979). Measuring the number of unemployed women in the Japanese economy is nearly impossible because most women did not go on unemployment insurance, but rather were absorbed into their parents' or husbands' households. It is estimated that between 700,000 and 800,000 women left the labor market during this period, demonstrating a decisive "discouraged worker" effect (Mizuno 1988).

The fact that Japan pulled through the 1970s recessionary period with only a moderate level of unemployment among the male working-age population can be attributed to the adjustments in the labor force described above: large firms' greater enforcement of the retirement age, restrictions on the hiring of new graduates, and layoffs of young female full-time workers and middle-aged part-time female workers.[10]

By the late 1970s the labor market had once more shifted in complex ways for different types of workers. With the contraction of the economy, young male graduates faced a more difficult employment situation than during the days of high economic growth. The large firms were hiring fewer new graduates, and furthermore, wage differentials by firm size had increased, thus making it more crucial for young men to compete for entrance into a large firm to attain high wages. The dualistic wage structure between large and small firms had softened from the late 1950s to the late 1960s with the labor shortage, but in the late 1970s and 1980s it was reasserted: workers in manufacturing firms of 100–999 employees in 1986 earned 77.2 percent of what workers in firms of 1,000 or more employees did. The figure for workers in firms of 10–99 employees was 69.6 (Kurosaka 1989). These 1986 figures were at about the same level as they had been in 1962, thus evidencing no net improvement over this 25-year period.

Ironically, as the labor market became ever more competitive for men, new opportunities opened up for women willing to work as part-

---

[10] Some observers have also cited Japan's bonus system as providing an additional measure of flexibility. Twice-yearly bonuses have typically constituted about 25 percent of the total yearly cash payments made to workers since 1960. But econometric work done by Mizuno Asao shows that the flexibility during recessions that is attributable to wages is not a result of manipulation of bonus payments as much as it is a reflection of adjustments in contract earnings (Mizuno 1988). Furthermore, unions oppose bonus cuts, and during the post–oil shock recession, it appears that such cuts were extended to all personnel only in cases where the company was on the brink of bankruptcy. Reports of temporary salary and bonus cuts were more common for management-level employees (Rohlen 1979). Thus it is hard to attribute a major adjustment role to a reduction in bonuses.

TABLE 4.2

MALE AND FEMALE PARTICIPATION AS
MANUFACTURING WORKERS, 1960–1980

	Age			
	Proportion under 25	*Proportion 25–34*	*Proportion 35 and over*	*Proportion all ages*
1960				
Male	.22	.19	.26	.67
Female	.18	.06	.09	.33
Total	.40	.25	.35	1.00
1970				
Male	.15	.20	.29	.64
Female	.13	.07	.16	.36
Total	.28	.27	.45	1.00
1980				
Male	.06	.18	.39	.63
Female	.05	.08	.24	.37
Total	.11	.26	.63	1.00

SOURCE: Office of the Prime Minister, Japan, *Kokusei chōsa* (Population census), 1960, 1970, 1980.
NOTE: Figures represent proportions in each age-sex category.

time or temporary workers. Slower economic growth rates during the late 1970s inspired companies to hire a larger number of part-time workers at low wages. With fluctuation in the wage levels of household heads, middle-aged women were willing entrants into the labor force as part-time workers in the manufacturing and service industries. This was heightened by another factor too: as more and more young men went on to higher education, the supply of male junior high school graduates for manufacturing jobs grew short. This had occurred by the mid 1970s: the ratio of job offers to junior high male job seekers in 1960 was 1.9, whereas it had reached 6.2 in 1975 (Sakuma 1988). This condition became greatly exacerbated by the 1980s.

Table 4.2 shows changes in the age and sex distribution of manufacturing workers since 1960. Two-thirds of manufacturing workers were male in 1960, a figure that had declined slightly by 1980. More important, however, the age structure of the total manufacturing sector had shifted dramatically by 1980. Initially, about one-quarter of the labor force was in the 25–34 age group, and the rest was distributed more or less evenly among very young workers and workers above age

35. By 1980, the 25–34 age group still comprised about one-quarter of all manufacturing workers, but another two-thirds of workers were in the older group, and the participation of young workers in the manufacturing sector was down to about 10 percent. Thus, the average manufacturing worker in 1980 was much older than in 1960. The increased participation of older women in manufacturing was particularly marked. While the manufacturing share made up by men 35 and over increased by about one and a half times between 1960 and 1980 (from .26 to .39), women's share nearly tripled (from .09 to .24).

These figures reflect the extreme shortage of junior high school graduates that had developed by 1980 in the Japanese economy. Traditionally, graduates at this level had entered manufacturing jobs in large numbers. With high school attendance nearly universal by 1980 and rates of university and junior college attendance up as well, the supply of new graduates willing to take manufacturing jobs had sharply declined. Part of the increased demand for factory workers was met by women reentering the labor force in their late thirties after their children had reached school age.

SECONDARY WORKERS

Temporary and Part-Time Work   The employment gains of male employees from the 1950s onward were in part a result of the bargaining power that resulted from the labor shortage. Temporary and daily employment became less and less common for men. By the late 1960s, the proportion of male temporary employees in large firms was under 5 percent. But as male temporary employment declined, part-time work for women increased. In government publications in the late 1960s, the new term *pāto-taimu* (part-time worker) appeared (Gordon 1985). Whereas only 8.8 percent of married women worked in the labor force as employees in 1960, 30 percent were employees in 1987 (Ministry of Labor, Japan, 1988) and much of this growth was in part-time work. Figure 4.1 shows the shift in the proportions of men and women in temporary, daily, or part-time employment since 1960, when slightly fewer than 10 percent of men and slightly more than 10 percent of women were in such employment. The rate of non-regular employment (temporary, daily, and part-time) among men declined and stabilized at around 5 percent, but that among women increased, particularly after 1975. By 1987, 19.3 percent of all female employees

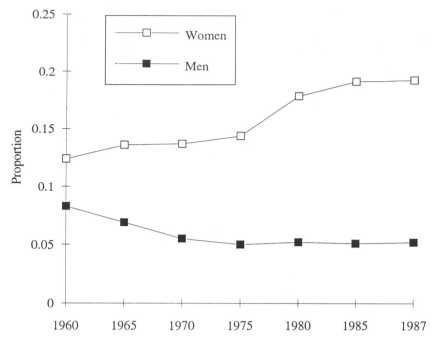

Figure 4.1. Proportion of Men and Women in Temporary, Daily, or Part-Time Employment

SOURCE: Office of the Prime Minister, Japan, *Rōdōryoku chōsa* (Survey of the labor force), 1988.

were in this category. The figure is considerably higher for married women. Fully 41 percent of all married female employees in 1987 were part-time workers, and the figure was even higher for middle-aged married women (Office of the Prime Minister, Japan, *Rōdōryoku chōsa*, 1988).

Individual companies designate what constitutes part-time work in Japan, and great variation exists across companies as to how they choose to define it. The categories *pāto* and *pāto-taimu* include not only those who work short hours but may also include employees who work nearly as many hours as full-time workers. The characteristics of male and female part-time work vary considerably: women who are *pāto-taimu* tend to have hours that are much closer to full-time than men do. About half of male part-time workers work at least 40 percent fewer hours than full-time workers, whereas this is true of only 32 percent of female part-time workers (Ministry of Labor, Japan, 1985b). For both sexes, small companies have a higher percentage of part-time workers whose hours are similar to those of full-time work-ers. About 10 percent of women part-timers work approximately the same number of hours as full-time workers. A report by the Japan Institute of Labor (1989) stresses both the positive and the negative aspects of female part-time work: "Firms seem to respond in a rela-tively flexible manner to employment of part-time workers (days and hours of work). Also, it can be observed that women part-time workers choose the hours to start and finish work according to their age." Yet the same report notes the nearly flat hourly wage curve for women part-time workers, reflecting the fact that wages are barely altered with years of work experience (see Fig. 2.10 above).

As temporary work became less common for Japanese men, one of the "buffers" in the economy became thinner. It is hard to avoid the conclusion that the part-time work of married women has provided an extra cushion. The symmetry between the substitution of part-time married female workers for temporary male workers may not be per-fect on the level of the individual firm (Gordon 1985), but the wage bill is substantially cut by the hiring of temporary part-time workers. The reasons to employ part-time labor differ somewhat by firm size. In government surveys, small firms are more likely than large ones to mention that their reliance on part-time workers is partly owing to the difficulty of hiring regular workers. This makes sense, given that large firms with their higher wages and better employment security can at-tract the best graduates. On the other hand, large firms are more likely than small ones to mention that savings in personnel costs are a major reason for hiring part-time workers (Ministry of Labor, Japan, 1983). In 1985, female part-time workers in large firms were much less likely to have open-ended contracts than those in smaller firms. Regardless of the size of firm, fewer than 10 percent of female part-time workers had employment contracts that specified a duration of more than one year. In the largest firms, nearly one-third of the part-time workers with fixed employment contracts had been hired for two months or less! (Ministry of Labor, Japan, 1985b).

Ethnographic data put meat on the bare bones of government re-ports and statistical observations on women's part-time and temporary work. During my fieldwork in Tokyo in 1984, a supermarket manager explained the conditions of female part-time workers as follows:

It is hard to get married women to work early in the morning or at night (after 4:00 P.M. or so). They have their household responsibilities to take care of at those hours, so we try to be flexible. It works out well for everybody if women come in during the middle of the day and make fruit salads and box lunches [*bentō*] and so forth—they really enjoy that kind of work and they're good at it. . . . It's true that some women do want to work longer hours but it becomes kind of a liability for us, you know.

This manager clearly had a certain amount of pride in the fact that his company deals with middle-aged women in a flexible manner, setting up their work hours in such a way as to allow them to be at home during the hours when household work is most crucial.

Another implication of such policies is, of course, that in adopting a flexible attitude toward women and an inflexible one toward men, employers play a major role in perpetuating gender segregation in both household and market roles. The people who make decisions regarding the employment relationship—hiring, wages, layoffs, and so on—are almost all middle-aged married men.[11] They have a keen (if not necessarily carefully examined) understanding of the benefits to men, and the perceived benefits to women, of treating the sexes differently in employment. What would the middle-aged manager do if his wife were working the long hours he was? This is no joking matter in a country where most men readily admit that their cooking skills are limited to boiling water to make tea or instant noodles.[12]

An attitude similar to the one expressed by the grocery store manager quoted above is depicted by a manager at a major electronics corporation in Tokyo, who explained the reasoning behind the labor contracts for female part-timers that specify a set period of employment. In his company, contracts for male employees are open-ended. In the manager's words, "We assume that regular workers will work for the company for the duration of their working life—this is implied in their contract." Women's contracts are different. Many companies use two-month contracts for women, but this particular company starts women out on a two-month contract, then extends it to ten months and finally to twelve in some cases. Bonuses are paid to part-time workers but retirement benefits are not. For the manager with whom I spoke, the flexibility of the company toward women was asource of pride and an indication, in his mind, of a liberal posture. As he explained:

[11] Many of these men have at least one daughter. As more women go to four-year universities and employment options for them remain restricted, these men may reconsider their attitudes toward the recruitment of women into career tracks.

[12] Several middle-aged men with whom I talked about household and family matters paused for an embarrassed moment before they could tell me the age or grade level of their children. This is a memory lapse unimaginable for a Japanese mother.

> For the [part-time] worker as well as the company, in some cases it would be inconvenient or inappropriate to have a long contract because the worker may want to return to her homemaker role full-time [*katei ni hairu*]. Instead, if we would like her to work another year, we ask her if she is able to [*mō ichinen dekimasu ka*]. If so, then her contract is renewed.

In her study of a lingerie factory in the mid 1980s, Glenda Roberts reports that while nearly all of the part-time workers wanted to continue working until the normal retirement age for regular employees, they also expressed the opinion that the company would not go along with such a desire. In 1981 a hotline for *pāto* was set up in Osaka by a group of lawyers. Over a four-year period, about one-third of the incoming calls concerned part-time workers' problems of sudden dismissal from the company or the company's refusal to pay agreed-upon retirement money (Roberts 1986).

Self-Employment   Fewer Japanese women than men work as wage or salary earners across the life cycle, and within the ranks of such workers, women's work conditions are very different than men's. The character of self-employment also differs radically for men and women. The vast majority of both male and female self-employed workers, over 90 percent, are in the smallest firms in the economy (1–4 persons). Self-employed workers are older than employees. The average age of male self-employed workers is slightly higher than that of females: males average 50 years old and females 47 years old.

But beyond these rough similarities in self-employment for the two sexes lie important differences in the characteristics of the work they do. This has been outlined in previous chapters, but some further attention is in order here, in respect to the different industries in which male and female self-employed workers are located. Nearly one-third of the male self-employed population is in agriculture, while less than half that proportion (15 percent) of women are. Offsetting this is the heavy participation of the female self-employed in manufacturing, with the balance employed mainly in sales or services. The largest proportion (about one-quarter) of male self-employed urban workers are in wholesale or retail sales, operating small shops on their own. The rest of the male self-employed workers in the urban sector are quite evenly distributed across industries—manufacturing, construction, services, transportation and communication, and finance and insurance services. A further distinction between male and female self-employed workers is the following: nearly 30 percent of all of the self-employed females in the Japanese economy are home piecework workers in manufacturing. Fewer than 1 percent of the male self-employed fall into this category.

These figures show that self-employment signifies very different types of work for men and women. Men may inherit a small neighborhood shop from their father and employ other family members or a few employees. As Hugh Patrick and Thomas Rohlen put it: "Small business is the outlet and opportunity for those who are hopeful and ambitious and either not hired by large employers or not wanting to be" (1987: 382–83). Self-employment for women is much more apt to mean the assembly of electronic parts in their homes while their children are at school or napping, and the delivery of these parts to a subcontractor for a larger firm. Indeed, self-employment could hardly be more different between two groups of people than it is between Japanese men and women.

The discussion up to this point has focused on how the permanent employment system was consciously developed in twentieth-century Japan, especially after World War II, to meet the needs of both employers and of workers (though not always coterminously). Accompanying permanent employment for one class of workers has been the continued reliance on a secondary group of workers who are either in non–career track positions in large firms or who are in small firms or family enterprise employment. These dualistic trends in the economy have worked to the detriment of women in particular. If women are by definition to devote a part of their adult lives to childrearing, they will have difficulty maintaining unbroken records as full-time employees. Few women are considered by large firms to be candidates for permanent employment. If the central argument of this book is correct—that Japan's human capital development system systematically handicaps women as workers—we should expect to find much evidence of gender stratification in the contemporary labor force and especially in workers' careers as they develop across the life cycle. Chapter 5 looks in more detail at the fabric of individual men's and women's work lives in contemporary urban Japan.

FIVE

Gendered Work Lives

Japan's system of human capital development originated at a time when few married women were in the urban labor market. The reward structures in employment are better suited to the contours of men's than women's lives, a claim this chapter examines by following the employment experiences of individual men and women from the early to the middle stages of their working lives. Several questions are key. To what degree are young women continuing to follow the path set by older women, leaving the labor force at marriage or childbirth? Does greater education benefit women in the labor market as much as men? In other words, would greater acquisition of human capital by Japanese women in the future "equalize" men's and women's rewards in the labor market, or is discrimination built into the Japanese workplace at a more fundamental level?

The limitations of organizational case studies are frustrating when one tries to answer such questions, because these studies, from which so much of our knowledge about Japanese labor relations is drawn, generally focus on male workers and only briefly mention women's categorical exclusion from internal labor markets. On the other hand, surveys conducted by the Japanese Labor Ministry and the Prime Minister's Office are extremely helpful in viewing the employment of men and women at any one time. But they are not so useful in showing how people got to where they are in the employment structure, and how and why men's and women's work lives diverge over the life cycle. Because of these limitations of previous research and published statistics, I conducted a survey in 1984 of approximately 1,200 men and women in urban Japanese settings. The survey was carried out in Kodaira, Sapporo, and Toyohashi. Kodaira is a western suburb of Tokyo, and has a largely white-collar working population that commutes into central Tokyo. Sapporo is the largest city on Hokkaido, Japan's northernmost island, and has a working population broadly representative of large Japanese cities. Toyohashi is a smaller, older industrial city about 160 miles southwest of Tokyo and 40 miles southeast of Nagoya. A larger proportion of Toyohashi's population is employed in agriculture or manufacturing, especially the automobile industry. Respondents to the survey were drawn from two age groups of the populations of these cities, 25–29 and 40–44 year-olds. Although the sample is not a national one, it is quite representative of the urban Japanese population in these age groups. Details of sample selection and response rates are discussed in Appendix A.

The cohorts were chosen for two reasons. The first is age. The younger cohort represents people who have recently entered the labor market. The men in it have worked on average about seven years, and the women about six years. By studying them, we can see in detail what men's and women's early work experiences are like. The older cohort represents people who have potentially been in the labor force for close to twenty-five years (men in this group have worked an average of twenty-three years). The experiences of this cohort offer rich documentation of how men's and women's employment patterns diverge over the first decades of work life. Women aged 40–44 are an important group to look at, because by this point in their lives, most of those who eventually reenter the labor force will already have done so. Their experiences show the difficulties posed by an employment system that reserves the good positions for young people whose human capital will be developed in the work organization, with employers' expectation of the worker's continuous employment.

The second reason for choosing these particular cohorts is historical. The older cohort entered the Japanese labor market during the high growth period of the early 1960s, and the younger cohort entered in the post–oil shock period of the mid 1970s. As explained in chapter 4, these groups faced different structural conditions in the labor market, and it is therefore important to compare how women fared in the two settings.

Another reason for comparing the cohorts aged 25–29 and 40–44 is also historical. The older cohort is the first to have been educated entirely in the postwar educational system. By choosing that cohort, rather than an older one educated partially in the prewar system, we can hold constant the effects of the educational system when we make comparisons with the younger, postwar-educated cohort.

A wide range of employment experiences is represented by these people. Some respondents have spent their lives as self-employed or family enterprise workers, and others have been employees in large firms all of their lives. Respondents to the survey provided detailed information about their educational experiences, family backgrounds, work experiences, marriage and fertility histories (who and when they married, numbers and ages of children), and information about children's education and hopes for their children's future. In addition to these data, the discussions of men's and women's employment, educational, and family lives in this chapter and the next one are informed by my experience of living in two Tokyo neighborhoods for one and a half years, from 1983 to 1985. The conversations and social occasions of everyday life are reflected in the following pages.

The rest of the chapter describes the typical working patterns of Japanese men and women as they enter the workplace for the first time after leaving school, receive (or do not receive, as the case may be) training on the job, and accumulate work experience. These data show how the system of human capital development in contemporary urban Japan progressively stratifies the sexes as they move from the stage of being young to being middle-aged adults. Surprising similarities between the work experiences of the younger and older cohorts of women are also revealed, suggesting the reproduction of gender stratification patterns in urban Japan at least through the mid 1980s, the time of the survey. Similarities in working patterns among women of different educational backgrounds are also striking, suggesting that additional amounts of human capital do not create the strong advantages for women in the labor market that they do for men.

The focus here is on the interpretation of the social-institutional and cultural context of Japanese gender stratification, rather than the statistical techniques that can be used as partial tools in this interpretation. Technical points are relegated to the Appendices, and readers interested primarily in the theoretical or qualitative side of the discussion will probably require little reference to them. Readers who want the details of survey design should refer to Appendix A. The tables in Appendix B show the measurement of variables and the results of statistical analyses. Tables sprinkled throughout the body of the text

TABLE 5.1

PERCEPTIONS OF HOW WOMEN
ARE TREATED IN THE WORKPLACE

	In hiring	In job rotation and promotion
Percentage whose response is:		
"Very disadvantageously"	22.2	34.6
"Somewhat disadvantageously"	57.4	49.0
"Not at all disadvantageously"	11.7	6.9
No answer	8.7	9.5
Total	100.0	100.0

SOURCE: *Yomiuri Shinbun*, May 14, 1984.

in this chapter and the next one are primarily restricted to descriptive statistics.

GENDER AND EDUCATION AS SCREENING DEVICES

The Japanese public perceives gender as a major screening device used by employers in their recruitment and hiring of school graduates. A national opinion poll of 3,000 people conducted by the *Yomiuri* newspaper in Japan in April 1984 gave evidence of widespread perception of sex discrimination in Japanese workplaces (Table 5.1). Almost 80 percent of respondents believed that women are treated in a "disadvantageous" way in regard to hiring, and about 84 percent felt that this also applies to job rotation and promotion. Results from my own survey also indicated widespread perception of discrimination at various stages of the work process (Appendix Table B.1).

The results from the *Yomiuri* report indicate that perception of discrimination is related to respondents' educational level. Whereas 16 percent of respondents with a high school or lower educational background felt that women were treated "very disadvantageously" at the hiring stage, nearly twice as many respondents with a higher education felt that way. The strong perception of sex discrimination among university graduates in particular is mirrored in other studies and in ethnographic observations. A mid-1980s survey by a private research organization in Tokyo surveyed young women's opinions on the correspondence between education and success in finding a job. Respondents to the survey were women graduating the following March, and at the time of the survey, they were busy searching for a job. Whereas 12 percent of junior college women felt that their education was more of a disadvantage than an advantage, fully one-fifth of university women felt that way. About equal proportions (one-half) of junior college and university women felt that their education helped them in the job market (Nihon Recruit Center 1984).

In the three-city survey I conducted, there was also variation in the perception of discrimination according to the educational level of the respondent. The relationship between education and perceptions of sex discrimination is not linear; that is, it is not the case that such perceptions uniformly increase with educational level or, for that matter, uniformly decrease. One would intuitively expect such a linear relationship to exist. Women with more education might be expected to be more sophisticated and thus more aware of structural forces such as discrimination, or conversely they might experience less discrimination because they are better-educated and have greater opportunities. In fact, young university-educated women are significantly *more* likely ($p < .001$) than young women of other educational backgrounds to perceive that strong sex discrimination exists in Japanese hiring practices; 65 percent of university-educated women report this. But in contrast, junior college–educated women are significantly less likely ($p < .001$) than other women to feel this way—only 21 percent perceive strong sex discrimination in hiring practices. Junior high school graduates and high school graduates fall in between, at 25 and 45 percent. Interestingly, young men and women do not differ in their perception of discrimination against women in the labor market: Japanese men recognize as much discrimination against women as women themselves recognize.

In chapter 2 it was shown that female university graduates have consistently had a lower rate of job-seeking than high school or junior college graduates. The industries that female junior college and four-year university graduates enter are surprisingly similar, which is not what one would expect given their different educational qualifications. About equal proportions go into manufacturing (16 percent), and the proportions for all other industries are also similar, with three exceptions: finance/insurance, service industries, and government. More female junior college graduates than university graduates enter the finance/insurance industry (18 versus 7 percent), and fewer enter government service, although the numbers here are quite small in any case. Female university graduates are more likely than their junior college counterparts to enter service industries. But this is largely because one-quarter of all female university graduates become teachers, compared to only about 10 percent of junior college graduates (Ministry of Education, Japan, 1987). There has been little shift in the relative destinations of junior college and university graduates in the 1970s and 1980s.

Ethnographic evidence suggests that young Japanese women and their parents are well aware of companies' restrictive recruitment policies for university-educated women. People interviewed during my fieldwork in 1984 indicated that education for daughters was good up to a certain point, beyond which further education might actually inhibit the likelihood of getting a good job. A middle-aged mother who worked in the role of greeting customers at a Tokyo branch bank in Kodaira, where I lived for nine months, commented as follows:

> Now my daughter is debating about whether to go to junior college or to university. She says that getting a university education will be a handicap [furi] when she looks for a job; it's true that the situation for women university graduates is very bad and that close to 100 percent of women junior college graduates can get jobs. But even so, I think she should go ahead and go to university. It's a hard situation—and it's hard for me to give advice to my daughters.
>
> (Brinton 1989: 552)

How accurate are these popular perceptions of discrimination? Many employers ask women during the job interview whether they plan to quit when they get married, although such questioning is now formally illegal as a result of the passage of the Equal Employment Opportunity Law by the Japanese Diet in 1985. Young women I talked with during my fieldwork generally reported that their friends who had entered the job market a year or two earlier advised them to tell employers they would quit when they married, because this would increase the chance that they would be hired. If they quit, they will provide the service to employers of forming a cushion in an employment system that could otherwise be fiercely rigid under the weight of too many "permanent" employees. Yet at the same time that employers encourage this behavior, many claim that the reason they do not give women the training or promotion opportunities they give to men is precisely because they fear women are not serious about working and will get married and quit. The firm-internal labor markets and on-the-job training practices of Japan's top companies work as institutional barriers to women.[1]

The circular processes of sex-stereotyped expectations on the part of employers and the responses by women make it very difficult to see which comes first, the chicken or the egg. Employers' expectations and behaviors feed back to young women's attitudes and behavior, as well as to their parents'. This is especially meaningful in a context where parents are almost uniformly responsible for financing their children's education and are closely involved in the educational decision-making and investment process. As poignantly illustrated in the quotation above, parents have reason to wonder whether sending a daughter to university is "worth it." By contrast, they do not pause to wonder whether such an aspiration for a son will pay off or not.

Confusion over the processes entering into women's quitting behavior was expressed well in the comments of labor union officials with whom I spoke. In the words of a man in a large union that organizes unions in firms dealing with metalworking: "We usually think about women's situation *after* they enter the labor market (for example, they want to quit working, their job consciousness is low, etc.), not before. But sometimes I think, 'Oh—we can look at the problem from the viewpoint of socialization and education too.' Still, that kind of perspective is rare." Another official in the same union had a less sanguine view. He had become a union officer after having been a middle-level manager at a major automobile manufacturing firm for several years, and spoke on the basis of his managerial experience.[2] He expressed his frustration over female university graduates' work habits to me, citing a comparison between two people who had worked for him: "I always have the feeling that she [a female graduate from a four-year university] does only about 60 percent of the work I give her. The woman who worked in her position before [a junior college graduate] did everything that was required and a little more. . . . Female university graduates are spoiled."

In sum, attitude surveys and ethnographic data suggest strong discrimination against women in their first jobs and a particular percep-

---

[1] See Roos and Reskin 1984 for a general discussion of institutional barriers. Although Roos and Reskin's implicit point of reference is the U.S. economy, the practices they describe operate to varying degrees in other industrial economies as well. They provide a useful categorization of organizational processes that restrict women's access to preemployment training, access to certain jobs, mobility among jobs, and retention in jobs.

[2] This is not an uncommon career trajectory; after several years of working primarily in the union, officers customarily return to their managerial responsibilities.

tion that the marginal utility of university education for women may be quite low. The role of education in explaining work patterns is clarified below as individual work lives are traced from their starting points: first jobs.

FIRST JOBS

Women in both survey cohorts, 25–29 and 40–44 years old, are less likely than men ever to have worked.[3] As one would expect, over 99 percent of men have labor force experience. But about 10 percent of the older women and 7 percent of the younger women have never been in the labor force in any capacity, including unpaid family enterprise work.

Among all those with work experience, there are few distinctions on the surface between men's and women's early employment experiences. Over 90 percent of those surveyed entered the labor force within two years of leaving school. So it is clear that later gender differentiation in occupation or wages is not because Japanese women delay their initial labor market entry. Nor are there significant differences between men and women in their initial employment status. In the older cohort, between 75 and 80 percent of both men and women entered the labor force as employees; this rises to over 85 percent for men and women in the younger cohort. The overwhelming percentage of respondents of each sex began their work lives as full-time employees.

In chapter 2 it was shown that in every cohort born since 1970, at least 30 percent of women have worked in large firms when young, a proportion similar to that for men. Table 5.2 shows the proportions of men and women in the younger and older cohorts in Sapporo, Kodaira, and Toyohashi who entered firms of different sizes on their first job. The difference in the distribution of men and women across firms of different sizes is not statistically significant in either cohort: women were not initially excluded from large firms or government when they left school. (This table includes workers of all employment statuses including employees, self-employed, and family enterprise workers. The results are very similar if we restrict the comparisons to employees only, or to full-time employees only.) Thirty percent of older women and 38 percent of younger women originally entered this sector of the economy.

[3] Some of the material in this section has appeared in Brinton 1989.

TABLE 5.2
FIRM SIZE OF MEN'S
AND WOMEN'S STARTING JOBS

| | Number of employees | | | | | Govern- | |
	1–9	10–99	100–299	300–999	1000+	ment sector	Total
Younger cohort (25–29)							
Men							
%	15.8	26.9	11.7	11.1	20.5	14.0	100.0
N	(27)	(46)	(20)	(19)	(35)	(24)	(171)
Women							
%	13.1	20.5	16.0	12.3	25.0	13.1	100.0
N	(35)	(55)	(43)	(33)	(67)	(35)	(268)

$X^2 = 4.90$, $df = 5$; not significant

Older cohort (40–44)							
Men							
%	22.8	24.6	10.3	8.6	21.6	12.1	100.0
N	(53)	(57)	(24)	(20)	(50)	(28)	(232)
Women							
%	20.5	28.9	11.7	8.8	17.8	12.3	100.0
N	(70)	(99)	(40)	(30)	(61)	(42)	(342)

$X^2 = 2.56$, $df = 5$; not significant

SOURCE: Survey conducted by author.

The characteristics that predict whether an individual will enter a large firm or the government after leaving school are also quite similar for men and women, as shown in Appendix Table B.4. (For convenience, the term *large firm* is used from this point on to refer to private companies that employ at least 1,000 people or to the government sector.)[4] A description of the variables used in this analysis is given in Appendix Table B.2; Appendix Table B.3 shows means and standard deviations. Both high ability and higher education increase the probability that a person will enter a large firm, and one's family background

[4] This definition corresponds to Hashimoto and Raisian's (1985) conceptualization and is consistent with several classic studies of Japanese companies such as Cole's *Work, Mobility, and Participation* (1979), as well as with published government statistics on firm size. A further justification for considering large firms to be ones that employ at least 1,000 workers lies in Hashimoto and Raisian's empirical findings. Median tenure and estimated eventual tenure of currently held jobs differs substantially between medium (100–999 employees) and large (1,000+) firms. Median tenure increases by a factor of 1.5 between these two firm sizes, and estimated eventual tenure increases by a factor of 1.3. Meanwhile, the distinctions between tiny, small, and medium firms are much smaller in magnitude.

(father's type of employment and mother's work status) does not matter. However, a greater number of male high school graduates enter large firms than junior college/vocational school graduates or men from low-ranking universities. Men from medium- / high-ranking universities fare best of all. In the case of women, education improves the chances of getting hired by a large firm. High-ability men are nevertheless significantly more likely than high-ability women to enter large firms. Also, male high school graduates have a significantly greater probability of entering large companies than female high school graduates. (These substantive conclusions stem from the finding of statistically significant interaction effects between sex and ability and between sex and high school graduation.) The historical period in which people entered the labor market (reflected by the "cohort" variable) is not related to the probability of entering the large firm/government sector.

While these results argue for strong similarities in the early work experiences of men and women and in the determining factors of these experiences, a closer look reveals important differences. Clear sex differences exist in the starting occupations of respondents. In the younger cohort, over half of female respondents report having been engaged in strictly office work (clerical work or assistant clerical work), whereas only 15 percent of men started out in that capacity. In contrast, men are more likely than women to have entered manufacturing or sales jobs. In the older cohort, office work was a less common point of origin and manufacturing a more common starting point. But the sex differences are virtually identical to those evident in the initial employment experiences of the younger cohort.

Because employment in large firms or the government is viewed by many workers as so desirable, it is especially important to determine how men's and women's starting jobs differ in these workplaces. This is best summarized by the proportions of men and women who enter firm-internal labor markets.

FIRM-INTERNAL LABOR MARKETS

Permanent employment in a Japanese company is not a formal legal status, but simply means that the individual is located in a career-track position inside the firm, from which the vast majority of promotions occur. Measuring such employment is difficult. I have defined individuals' first jobs as being in a firm-internal labor market if they reported:

(1) starting their work life as full-time employees or managers in a firm of 1,000 or more employees or in the government sector, *and* (2) starting in a nonprimary industry (primary being agriculture, mining, or fishing), *and* (3) starting in other than an agricultural occupation or an "assistant clerical" position (worded *hojoteki jimushoku* in the survey), *and* (4) perceiving a possibility of promotion to section chief or higher. The justification for this definition is given in Brinton 1989.

At the beginning of their working lives, 22 percent of men and only 7 percent of women held firm-internal labor market jobs. Furthermore, women in the older cohort had a significantly *higher* chance of entering such a job when they left school than women in the younger cohort. Although this may seem counterintuitive, it in fact makes sense when one considers that most of the younger cohort of women entered the labor market between 1973 and 1978, a time when Japan was in its worst recessionary period since World War II. As discussed previously, during this period, permanent employment for men was preserved at great cost. Large numbers of women left the labor force, and employers' willingness to place women in career-track slots became even slighter than in the high-growth phase of the economy (Rohlen 1979).

Combining the figures on large firms and permanent employment in a slightly different way yields the finding that 71 percent of men who started out in large firms were in internal labor markets, compared to 23 percent of women. This can be better understood by looking at the occupations of men and women in large firms. About one-third of the men were in clerical slots, and only 7 percent were in "assistant clerical" positions. By contrast, nearly two-thirds of women in large firms were clerical workers; among them, three-quarters were "assistant clerical" workers (ten times the figure for men). Several terms in Japanese reflect this phenomenon. *OL* ("office lady") refers to young women in white-collar jobs; bookstores routinely stock volumes on how to become a good *OL*. Even more revealing than this appellation is the expression *shokuba no hana* ("the flower in the workplace"): pretty, decorative, fresh-faced young women who work as receptionists or serve tea and operate the xerox machine. Susan Pharr describes tea-serving, one of the ubiquitous duties of Japanese female employees:

> The interesting thing about the ritual of providing tea to office members is that all the activities relating to it except the drinking—heating the water, pouring it in the teapot, pouring the tea into cups, serving the tea, remembering which cup belongs to whom (since personal cups are generally used),

gathering, washing, and arranging the cups afterward, cleaning up the counter where the tea was made, buying the tea or making sure that it is bought—are assigned to women employees by virtue of their ascribed status as women. It is true that most offices hire certain women to do little other than to prepare tea. These women, however, known as *ochakumi*, are generally reserved for "up front"—that is, for serving tea to high-ranking officials who are in regular contact with the public and for their guests. Quite apart from the *ochakumi* and their duties, it is the general expectation of everyone in the office that if a woman employee is present when tea is wanted by male employees, it is she who will be responsible for its preparation.

(Pharr 1984: 221–22)

Would more women be in firm-internal labor markets (rather than in the ranks of *OLs*) if only they had enough education or ability? Appendix Table B.5 suggests not. Men who have high ability and who graduated from a top- or medium-ranking university are significantly more likely than other men to enter the ranks of permanent employment. Ability heightens women's chances too, but education does not. University graduation does *not* substantially increase women's chances of entering an internal labor market position, which is precisely what the ethnographic data cited earlier would suggest. Also, women who had plans in adolescence to work more or less continuously throughout their lives are more likely to enter internal labor markets. This makes sense given employers' often-cited reluctance to place women on career ladders because of their lack of attachment to work.

The family backgrounds of Japanese men and women also have something to do with whether they enter an internal labor market in a large company, although such factors do not affect whether they enter a large firm per se. Young men and women whose fathers are self-employed are less likely to enter internal labor markets than their peers whose fathers are wage earners. This may be owing to some disadvantage faced by these individuals (a disadvantage we are not able to measure in other ways), or it may reflect less motivation to be in a career-track position in a corporate or factory setting if one's father is self-employed. Some men with self-employed fathers might, for example, eventually inherit the family business.

A mother's participation in the paid labor force also dampens the possibility that her daughter will achieve a career-track position. This can be understood in the context of a highly sex-discriminatory environment: daughters whose mothers worked are likely to have been aware of their mothers' difficulties, and may not aspire to "fight it out" in competition with men by trying to have a career rather than a temporary job.

A closer look at the people who entered internal labor markets reveals another important distinction between men and women in addition to the different effects of education: women who entered internal labor markets were more likely than men to be employed in government. For the older cohort, this sex difference was particularly strong: 41 percent of women who initially entered internal labor markets were in government service, compared to only 23 percent of the men. This suggests that government may be more hospitable to women than the private sector, a distinction not apparent for men.

STARTING WAGES

Neither the monthly nor the yearly starting wages of the older cohort, who entered the labor force in the 1960s, differed significantly by sex. This contrasts with the starting wages of the young men and women in the survey. Among those who graduated from school and entered the work force as full-time employees in the late 1970s and early 1980s, men earned significantly more than women on both a monthly and a yearly basis.[5] For example, men entering the labor market in 1980 started out on average at ¥126,500 per month, whereas women began at ¥101,974.

Appendix Tables B.7 and B.8 show the effect on wages of human capital variables such as education and ability and workplace variables such as size of firm and internal labor market position. (Appendix Table B.6 shows the means and standard deviations of the variables.) Logged monthly wages is the dependent variable.[6] The only factor that

[5] Because respondents to the survey entered the labor market in different years, I standardized wages by the consumer price index of each year. I used monthly rather than yearly wages in order to include all individuals who had ever worked. (A few women had worked less than a year, in which case they did not have yearly wages to report.) In analyzing wages, I do not consider nonemployees (the self-employed, home handicraft workers, and family enterprise workers). Family enterprise workers are generally unpaid, home handicraft workers work short and often irregular hours, and it is problematic to ask self-employed workers about their monthly wage rates. In any case, this does not seriously restrict the analysis, because over 90 percent of the younger cohort entered the labor force as full-time employees.

[6] In these equations, the dependent variable is logged monthly wages before taxes and including bonuses. Wages are typically logged in wage determination equations in order

affects women's starting wages is ability. Higher levels of education do not significantly affect starting wages, and neither do the size of the firm women enter, the location of the firm in the core or peripheral industrial sectors of the economy,[7] nor the characteristics of the job (white-collar or not, percentage female in the job category, or internal labor market). Only about 7 percent of the variance in women's wages is explained by the combination of all of these factors.

But for men, the effects of education reign supreme: successive levels of education bring greater monetary rewards (Appendix Table B.8).[8] In contrast to the effect of ability on women's wages, ability has no significant net effect for men. None of the industry or job variables contribute to men's earnings either.[9] In total, 17 percent of the variance in men's wages is explained, owing primarily to education.[10] In sum, while the utility of higher education is clear for a Japanese male, it is less clear for females. Women with higher education do not receive significantly higher starting wages than their less-educated counterparts, whereas men

---

to normalize the distribution. This is also advantageous because it renders the regression coefficients easy to interpret: the coefficient for a given independent variable indicates the percentage change in salary for a unit change in that variable (Halaby 1979).

[7] The industrial sector is included as a variable in order to test the assertion of some American sociologists and economists that wages and working conditions in general are better in the core sector. Industries were scored as being in the core (or monopoly) sector or in the periphery sector according to the classification used by Kawashima and Tachibanaki (1986). Core industries are: manufacturing, finance/insurance/real estate, transportation and communication, utilities, and the civil service. Industries in the periphery are: agriculture, construction, wholesale and retail sales, and services.

[8] Inspection of the regression equation shows that the effect of education is not perfectly linear: the benefits of a low-ranking university education are slightly higher than those of a medium- /high-ranking university education, and the benefits of a high school education show up as being higher than those of junior college/vocational school. Statistical tests were conducted to see whether the returns to different ranks of university were significantly different, and likewise for the effects of high school versus vocational school. These tests revealed no significant differences in these pairs of coefficients. We can therefore describe the effect of education as generally linear.

[9] These findings may seem to fly in the face of the widespread knowledge that large Japanese firms pay higher wages than smaller firms—here I have found no demonstrable effect of large firm size on wages. Yet this is consistent with the thesis of specific human capital, which argues that employees in large firms accept relatively low wages at the *start* of their careers in exchange for on-the-job training that involves costs to employers. Wages in large firms increase rapidly as the worker gains experience and becomes more valuable to the employer. In effect, employers and employees have an implicit contract that work experience (viz., commitment to the firm) will be rewarded with a steep age-earnings profile. The results for the survey respondents square with other research showing that Japanese firms of under 30 employees actually offer higher mean *starting* wages than firms of over 400 employees (Ono 1980).

[10] This finding might be partially accounted for if the variance in men's wages was higher, and there was thus more variation for the independent variables to explain. However, the variance in women's wages is actually higher.

TABLE 5.3

SEX SEGREGATION IN INITIAL JOBS
OF MALE AND FEMALE EMPLOYEES

	First job	
	White-collar	Blue-collar
Younger cohort (25–29) % female incumbents in job held by average woman	21.8	28.5
% female incumbents in job held by average man	4.4	4.9
	$t = 9.82, p < .001$	$t = 7.84, p < .001$
Older cohort (40–44) % female incumbents in job held by average woman	15.1	22.7
% female incumbents in job held by average man	6.1	3.0
	$t = 6.35, p < .001$	$t = 9.39, p < .001$

SOURCE: Survey conducted by author.

do. And when the difference in men's and women's education is held constant, men still earn significantly more than women.[11]

SEX SEGREGATION OF STARTING JOBS

The degree of sex segregation in the jobs men and women enter is also striking. William Bielby and James Baron (1984) have shown that in U.S. firms, men and women are almost totally segregated by job title. In the three-city survey, I asked respondents to estimate, for their workplace, the proportion of women in jobs similar to their own. This question was asked of employees only, because family enterprise workers, the self-employed, and home handicraft workers would be hard-

[11] Tests for the statistical significance of differences in the effect of education and ability for men and women verified this interpretation. The coefficients for education and ability are all significantly different for men and women at the .01 level or, in some cases, the .001 level.

pressed to know the universe of jobs to which they should be comparing their own. But as I have discussed so far, these nonemployee jobs are even more highly sex-segregated because family enterprise workers and home handicraft workers are almost always female.

Respondents' answers reveal a very high degree of sex segregation in all starting jobs, regardless of the size of firm or whether jobs were white- or blue-collar (Table 5.3). Younger women in white-collar jobs reported an average female incumbency rate of about 22 percent, whereas men in white-collar jobs reported a rate of only 4 percent. Sex segregation in the jobs of women remained consistent across size of firm, but men in the largest firms (not shown in the table) reported that only 1 percent of the individuals in their job type were female! The degree of sex segregation in the first jobs of the older cohort was also statistically significant, although not as extreme as in the younger cohort. There, women in white-collar jobs reported that only 15 percent of incumbents were female, whereas men reported a rate of 6 percent. Sex segregation was similar in firms of different sizes. Blue-collar jobs were even more highly segregated for both cohorts, with women reporting that their jobs were 20–30 percent female, and men stating that their jobs were less than 5 percent female.

These results show that the starting jobs of Japanese male and female employees in both cohorts were heavily sex-segregated, and this was especially true for white-collar jobs in large firms for the younger cohort. This adds yet another piece of evidence that the internal labor market structure of Japanese firms adversely affected the younger cohort of women even more than it had their predecessors.

Qualitative data add vivid illustration to the statistical description of hiring and recruitment of the sexes presented so far. Young women are hired into large companies to perform fundamentally different work than young men. In her late 1970s study of a small-scale protest by female municipal office workers in Kyoto, Pharr (1984) observed the interview process for female clerical workers. Both female and high-ranking male employees reported that after passing the civil service examination, female job applicants were routinely asked how they felt about serving tea to co-workers. If they objected, their chances of being hired went down. (A number of female employees objected in the 1960s to the implicit expectation that they prepare and serve tea no matter what their rank, but the Kyoto City Employees' Union did not consider the absence of this in their job description to be sufficient basis for complaint, and the "tea-pourers' rebellion" was squelched.)

TABLE 5.4

VARIATIONS IN INITIAL
CONDITIONS OF EMPLOYMENT FOR
NEW UNIVERSITY GRADUATES

Condition	% of firms
Type of work differs by sex	53.1
Women are transferred within regions of the country and men are transferred throughout the country	27.0
Women must commute from home and/or are not permitted to live alone in an apartment	17.9
Requirements for qualifications, major, or technical ability are different for men and women	16.6
General way of hiring men and women is different	8.1
Men are hired for the head office and women for regional offices	7.4
Married women are not hired	6.1
Age requirements differ for men and women	4.8
In the case of women, university graduates are treated the same as junior college graduates	3.5
Women must have someone introduce them to the company	2.3

SOURCE: Ministry of Labor, Japan, 1985a.
NOTES: Figures are based on responses from firms surveyed by the Ministry of Labor that report that conditions of employment differ for male and female university graduates. Figures do not sum to 100 percent because the question permitted multiple responses. The same question was asked about graduates from other levels of education, but because the answers vary little by education the university case is taken as representative.

In the course of my own fieldwork, a personnel manager in a major electronics corporation (who asked that his company remain anonymous) explained company policy toward women:

> As a major company, it is our responsibility to go along with the dominant ideology in society [*shakai tsūnen*]. Parents give us their daughters to take care of for a period before marriage, and we are responsible for them. Business trips, transfers, and so on are difficult for women—who will take care of them if something goes wrong? Rather than risk the possibility of an auto accident or whatever, we feel it is better to create a hands-off policy to begin with and go along with society's responsibility to protect women.

These comments represent an extreme conservatism that by no means pervades all corporate environments in Japan but is, by the same token, not unexceptional. The Labor Ministry asked employers in 1985 how

men's and women's initial employment conditions differed (Table
5.4).Employers most frequently stated that the nature of the work differs
for the sexes. Other frequently cited differences are that women are not
transferred as widely as men (27 percent of employers), women are not
permitted to live alone (18 percent), and the job requirements are different for men and women (17 percent). Many of these conditions appear
sex-discriminatory to Western eyes. Others simply seem rather foreign,
such as the restrictions on living arrangements for women or the necessity
for an introduction to the company by another party. Some large, prestigious companies feel that unmarried women living alone are socially
suspect, and that they should be living at home with parents or relatives.
The requirement of a personal introduction by a superior such as a teacher or family friend provides another means of screening out women who
may not "fit in" properly to the company.

"Fitting in" often has a very particular meaning for women. Some
large companies view young female employees mainly as a pool of
potential marriage mates for their up-and-coming young male employees. This was first brought to my attention when a middle-level manager in a major corporation mentioned to me that his company kept
an eye out for job applicants from one of the major private Catholic
women's universities in Tokyo. When I inquired as to the reason, he
replied: "Such women make good wives for the young salarymen in
our company, whose work leaves them little time to date or to look
for a suitable mate."[12]

Support for the notion that prestigious firms place a high value on
attractiveness and good upbringing in their young women workers
comes from other sources as well. A graduate student in his late twenties suggested to me that I should have asked in the survey where
university-educated women had lived during their college days. He
explained:

> Female job candidates for large corporations must have impeccable "rep-
> utations." I have a close friend who works for _____ Heavy Industries.
> In his first year, he was chosen to be what they call a "recruiter," which
> means that he, along with senior recruiters, screens all the job candidates
> from his alma mater and decides who gets official job interviews. According

---

[12] Based on his study of a large general trading company, McLendon writes: "In de-
ciding which company to join, a young man takes into consideration its reputation for
the beauty, charm, education, and personal cultivation of its women." He emphasizes
that female employees, faced with "almost no possibility of developing long-term work
careers that would bring them into a closer identification with the organization's goals,"
also use the company as a place to search for a mate (McLendon 1983: 158–59).

to him, _____ never hires women who lived alone during their college days. Because such women are under less parental supervision than those who live in their parents' home, they may possibly have less than "reputable" social (and sexual) lives prior to recruitment, which may not be suitable for their male workers. So they [the firm] engage in an act of statistical discrimination and altogether avoid hiring women who are from other parts of the country and thus lived away from their parents during their college days in Tokyo. Consequently, female workers in the main office of _____ Heavy Industries consist exclusively of those from the Tokyo metropolitan area.

A conversation with three women in a large pharmaceuticals company in Tokyo is indicative of women's perception of the relative employment conditions of males and females:

> A: "In our company, men and women aren't treated equally—from hiring to retirement. When a single man enters the company, the company provides him with housing in a dormitory at very low cost, and when he marries, he and his family can move into company housing. But you know what happens in the case of a woman? There is no women's housing, and the company does not subsidize her housing in any way. And when she marries, well, she must quit. . . . Of course, it isn't written in her employment contract; that would be illegal. But the manager tells her that that's the way it is. Isn't that right, Ms. B?"
>
> B: "Yes, when I was hired five months ago, I was told that I would have to quit when I got married."
>
> Me: "Ms. A and Ms. C, are you married?"
>
> A: (Laughter) "Oh, no, of course not. I've worked in this company for eleven years, and Ms. C has been an employee for thirteen years. We are pharmacists."

Although the pharmaceutical field is often held up to women as having good opportunities for advancement, the two women in the scene sketched above who *were* pharmacists and had worked continuously had never married. Ms. B has yet to face such a decision.

Ethnographic data and statistics on the wages, internal labor market status, and sex segregation of the starting jobs of men and women all belie the superficial similarity in starting jobs suggested by the equivalence in numbers of men and women entering large firms. They are hired under different conditions, and employers have different expectations of their subsequent behaviors. Moreover, there is a striking lack of improvement between the two cohorts in the conditions of women's first jobs relative to men's, measured by internal labor market placement, wages, and job-level sex segregation. University education also

TABLE 5.5

TYPES OF ON-THE-JOB TRAINING
GIVEN TO NEW SCHOOL GRADUATES
(%)

Companies' training practices	Given equally to men and women	Different for men and women	Men only	Women only	Total
1. General improvement in attitude (54.6% of companies)	75.8	6.4	3.9	13.9	100.0
2. General orientation and transmission of basic knowledge (58.1% of companies)	83.3	6.5	8.5	1.7	100.0
3. Transmission of basic knowledge and skills for the organizational division and its type of work (67.7% of companies)	72.1	12.3	14.2	1.4	100.0

SOURCE: Ministry of Labor, Japan, 1985a.

contributes less to women's internal labor market placement and wages than to men's.

The sexes' workplace experiences diverge further as they are exposed to the training and promotion practices of firms.

MEN'S AND WOMEN'S EMPLOYMENT EXPERIENCES OVER THE LIFE CYCLE

TRAINING AND JOB ROTATION

A point often overlooked in the Western praises sung to Japanese-style management and on-the-job training is that gender differentiation is further accentuated in the training process. Managers, who are almost universally men, make judgments about workers' inherent skills and preferences. They frequently perceive that men and women differ on both counts, and these judgments have major ramifications for the differentiation of skills, work commitment, and income of men and women over time. Managers and foremen also make judgments about the role conflict married women feel between their family and workplace responsibilities.

TABLE 5.6
TYPES OF ON-THE-JOB TRAINING
FOR CURRENT EMPLOYEES
(%)

Companies' training practices	Given equally to men and women	Different for men and women	Men only	Women only	Total
Improvement of knowledge and skills for current job (66.1% of companies)	57.7	9.6	32.1	0.6	100.0
Transmission of knowledge and skills for transfer to position with same degree of complexity as current job (32.9% of companies)	49.3	10.4	39.9	0.4	100.0
Transmission of knowledge and skills for transfer to higher-level job (34.3% of companies)	40.9	13.3	45.6	0.2	100.0
Transmission of knowledge and skills after transfer to higher-level job, for purposes of carrying out that job (36.1% of companies)	40.1	10.4	49.5	0.0	100.0
Transmission of knowledge and skills for promotion to position that has subordinates (36.1% of companies)	36.2	6.1	57.7	0.0	100.0
Transmission of knowledge and skills after promotion to position that has subordinates, for purposes of carrying out that job (33.6% of companies)	35.7	5.9	58.4	0.0	100.0

SOURCE: Ministry of Labor, Japan, 1985a.

Tables 5.5 and 5.6 show figures on on-the-job training collected by the Japanese Labor Ministry in 1985 for a sample of 4,800 firms ranging in size from 30 to 1,000 or more employees. Table 5.5 gives information on the types of training given to male and female employees (new graduates) when they enter the firm, and Table 5.6 shows training statistics for employees already in the firm.

TABLE 5.7
APPLICATION OF POLICY OF
ROTATION AMONG WORK POSITIONS
(%)

	(1)	(2)	(3)
Applies equally to men and women	57.5	46.4	7.2
Applies only to men	19.2	40.1	86.6
For women, policy is restricted to certain jobs	20.3	10.0	0.7
For women, policy is practiced only if they request it	2.1	2.6	4.7
Other	0.9	0.9	0.8
Total	100.0	100.0	100.0

SOURCE: Ministry of Labor, Japan, 1985a.
NOTE: (1) Rotation within workplace, carried out by 46.1 percent of companies; (2) Rotation between offices or branches that does not require a change of residence, carried out by 24.3 percent of companies; (3) Rotation between offices or branches that requires a change of residence, carried out by 19.0 percent of companies.

Training designed to shape general attitudes is given to new employees by 55 percent of companies; 58 percent provide training for general orientation and to transmit basic knowledge; and 68 percent do so to transmit basic knowledge and the skills specific to each division in the company. The distribution of each type of training by gender is revealing: the likelihood that training will be given only to men increases as the training becomes more sophisticated (from level 1 to level 3 in Table 5.5). Fewer than 4 percent of firms restrict general training to men, whereas 14 percent limit division-level training to men. Almost 14 percent of companies give general attitude training only to women, and fewer than 2 percent give basic knowledge and specific division-level knowledge to women only. The least gender-differentiated type of training involves the imparting of general knowledge.

Table 5.6 shows that greater sex differentiation emerges as employees move through the company. Approximately 58 percent of firms give equivalent opportunities for training to men and women in order to help them improve their performance in their current positions. But the proportion of firms giving training to both sexes declines (and the proportion giving training only to men increases) as the training becomes more and more oriented to job changes and promotions in the firm. (The trend is strikingly linear as we move down the table in column 3, showing training given to men only.) These figures move in tandem with the rarity of Japanese women's advancement in the organization.

Job rotation involves moving the employee through different sections and divisions of the firm to increase his or her familiarity with various work activities and to allow the employer gradually to make an informed assessment of the individual's special talents. Table 5.7 shows Labor Ministry data on gender differentiation in job rotation in Japanese companies. Rotation within the workplace is carried out by nearly half of all companies, rotation among branches of the same firm is carried out by about one-quarter of companies, and rotation requiring a residence change is carried out by about one-fifth. Nearly 60 percent of companies apply a policy of rotation within the workplace equally to male and female employees. The figure falls markedly as rotation moves outside the office, to less than 10 percent in the case where a change of residence is necessary. In summary, job rotation opportunities are heavily oriented toward male employees, and this tendency is strongest when rotation occurs outside the confines of the immediate work setting.

Ethnographic data illustrate the distribution of training and the assignment of job responsibilities based on sex. In an organizational training chart used in a class taught by a young assistant professor in economics at my Japanese host university, one category of workers was labeled "female employees" (*joshi shain*). Part of their training was listed as "mutual discussion and support," and I noticed that this was not included under the list of training requirements for other employees. I asked my friend what the phrase meant. Laughing ruefully, he said: "It probably means they have to learn how not to complain."

An interview with a branch manager of a Japanese supermarket chain provides a graphic illustration of sex differences in training. When new school graduates entered the company, they went on a five-day retreat (*kenshūkai*) to "wash off the dirt" (*aka o otosu*) from their school life and to experience a transition to the next stage of life: work. For men, this was followed by a two-month training period during which they were rotated among various jobs to gain familiarity with the overall work process. Women's training, on the other hand, lasted two weeks and focused on how to operate the cash register. The branch manager explained that after one year, the supermarket surveys the new employees and asks them what they would like to do. Curiously, women always seem to pick the same things: "They like to deal with fruit or candy because it's pretty." A similar scenario was repeated by a foreman at an auto parts factory, who stated, "Women are skilled at repetitive work. After three years, men can do some repair work, and so differences start to emerge." These examples from a supermarket and a factory suggest that the different training and socialization men and women experience on the job play a role in their development of different preferences and skills.

In the three-city study, more men than women report having received on-the-job training: 47 percent of men and 21 percent of women in the older cohort had had such training at some point during their work careers (a difference that is statistically significant at the .001 level). Since some on-the-job training is actually socialization into the workplace, it occurs soon after the individual starts working. So it also makes sense to look at the younger cohort, to see if men and women have already had different training experiences after working for several years. Indeed, the difference between the sexes has already appeared by the time people have been in the labor market for five to ten years: 46 percent of men and 35 percent of women report having had on-the-job training (a difference significant at the .05 level).[13] It is surprising that even without specifying the type or amount of on-the-job training, fewer women than men report having received *any* training at all.

In contrast, more young women (about 14 percent) than young men (7 percent) in the survey have had some job-applicable training in school (statistically significant at the .05 level). Men and women in the older cohort are less likely to have gotten such training, but here again, about twice as many women (5.4 percent) as men (2 percent) had any kind of job-related training while they were in school (a difference significant at the .05 level). Thus while men have a greater propensity than women to receive on-the-job training, women are more likely than men to receive job-related training in school. School-based train-

---

[13] These figures were calculated for everyone in the sample who had work experience. We could also exclude the few people who entered the labor market as self-employed or family enterprise workers, for the issue of on-the-job training is not really relevant for them. When we exclude this small group and recalculate the figures, the sex differences in probability of training remain the same. That is, even among people who started out their work lives as full-time employees, men are more apt to receive on-the-job training than women.

ing prepares women for professions such as teaching and nursing, or personal services such as hairdressing.

Job rotation experiences were also examined via the survey data. Because the purpose of job rotation is to give some experience in different parts of the company to employees who will presumably remain with the firm over a long period of time, it can be viewed as an employer investment that is more specialized than on-the-job training. An analysis of job rotation was carried out with the survey data, and was restricted to those workers who began their work lives in situations where job rotation practices were most likely to occur. Excluded, then, are people in occupations where job rotation is not really a relevant concept: people in professional occupations such as teaching or medicine; in occupations related to agriculture, forestry, fishing, or mining; in protective services (police and firemen); and in personal services (such as hairdressing or housecleaning). Also excluded are self-employed workers, family enterprise workers, and piece-rate (home handicraft) workers.

Appendix Table B.10 shows the determinants of whether people are rotated among jobs in their first workplaces or not. (Appendix Table B.9 shows the means and standard deviations of the variables.) About one-third of men, compared to 14 percent of women, have had job rotation experience (a difference statistically significant at the .001 level). (Again, these figures are relatively high because they are restricted to people in the subset of occupations where job rotation is likely to be practiced.)

The first equation in Table B.10 includes characteristics of the individual (sex, cohort, ability, and education) and in the second equation characteristics of the worker's first job and workplace are added (full-time employee, starting wages, firm size, internal labor market, and industrial sector). The effects of ability and education are what we would predict. High school education and education at a medium- / high-ranking university have the strongest effect on job rotation. Once job and workplace characteristics enter the equation the significance of ability and education diminish, with ability in particular becoming statistically insignificant. It is clear that part of the contribution human capital makes to enhancing the probability of receiving job rotation experience lies in helping the individual to get into the type of job and firm where such experience is offered. Job and workplace characteristics contribute significantly to the variance explained in job rotation.

Being a full-time worker significantly increases one's chances of being rotated among jobs in the workplace, as does being in a large firm. Moreover, an internal labor market position contributes significantly to the probability of job rotation even when full-time employment and firm size are controlled. Starting wages are not significantly related to job rotation. This is to be expected, given that starting wages are not higher in large firms (and it is large firms where job rotation is most common). Being in industries such as finance or utilities contributes to the probability of job rotation, but being in certain others, such as sales, does not. (These industries were all of particular interest because more employers there have reported using job rotation practices than employers in other industries; see Table 4.1.) No significant differences in the qualifications for job rotation exist between men and women.[14] This means, for example, that higher education does not raise the probability of men being rotated among jobs in the workplace significantly more than it does for women, or vice versa. All else held equal, women are simply less likely overall than men to experience job rotation, as shown by the persistently significant effect of sex after other variables are controlled. When statistical interactions with sex were tested, no significant results were found.

Appendix Table B.11 follows up this analysis with an examination of the determinants of employer changes in the course of individuals' working lives.[15] Given that seniority contributes so highly to wages in Japan, it is important to see what determines continuous tenure with one employer; we would expect job rotation in the first workplace to be one such factor. In the first equation, individual characteristics (including years spent in the labor force) and job and workplace characteristics are considered. In the second equation, I add job rotation to see if it has an additional impact once other variables are controlled.

---

[14] It could be argued that the population "at risk" for job rotation includes only those who remain with the employer for a minimum period of time. People who are in a workplace for only a short period may not even reach the point of being considered for this type of training. In light of this, the analysis was also conducted for individuals who remained with their first employer for at least two years. This reduced the sample size from 749 to 681. The only differences between this analysis and the analysis across all workers were that two variables that had been significant at the .05 level (low-ranking university and full-time employee) dropped just below significance.

[15] In preliminary analyses, the equation was dominated by the effect of an exit from the labor force. Such an exit is virtually coterminous with an employer change (except under the rare circumstance that the individual returns to the same employer). The analysis reported here is therefore restricted to people who had not experienced any employment interruption longer than six months.

Sex and ability have strong effects on whether one leaves the initial employer or not: men are more likely to stay, as are high-ability individuals. People who have been in the labor force longer are more likely to have switched employers, a logical outcome. While education has a negative effect, none of the education coefficients are significant. No workplace characteristics have any impact on employer changes, except that individuals in sales are more likely to have experienced an employer shift. Job rotation, net of the effects of all other variables, has a powerful impact on employer changes. Individuals who received job rotation experience in the first workplace are much less likely to switch employers. This is precisely what the theory of specific human capital would predict—workers who have been "invested in" by their employer are less likely to move (Becker 1964; Oi 1983).

This investigation of job rotation demonstrates that women are significantly less likely to receive this type of employer investment, even when we control for the difference in education between men and women and differences in their work status. The probability of job rotation is higher for men, and is also associated with higher education, full-time employment in a large firm and in an internal labor market, and employment in the finance/insurance or utilities industry. One result of job rotation experience on the first job is a higher probability of remaining with the same employer across the years of one's working life, a strong benefit in the Japanese labor market.

One could argue that women are consistently *choosing* positions that do not have long-term potential and training opportunities, but such an interpretation seems highly unlikely. As discussed in previous chapters, large Japanese firms tend to hire generalists straight out of school and assign them to positions in the company. Purposely eliminated from this analysis of job rotation were occupations (such as teaching or hairdressing) for which this would not be true. It would also be hard to argue that women are choosing school-related training and purposely forgoing workplace training; most of the women with school-based training are eliminated by default from this statistical analysis. In sum, it is difficult to avoid the conclusion that the results described here stem from employers' preferential allocation of training opportunities in the workplace to men.[16]

---

[16] Still, some might argue that there is another reason besides discrimination that only 14 percent of Japanese women in industry compared to 32 percent of men receive job rotation. Perhaps women do make this decision, not out of occupational choice, but out of a straightforward rejection of training opportunities offered them. Although here

TABLE 5.8
WOMEN'S RATES OF LEAVING
THE LABOR FORCE UPON MARRIAGE

	Left labor force within one year of marrying	Didn't leave labor force within one year of marrying
Younger cohort (25–29)		
%	43.1	56.9
N	(72)	(95)
Older cohort (40–44)		
%	43.4	56.6
N	(155)	(202)

SOURCE: Survey conducted by author.
NOTE: $X^2 = .000$, $df = 1$; not significant.

DIVERGING PATHS: EMPLOYMENT EXPERIENCES ACROSS THE LIFE CYCLE

By the time Japanese men and women reach their early forties, their experiences diverge in even more ways. Whereas the vast majority of men have worked continuously, an equally vast majority of women have not. In 1988, only 13.5 percent of married women workers in their early forties had been continuously employed since their early twenties (Ministry of Labor, Japan, 1988). In addition to differences in the length of employment, fewer women than men have spent the totality of their working lives as employees; more have switched instead to self-employment or family enterprise work.

Among the critical questions for understanding the divergence in men's and women's labor market paths, perhaps the most important is women's pattern of quitting upon marriage or childbirth.

Women's Quitting Behaviors: Who Leaves and Who Doesn't?   Table 5.8 shows that slightly fewer than half of each cohort of women in the three-city study left the labor force within one year after marriage. Surprisingly, there is no difference between the two cohorts: younger

---

again Japanese organizational case studies and ethnographic evidence argue heavily to the contrary, I attempted to test this alternative hypothesis by running the job rotation analysis separately for women. Here, I included information on whether they had aspirations at age 18 to work continuously once their education was completed. This variable, the best available measure of a woman's work commitment, had no effect on whether she received job rotation experience or not.

women are as likely to leave the workplace when they marry as older women were. This table is restricted to women who have married, so it could be that the younger group is a slightly more select group than the older one. In other words, the younger women represent those who have married already (about two-thirds of the younger cohort sample), and they may therefore be more "conservative" than their counterparts who have not yet married. To investigate this, I also constructed a table that restricted the young cohort to only the 28–29 year olds (72 percent of whom had married). But even after weeding out the young married women, 41 percent of the remaining group had quit the labor force when they married—almost as many as in the entire sample of young women. So the general conclusion about the behavior of young women remains.

The virtually identical behavior of two groups of women who are separated historically by a fifteen-year period is very interesting. The older group of women reached marriage age in the mid 1960s; the younger group in the early 1980s. Despite this historical gap, the link between marriage and leaving the labor force did not significantly alter during this period.[17] This reflects the first drop in the M-shaped age curve of female labor force participation that is unique to Japan in contrast to Western industrial countries. Recent opinion polls in Japan also show virtually no variation in attitudes among different age groups of women when they are asked whether it is best for a woman to leave the labor force when she marries or has her first child. About 15 percent of women in every age group surveyed feel that a woman should permanently leave the labor force when she marries, and an additional 10 percent feel instead that a woman should leave permanently when she has her first child. But over 50 percent of women

[17] Government statistics can be a bit misleading on this. The Labor Ministry reports the proportion of women aged 20–24 and 25–29 in the labor force. Were there to have been a major historical change from the 1960s to the early 1980s, we would see a smaller drop in labor force participation across these age groups. In 1965, 70.2 percent of women aged 20–24 were in the labor force, and five years later (after most of these women had probably married) 45.5 percent of that cohort were working. The figures beginning in 1980 were 70.0 and 54.1. The drop in labor force participation is thus in fact less substantial now, but during this period, women's mean age at marriage also rose a full year, from 24.4 to 25.5. Although government statistics do not report the *variance* in age at marriage, it is undoubtedly the case that a larger proportion of women aged 25–29 in 1985 were unmarried, compared to 25–29 year-olds in 1965. In other words, the labor force participation rate of 25–29 year-olds now includes more unmarried women than it previously did. It would therefore be erroneous to conclude from the increase in the labor force participation rate that fewer women are leaving the labor force upon marriage. It is still a little too early to accurately assess trends since 1985.

favor a third pattern: quitting at marriage or childbirth and returning to work when childrearing responsibilities are completed (Office of the Prime Minister, Japan, 1987a).

Quitting at marriage rather than at childbirth has been the most common pattern for Japanese women. In the older cohort of survey respondents, about 60 percent of women left within one year of either marriage or the birth of the first child; of this group, 80 percent left upon marrying. Unfortunately, it is not possible to compare the older to the younger cohort on this, as many women in the younger cohort have not yet had their first child.

What sorts of variations are there between the women who leave the labor force soon after marriage and those who do not? In particular, are highly educated women less likely to leave? More likely? How about women of high ability? Do the few women who enter internal labor markets in large firms or government have a lower probability of leaving? To look at these questions, I conducted an analysis of women in the three-city study to predict who left the labor force within one year after marriage and who continued working. This analysis was restricted to older women because some of the younger women have not yet married and faced this issue, whereas of course all of the older women have made their choices. In this analysis and others involving older women, university-educated women are considered as one group no matter what the ranking of their institution was. There are so few women in this age group who went to four-year universities that it is not statistically possible to retain the university "quality" distinction used in other analyses (to separate out people who went to low- and medium- /high-ranking universities).

Appendix Table B.14 shows the results. (Appendix Tables B.12 and B.13 describe the variables for the analysis and show their means and standard deviations.) Little predicts which women leave the labor force. Education is not a good predictor; all women educated above the junior high school level are more apt to quit than junior high school graduates, but of these, only high school graduates are *significantly* more likely to quit. Ability is unrelated to quitting behavior. In another analysis, I looked at whether the handful of women who had entered internal labor markets in either large firms or the government had been less likely to quit. As a group, they had not. I then investigated instead the size of the firm in which a woman initially worked, in tandem with her employment in the private or public sector. As Table B.14 shows, women who were in government service were less likely than other women to quit; in fact, this has the strongest effect of any variable. This finding is consistent with the common view in Japan that the government sector is more meritocratic than the private sector, and that women of high ability should set their sights on it (Lebra 1981).

In general, if a woman's participation in the labor force was as an employee, she was more likely to quit upon marriage (all else held equal). This makes sense intuitively because it contrasts with the behavior of women engaged in family businesses or piecework, statuses more traditionally compatible with marriage because of the location and hours of work.

The characteristics of the woman's husband have little predictive value. In the absence of information on husband's income or occupation at the time of marriage, education was used as a proxy. Better-educated young men are likely to have higher incomes and to be employees, often in white-collar jobs, and one might expect their wives to be more likely to quit work (because they can afford to). But whether or not her husband was a university graduate does not serve to predict a woman's quitting behavior. Nor is a woman's exit behavior from the labor force at marriage very much affected by her husband's employment conditions. (Of course, whether a woman *eventually* leaves the labor force and stays out for a long time may nonetheless be affected by her husband's earning power; this is a separate question.) Women who married at later ages had a greater tendency to quit work when they married than those who married young. These later-marrying women are more likely to be ready to settle into domesticity and begin childbearing. One might argue in the context of the United States that late-marrying women are more committed to their careers. But given the strong norm for Japanese women to have children by their late twenties, late marriers are likely to begin childbearing soon after marriage. Morgan, Rindfuss, and Parnell (1984) found that late-marrying women in Japan were more likely than other women to give birth within the first fifteen months of marriage, although the difference between early and late marriers was not substantial enough to be statistically significant. The pattern is reversed in the United States: women who marry *young* are more apt to bear a child within fifteen months of marriage.

The weak relationship between education and the likelihood of leaving the work force upon marriage is consistent with findings for a large sample of Tokyo women reported by Tanaka Kazuko (1987), who found high rates of withdrawal from the labor force after marriage, especially for recent cohorts. This held at all levels of education. Life-cycle employment patterns for highly educated women in her sample had changed little over eight successive cohorts. The most recent Japanese national fertility survey in 1987 also found that even women in the youngest cohort showed a strong tendency to withdraw from the labor force soon after marriage, regardless of their level of education (Japan Institute of Labor 1990). Instead of being an investment that "pays off" for Japanese women in terms of work continuity, education may pay off in what Arleen Leibowitz (1975) has called "home productivity" by allowing women the opportunity to care for their own children rather than using daycare. Japanese women become strong investors in the human capital of their children, a subject taken up in the next chapter.

The complexity of the relationship between a woman's educational level and her long-run work patterns shows up in other areas besides the behavior of quitting upon marriage. In the younger cohort, women at either end of the educational spectrum—junior high school or university—are significantly more likely than high school or junior college graduates to be in the labor force. But among women in their mid forties, the university-educated are the *least* likely of any group to be working, and junior high school graduates are the most likely. Junior high school graduates have spent more years on average in the labor force than other women, and this is a highly significant statistical difference ($p < .001$). Of course, in a sense, they got a "headstart" on other women because they entered the labor market at an earlier age, after junior high school graduation. But even after the age at entering the labor market is statistically controlled for, junior high school–educated Japanese women have worked more years than other women. The university-educated have spent the fewest years in the labor force, although their behavior is not so very different from that of women who have completed high school or junior college.

Years of Employment   Partly because it is so common for Japanese women to withdraw from the labor force after marriage, men and women on average accumulate very different amounts of employment experience. Men in their early forties have spent an average of 22.7 years in the labor force, whereas women have spent an average of only 12.6 years. Figure 5.1 shows the proportions of different types of employment experience reported by middle-aged Japanese men and wom-

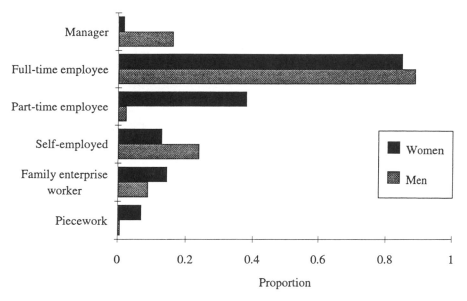

Figure 5.1. Proportion of Japanese Men and Women Aged 40–44 with Experience in Various Types of Employment
SOURCE: Survey conducted by author.

en. The vast majority of both sexes (89 percent of men and 85 percent of women) have at some point worked as full-time employees. Other than this, there are virtually no similarities between the work experiences of middle-aged men and women. (The contrasts shown in the figure are all statistically significant at the .001 level). Among men, 16 percent report having had some managerial experience, compared to only 2 percent of women. Experience as a self-employed worker is twice as common among men as among women. In contrast, nearly 40 percent of women have had the experience of working part-time, compared to only 2 percent of men. Experience as a family enterprise worker or pieceworker is also much more common for women than for men.[18] As is clear from looking at the younger cohort (Fig. 5.2),

[18] Figures showing the proportion of working life spent by each sex in different employment statuses complement this analysis. All of the gender differences are significant, including the proportion of working life spent as a full-time employee: men have spent an average of 73 percent of their working lives in that status compared to 63 percent for women. This basis of comparing the experiences of the two sexes is less satisfactory than that discussed in the text, however. The reason is that most women exited the labor force for some period of time, and this was not true of men. Comparing the proportion of *working life* spent in each status for men and women therefore understates the actual difference in adult life experiences between the sexes.

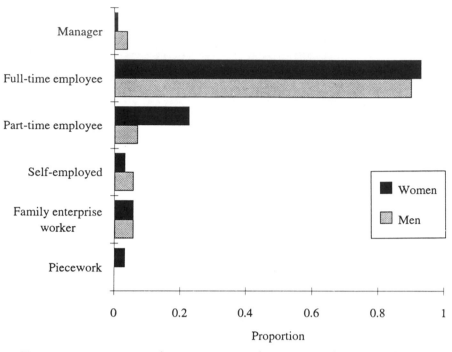

Figure 5.2. Proportion of Japanese Men and Women Aged 25–29 with Experience in Various Types of Employment
SOURCE: Survey conducted by author.

the differences between men's and women's experiences start to emerge early in the life course, but are not yet very substantial at that point. Young men have worked an average of 6.8 years, compared to 5.6 years for young women (statistically significant at the .001 level). The only statistically significant differences in employment status are that more young women (9 percent) than young men (3 percent) have spent some of their work life as part-time employees, and the same holds true for piecework (although a trivial proportion of young women— 2 percent—have such experience). The weak sex differences in experience observed for the young group are greatly magnified in the older group. Based on the data presented in this book from a variety of sources, we can say with confidence that this represents a combination of both age and cohort effects. Slight differences have emerged very early in men's and women's working lives, and these will become greater across time. They may not reach the magnitude evident for the older cohort, but they are likely to be strong and significant.

TABLE 5.9
CHANGES IN SEX SEGREGATION FROM
INITIAL TO CURRENT JOB OF
MALE AND FEMALE EMPLOYEES

	White-collar	Blue-collar
Younger cohort (25–29)		
% female incumbents in		
job held by average woman		
First job	21.8	28.5
Current job	25.0	26.3
% female incumbents in		
job held by average man		
First job	4.4	4.9
Current job	3.4	3.4
Older cohort (40–44)		
% female incumbents in		
job held by average woman		
First job	15.1	22.7
Current job	17.3	26.5
% female incumbents in		
job held by average man		
First job	6.1	3.0
Current job	1.9	1.6

SOURCE: Survey conducted by author.

Although a high degree of sex segregation exists in starting jobs, it increases as men and women gain more work experience (Table 5.9). Little change occurs by the late twenties, when men and women have been in the labor force for only 5–10 years. But in the older cohort, current jobs reflect potentially 20–25 years of work experience. By that time, fewer than 2 percent of the incumbents in the job categories that men occupy are female.

What is most striking about the sex segregation of jobs is its stability—across cohorts and across the jobs people hold at different points in their lives. The typical female composition of the job category occupied by a Japanese woman employee, whether white- or blue-collar, varies from 15 to 29 percent. Japanese men's job categories are never more than 6 percent female and are sometimes as low as under 2 percent female. These figures would be even more extreme if we could reasonably measure the sex segregation of other types of workers—the self-employed, family enterprise workers, and home handicraft work-

TABLE 5.10

CURRENT EMPLOYMENT STATUS
OF OLDER COHORT (40–44)

	Full-time employee or manager	Part-time, temporary, or daily employee	Self-employed	Family enterprise worker	Piece-worker	Total
Men						
%	76.6	1.7	20.5	1.3	0.0	100.0
N	(183)	(4)	(49)	(3)	(0)	(239)
Women						
%	31.1	34.0	16.0	15.1	3.8	100.0
N	(74)	(81)	(38)	(36)	(9)	(238)

SOURCE: Survey conducted by author.
NOTE: $X^2 = 154.29$, $df = 4$; $p < .001$.

ers—or if we were to count "housewife" as a job that is 100 percent female.

Employment Status   By the time Japanese women reach their early forties, nearly 70 percent have reentered the labor force after having spent several years at home raising children (Ministry of Labor, Japan, 1988). The three-city survey complements this national statistic: 66 percent of women aged 40–44 participated in the work force in some capacity. Table 5.10 shows the employment status of the survey sample of men and women in their forties, excluding women not currently in the labor force. Women are quite evenly distributed across the categories of full-time employee, part-time employee, and the combined category of family enterprise worker/pieceworker/self-employed worker. Much less variation exists in men's roles: almost 80 percent are full-time employees, and nearly all of the remaining men are self-employed. Very few are engaged as part-time employees or as family enterprise workers. The difference between the distribution of employment statuses for the two sexes is demonstrated by the very large X^2 value for the table.

Log-linear analyses of the movement (or stability) of men and women from one employment status to another also show that men are more apt to remain employees than women (Table 5.11). In modeling men's mobility between their initial employment status and the one they hold in mid-life, we need to include a term for persistence in the status of employee in order to find a model that fits the data well. This

TABLE 5.11
EMPLOYMENT-STATUS MOBILITY,
OLDER COHORT (40–44)

Destination

Origin	Men				Women			
	Employee	Self-employed	Family enterprise worker	Total	Employee	Self-employed	Family enterprise worker	Total
Employee	163	32	0	195	141	19	27	187
Self-employed	11	13	0	24	4	13	1	18
Family enterprise worker	11	2	3	16	5	4	14	23
Total	185	47	3	235	150	36	42	228

Models	Log-linear analysis					
	Men			Women		
	G^2	ΔG^2	df	G^2	ΔG^2	df
1. [R] [C]	30.88	—	4	60.16	—	4
2. [R] [C] [D]	9.01	21.87[a]	3	2.91[a]	57.25[a]	3
3. [R] [C] [D] [Z]	5.57[a]	3.44[a]	2	2.70[a]	.21	2

NOTE: R = row effect; C = column effect; D = diagonal effect; Z = effect of persistence in employee status.
[a]$p < .05$.

is not so for women: it is sufficient to take into account women's overall distribution in their initial employment, their current employment, and the persistence of some women in the employment status in which they started out (the diagonal effect in a mobility table). Many women become nonemployees as they age, and it is essential to ask why. About 20 percent of middle-aged men are also nonemployees, and their experiences constitute a baseline against which to compare women's experience.

Appendix Table B.17 shows the determinants of self-employment for older men. (Appendix Tables B.15 and B.16 give information on the variables.) Men who are currently self-employed are lower in native ability than other men, are more likely to have begun their work life as self-employed workers, and are unlikely to have started out in internal labor markets in large firms or government. Neither education nor father's employment status have a significant influence on this outcome, although a father's self-employment is positively related to his son's.[19] The family circumstances of men in their forties—notably whether they are married or not, and the age at which they married—do not affect their current self-employment either. (These variables were tested in models not shown here.) Thus, little predicts whether a man will be self-employed in middle age except the fact that he began his work life in self-employment.

Women's employment destiny by mid-life tells a different story. For one thing, women are distributed across a full range of employment statuses. While Japanese women's mid-life employment situations are more varied than men's, they are also more varied than American women's. As Anne Hill has demonstrated (1983, 1984), the decision to work is not as straightforward for married women in Japan as in the United States, where women have historically been much less likely to be employed in family-run enterprises. The employment decision for middle-aged Japanese women involves several possibilities. The analysis of this is shown in Appendix Table B.18, which is restricted to currently married women with children because they constitute the great majority of the sample.[20] (A very high proportion—97 percent—of all

[19] These results are somewhat surprising. But as Appendix Table B.16 shows, 27.4 percent of men currently in their early forties had fathers who were self-employed in business. An additional 16.5 percent had self-employed fathers in agriculture. These were not aggregated together with self-employed fathers in business because it is much more unlikely that the urban sons in the sample have inherited rural self-employment, and it is inheritance of employment status with which we are concerned here. So these results partially demonstrate the amount of mobility *away* from self-employment in the generation we are looking at, where only about 22 percent of men were engaged in *any* type of self-employment, including agriculture.

[20] Only eight older women never married, another seven are widowed, and six are separated or divorced. All of these twenty-one women work, sixteen of them as employees. The salience of marital status was demonstrated in a log-linear analysis of women's age, marital status (married or not), year (1970, 1975, 1980, or 1985), and employment status ("regular employees"—generally full-time; temporary and daily employees—including most part-time workers, family enterprise workers, and self-employed workers). This analysis was done on population data from the *Shūgyō kōzō kihon chōsa* (Office of the Prime Minister, Japan, 1987b). The fact that it was carried out on population data means that the X^2 values themselves are all significant (i.e., all models show a significant fit). The important question is what combination of two variables can best account for the joint distribution in the table. In the analysis, the relative contributions of four different combinations of variables were compared: employment status and year; age and employment status; age and marital status; and marital status and employment status. Of these, the interaction of marital status and employment status was the most

men and women in the survey cohort aged 40–44 are currently married or have been married.)[21]

Four employment statuses are considered: full-time employment, part-time employment, self-employment or employment as a family enterprise worker, or full-time housewife (not participating in the labor force). The equations in Appendix Table B.18 contrast full-time housewives with each of the other statuses. Women are more apt to be self-employed or family enterprise workers than housewives if they started their working life in that status; they are married to a man who is self-employed; they live in a household that includes parents, parents-in-law, or other adult relatives; and their youngest child is older than twelve. Both the circumstances of these women's original participation in the labor market and the circumstances of their marriages differentiate them from full-time housewives. Considering housewives and self-employed/family enterprise workers as one group would indeed be misguided. Women who started out in a large firm or in government service are also less likely to be self-employed/family enterprise workers than housewives, although these are not statistically significant differences.

Part-time employees and housewives also differ from each other. Part-time female workers have less-educated husbands than their counterparts who are housewives. This effect on part-time work probably reflects the low-paying nature of such jobs. Japanese women who can afford to stay at home are likely to do so, and their husbands' education is a good proxy for this. (Since we are using the husband's employment status as a major explanatory variable, and since the earnings of the self-employed are unreliably reported even in the best of surveys, the husband's wages are not included in these equations.) Women whose husbands are self-employed are also less likely to work part-time than to be housewives, and women in extended family households are more likely to work part-time. Women who started out in medium-sized firms are more likely than other women to have gone back to work part-time, although this difference is not quite statistically significant.

---

important. This demonstrates that changes in women's employment status are more contingent on changes in marital status (from the unmarried to the married state) than on the historical time point or on women's age. This points to the salience of women's marital situation for their employment.

[21] The mean age at marriage for women was 24.1 years, and for men, about three years older, at 27.4. This age difference is statistically significant ($p < .001$), as is the difference in variances, with men demonstrating a greater range of marriage ages. Inclusion of the unmarried and the childless would make for a complicated analysis because a number of important variables such as husband's employment status and the number and ages of children pertain only to married women.

Full-time employees also contrast with full-time housewives, but differ in some respects too from part-time employees and the self-employed. Women are likely to be full-time employees rather than housewives if their husbands are less educated and if they live in an extended family household. These variables, as with part-time workers, reflect women's "opportunity costs"—the costs of entering the labor market or staying out. Overall, middle-aged Japanese women are more likely to work in a wage labor situation, either part-time or full-time, than to stay out of the labor force if their husband is less educated. This probably indicates both a need for money in the household and greater acceptance on the husband's part that it is alright for his wife to work. Being in an extended family household is also related to all types of participation in the labor force for women. While additional relatives in the household could mean a greater burden on the family financially, it also eases some of the childcare pressures on the wife. Children enter in as a factor for full-time employees: female full-time employees are less apt than full-time housewives to have a child under twelve. Number of children, though not indicated in the equations in Appendix Table B.18, has no separate impact on employment status. Rather, it is the age of the youngest child that is important: women with younger children are generally less likely to participate in the labor force.

Several factors are conspicuous in *not* having much to do with women's employment status. Neither native ability nor education have a significant impact on what women are doing in their early forties.[22] Likewise, the way in which women originally entered the labor market—as employees or not, and in different-sized firms—has little impact on their current employment except in two cases. Currently self-employed workers are less likely to have a history as employees, and full-time employees are more likely to have such a history. Being a full-time employee is positively related to having started out in the government, and negatively related to having started out in a large firm, although these relationships are not statistically significant.

[22] In preliminary analyses, it became clear that none of the female self-employed or family enterprise workers were university-educated, making that equation impossible to estimate, and junior college graduates and university graduates therefore had to be considered together as one group. The only loss of information is entailed in the estimation of the equation for part-time employees; university-educated women were significantly less likely to be part-time employees than to be housewives, whereas the same was not true for junior college graduates. In the equation for full-time employees, the effects of junior college graduation and university graduation were both insignificant.

These results show the strong connection between women's mid-life employment status and their family responsibilities. Women's adjustment of their work schedules to the demands of the household can be seen not just in labor force quitting behaviors, in the greater prevalence of part-time work for middle-aged than for younger women, and in greater involvement in the labor force in family enterprise and piecework labor, but also in how close to home they work. In the three-city survey, young single male employees in Kodaira were found to commute an average of 75 minutes to work, whereas the figure for single women is 97 minutes.[23] Young, single women thus commute *farther* to work than men. (As nearly all the men and women in this age group are employees, the results were similar when the analysis was restricted to employees only.) A different picture is produced by married men and women in the older cohort. Here, working men spend an average of 68 minutes getting to work compared to only 37 minutes for working women ($p < .001$). Even when we eliminate the self-employed and family enterprise workers, the categories in which women are more heavily concentrated and where home and work are likely to be spatially coterminous, a significant sex difference remains: male employees commute to work an average of 75 minutes and female employees an average of 38 minutes ($p < .001$). Female part-time employees commute even shorter distances than female full-time employees: part-time workers travel 19 minutes, and full-time workers 40 minutes ($p < .01$). Among the married women in the older cohort, those who used to work but are not currently working report commuting times substantially longer than those who currently work (67 minutes as opposed to 37 minutes, a difference significant at the .05 level), suggesting that commuting distance may very well be a factor in leading women to quit their jobs.

Married Japanese women who work outside the home do much to adjust their schedules to the demands of the household. Housework and childcare responsibilities far outweigh any other reasons cited by women in the survey for not working. Three other reasons are more

[23] The comparison was carried out only within Kodaira in order to control for the distance of the community to employment opportunities. In other words, we would not want to make a comparison by sex using the pooled sample of Kodaira, Sapporo, and Toyohashi because it does not make sense to compare men and women in different communities, with different potential commuting distances. Comparisons of the sexes across communities would conflate the effect of sex and the distance of the particular city from employment opportunities rather than allowing a focus on sex as an explanatory factor.

or less equivalent in ranking second in importance: one's husband objects, it is too physically demanding to work outside as well as take care of the household, and there are no suitable jobs available. A female government worker in early middle age, herself on a career ladder within one of the government ministries, commented candidly to me: "When I got married, my husband asked me to quit working. I didn't quit, but every year he still tells me he wishes I would. Many of my friends say their husbands say the same thing—so I think it is not an unusual experience." A young housewife pointed out a central issue: "Many men think of work as something painful, so they consider it a good thing or as something to be grateful for if their wives don't have to work. They can't understand why many women, if given the choice, would actually *like* to work outside the home."

A recent opinion poll (Office of the Prime Minister, Japan, 1987a) indicates that women in their thirties are the most likely of any age group to feel that contemporary Japanese women face a situation where it is difficult to work outside the home (*hatarakiyasui jōkyō ni nai*). More than half of women in that age group feel this way, whereas women in their fifties and sixties are much more likely to say that it is easy for women to work. This is probably a life-cycle effect, showing that women in the middle of their childrearing years perceive great difficulties in balancing their responsibilities. Among people who feel that women face a difficult employment situation, the major reason they give is that the number of workplaces for women is limited. In the minds of both men and women, this reason far outranks others, such as the deficit in childcare facilities, society's view that men should work and women should stay at home, and the difficulties that women face in gaining understanding at home. The same poll shows that men and women are in strong agreement over the good and bad points of women working. By far the most important justification for a woman to work, according to both sexes, is the financial one. When older working women in my survey were asked why they worked, the household budget was also the major reason. According to the government-conducted poll, men and women see two main problems as being related to a woman working: "She will not be able to take care of the house properly" and "She will not be able to raise and educate the children properly." But the presumed effect on children is a matter of some ambivalence, as about half of both men and women are undecided as to whether having a mother in the labor force affects children either for good or for ill.

TABLE 5.12
FIRM SIZE: MEN'S AND
WOMEN'S CURRENT JOBS

| | Number of employees | | | | | Govern- | |
	1–9	10–99	100–299	300–999	1,000+	ment sector	Total
Younger cohort (25–29)							
Men							
%	21.9	23.1	8.9	10.7	19.1	16.0	100.0
N	(36)	(37)	(15)	(17)	(31)	(26)	(162)
Women							
%	24.5	24.5	14.2	5.8	16.5	11.5	100.0
N	(34)	(34)	(24)	(8)	(23)	(16)	(139)
$X^2 = 7.35, df = 5$; not significant							
Older cohort (40–44)							
Men							
%	24.6	24.2	7.6	10.2	18.6	14.8	100.0
N	(58)	(57)	(18)	(24)	(44)	(35)	(236)
Women							
%	42.0	24.7	11.0	7.8	8.2	6.4	100.0
N	(92)	(54)	(24)	(17)	(18)	(14)	(219)
$X^2 = 29.15, df = 5; p < .001$							

SOURCE: Survey conducted by author.

Firm Size Women's movement out of large firms as well as out of employee status is dramatic as they age (Table 5.12). Among people in the *younger* cohort who are currently working, there is no significant difference in the distribution of men and women by size of firm (just as there was no significant difference in the size of the firms where they initially worked). But even though middle-aged men and women started out working in similar-sized firms when they were young, in their early forties they are distributed radically differently, with women more concentrated than men in the smallest firms and men more concentrated in the largest firms. As Table 5.13 demonstrates, the smallest firms are important in terms of what they represent for men and women. About two-thirds of the men who work in very small firms are self-employed, and the rest are mainly employees. Women in very small firms are fairly evenly distributed among employees, the self-employed, and family enterprise workers. Men in such firms are therefore much more likely than women to own and operate the business.

184   Women and the Economic Miracle

TABLE 5.13

EMPLOYMENT STATUS OF
OLDER COHORT (40–44) IN SMALL FIRMS

	Employment status				
	Manager or employee	Self-employed	Family enterprise worker	Piece-worker	Total
Men					
%	28.1	66.7	5.2	0.0	100.0
N	(16)	(38)	(3)	(0)	(57)
Women					
%	39.1	28.3	29.3	3.3	100.0
N	(36)	(26)	(27)	(3)	(92)

SOURCE: Survey conducted by author.
NOTE: $X^2 = 25.3$, $df = 3$; $p < .001$. The definition of small firms used in this table is
9 or fewer workers.

   Comparing the middle-aged women who are currently working with
those who left the labor force and have not reentered it shows that
many more women in the latter group were in large firms or government. In other words, women who have either come back into the
labor force or who never left are much more likely to be in small
businesses than their counterparts who worked for a while and then
left the labor force (Table 5.14). This reflects the entrance barriers to
internal labor markets in large firms for young women, and, in ironic
conjunction with this, the predilection of large firms to employ younger rather than older women. Women do not reenter large firms or
government at anywhere near the rate at which they leave.
   This conclusion is reinforced by Table 5.15, showing the firm-size
origin and current distribution of older men and women. In the lower
half of the table are the results of log-linear analyses. For women,
simply knowing the original distribution across firms of different sizes
and knowing the overall distribution of destinations (row and column
effects), we can understand the table quite well. Adding a term for the
diagonal effect (women's persistence in firms of the same size) improves the fit of the model, but this term is not necessary to reach a
good fit. In contrast, neither a model with row and column effects nor
a model with row, column, and diagonal effects provides a good fit to
the male data. The addition of a parameter (Z) for the effect of men's
persistence in the large-firm/government sector of the economy, how-

TABLE 5.14
FIRM SIZE: OLDER WOMEN'S
CURRENT OR MOST RECENT JOB

| | | Number of employees | | | Govern- | |
	1–9	10–99	100–299	300–999	1,000+	ment sector	Total
In labor force (current job)							
%	42.0	24.7	11.0	7.8	8.2	6.4	100.0
N	(92)	(54)	(24)	(17)	(18)	(14)	(219)
Out of labor force (most recent job)							
%	20.4	24.7	9.7	8.6	21.5	15.1	100.0
N	(19)	(23)	(9)	(8)	(20)	(14)	(93)

SOURCE: Survey conducted by author.
NOTE: $X^2 = 23.62$, $df = 5$; $p \leq .001$.

ever, yields a well-fitting model. This reflects the *immobility* of many men in the large-firm sector: men who start out in large firms or government are unusually likely to remain there.

Men's Wages   Finally, looking at the determinants of men's wages accentuates the importance of human capital and early work experiences in building a man's career. Appendix Table B.21 shows how men's ability, education, and early work experiences affect their current wages (before-tax wages in the past year, including bonuses). Tables B.19 and B.20 show definitions of the variables, and means and standard deviations. Because of the difficulty of accurately measuring the earnings of the self-employed (Patrick and Rohlen 1987), this table is restricted to male full-time employees. A number of variables have clear effects. Education is very important: having gone to a prestigious university is particularly significant for men's wages in mid-life. Ability no longer exerts a significant impact on wages at this point. The second equation considers whether having initially entered an internal labor market is important: it is.[24] The third equation adds the number of years spent in the labor force, and the proportion of working life spent

[24] The experiences of job rotation and on-the-job training are highly correlated with having entered an internal labor market (Pearson's $r = .511$ and .256, respectively), so they are not included in this analysis.

TABLE 5.15

FIRM-SIZE MOBILITY, OLDER COHORT (40–44)

	Destination							
	Men				Women			
Origin	1–99	100–999	1,000+	Total	1–99	100–999	1,000+	Total
1–99	74	16	16	106	77	17	13	107
100–999	23	16	5	44	24	12	6	42
1,000+	15	7	55	77	37	9	13	59
Total	112	39	76	227	138	38	32	208

	Log-linear analysis					
	Men			Women		
Models	G^2	ΔG^2	df	G^2	ΔG^2	df
1. [R] [C]	84.14	—	4	6.23[a]	—	4
2. [R] [C] [D]	14.64	69.50[a]	3	.54[a]	5.69[a]	3
3. [R] [C] [D] [Z]	1.28[a]	13.36[a]	2	—	—	—

SOURCE: Survey conducted by author.
NOTE: R = row effect; C = column effect; D = diagonal effect; Z = effect of persistence in the large-firm/government sector.
[a]$p < .05$.

as a full-time employee. These also increase wages. Finally, the size of firm in which the man is currently employed is important, and the effects of other variables decline once it is taken into consideration. The effects of education and early work experiences (such as being in a firm-internal labor market) seem to culminate in the position of being in a large firm in mid-career. As in the log-linear analysis above, it is quite unlikely that a man will be in a large firm in mid-career if he did not start out in one to begin with. It is also important to note that graduation from a good university is still exerting an effect on men's wages, even by middle age.

CONCLUSION

While Japanese men's and women's initial employment looks similar on the surface, this appearance is deceptive. Many more men than women are in firm-internal labor markets, and people's first jobs in general are highly sex-segregated. Men's and women's paths increasingly diverge as they move through the early and middle years of their working lives, and the processes producing these experiences for the two sexes are different as well. Men who received prestigious university educations and who started out in an internal labor market in a large firm or the government do predictably well—they stay in that sector of the economy, receive employer investment in training, are apt to remain with the same employer, and earn higher wages than other men. Men are not likely to shift from large to small firms unless they become self-employed. Whether they marry or not (and the vast majority do) does not strongly affect what happens to them employment-wise.

In contrast, women's employment patterns are very complex, and are neither affected by the same factors demonstrated for men nor exposited in the organizational literature on Japan. Human capital measures such as ability and education have *little* power in explaining Japanese women's employment over the life course. The most important early predictors of a woman's employment career are whether she started out as an employee and whether she started out in a government position. These starting points lead in opposite directions. Women who started out as *non*employees are more likely to keep working. They need to work to help support the household, they do not face the same types of discrimination as women working as employees in the private sector, and their hours and place of work probably accommodate family life better. Government workers make up a disproportionate share of the few women who started out in internal labor markets, and these women are less likely than any others to quit working upon marriage. Women's family responsibilities heavily influence whether they are employed in their mid forties, and their type of employment. The relative insignificance of education in predicting women's employment patterns is mirrored by the absence of marked change in the behaviors of young women in the mid 1980s compared to their counterparts nearly two decades earlier. Although the younger women are better-educated, employment discrimination against highly educated women and the force of strong marriage norms have perpetuated gender stratification.

The tight links that developed historically between the educational system and the labor market for men have structured parents' views of the relative value of education for sons and daughters. Having gone to an elite university smoothes the way for a young man to enter a large, prestigious firm or the civil service. Education at a prestigious junior college or women's university helps young women enter good companies in order to work for a few years and subsequently form a good marriage match (perhaps even with someone in their company). In short, a labor market that sorts men and women into different tracks from the very start has influenced parents' views of education, and has likewise influenced the macro-level evolution of an educational system that sorts young men and women into different tracks of higher education. This is the subject of the next chapter.

SIX

Gendered Education

Japan is a learning society of formidable dimensions.
U.S. Department of Education,
Japanese Education Today *(1987: 10)*

If there is any group or category of students who
consistently fare less well in the educational system in
Japan, it is women.
Estelle James and Gail Benjamin,
Public Policy and Private Education in Japan *(1988: 49)*

Japanese students consistently score at the top of the list in international achievement tests in mathematics and science (Stevenson 1989). These winning scores among young Japanese are not reached through heavy investment in private schooling at the elementary school level: 99 percent of Japanese elementary school children are enrolled in public schools. Nor can achievement be attributed to small classes in school and the consequent costs of a high teacher-student ratio. Japanese class sizes are larger than in most U.S. schools, and there is no system of tracking within schools. High international achievement has been attained at low public cost. The Liberal Democratic Party that has ruled Japan since 1955 has had the lowest rate of government expenditure and taxation in the postwar period among industrial countries.

Despite Western social scientists' and policymakers' attention to the achievement, efficiency, and egalitarianism of Japanese education, studies have rarely touched on the issue of women's education. This mirrors the status of women's education as a topic in Japanese policy circles. As James and Benjamin write: "While equality for women on the job is just beginning to be discussed in Japan, it will take many years before it reaches the forefront as a salient issue on the educational scene" (1988: 49).

The first part of this chapter examines how the role of women in the Japanese educational system has been affected by the historical development of the system. Just as I termed the development of the employment system a "conscious evolution," so too can the development of the educational system be seen as a result of policy decisions made by the government and by employers who developed close recruitment relations with schools. These social actors have shaped the fundamental context within which young Japanese men and women and their parents view the purposes and efficacy of education. By restricting the number of places at public universities throughout the postwar period, the government fueled the intense competition for these places. This has given rise to an educational race in which young men participate more than young women. The later part of the chapter shows that women are more active as *investors* in their sons' education than as students in whom investments for labor market success are made. They play an important indirect role in the economy through their own investments of hope and time in their sons' future success.

THE PREWAR EDUCATIONAL SYSTEM

The Japanese educational system prior to World War II consisted of two distinct parts: compulsory schooling at the elementary school level, and selective elite and vocational schooling at the post-primary level. Compulsory education had basically the same content for children of different classes and was oriented toward producing a literate population rather than a population trained for different vocations. Beyond the primary school level was a complex system of schools. Horizontal movement across different types of secondary schooling was very difficult, and remains so today (Cummings 1980; James and Benjamin 1988). For instance, an individual does not enter junior college with a plan to transfer later to a four-year university.

For those students continuing on to the post-compulsory level in the prewar system, sex-segregated tracks existed. Girls' academic track consisted of secondary schools and women's colleges, and the vocational track consisted of higher elementary schools and teacher training schools. Prior to World War II, only about 10 percent of women completed education past the elementary school level. Women were not eligible for entrance into most four-year universities. Most important, they were not permitted to enroll in the educational institutions of highest prestige: the government-sponsored imperial universities. Within compulsory schooling, too, the treatment of the sexes differed. After second grade, the sexes were segregated into different classes and girls' curriculum stressed domestic arts such as cooking, sewing, and flower arranging (Cummings 1980; Osawa 1988a). The main purpose of education for girls was to prepare them to be "good wives and wise mothers" (*ryōsai kenbo*), an expression that originated in the late nineteenth century and illustrated that women's role in nation-building was considered to be in the household.

Post-compulsory educational tracks for boys were more complicated, with a greater variety of technical and vocational schools as well as four-year universities. Boys' "ordinary" and "higher" middle schools were the forerunners of post–World War II high schools, and were created to offer preparation for entrance to elite universities. The ordinary and higher middle schools conducted highly competitive entrance examinations. The majority of young men who passed the examinations and attended these schools did not enter university, but instead were highly sought after as employees in business and government. Success on entrance examinations rather than mastery of specific subjects or skills was the hiring criterion. This emphasis on general learning as manifested by passing an examination established a historical precedent. As Thomas Rohlen succinctly states, "The formula has not changed in a hundred years" (1983: 59).

Japan had thirty universities by 1930, and over forty by the start of World War II. Not all university graduates found exactly the type of employment they sought, and many took jobs that probably did not require their level of education. But this meant that such jobs came to be defined (by employers and the public) as *requiring* a university education, leading in turn to increased public demand for higher education (Cummings 1980). In 1935 only 3 percent of elementary graduates went to university. Competition was intense, and about one-half of middle school graduates who were not accepted tried again the next year (Rohlen 1983). Thus originated the now-familiar *rōnin* ("masterless samurai") pattern: waiting out a year or more in order to retake a school entrance examination.

The pre–World War II educational system thus contained the seeds of many features of the contemporary one: (1) school-specific entrance examinations; (2) an emphasis on passing the examination to a "good" school in order to move on to another good school at the next level or to find good employment; (3) an emphasis on school admission rather than on the *content* of education in that school; and (4) sex segregation in tracking, by type of school as much as within schools.

THE DEVELOPMENT OF HIGHER EDUCATION
IN POSTWAR JAPAN

Just as the American Occupation leaders sought to democratize the Japanese workplace (e.g., by encouraging worker organization and unions), they sought to democratize the educational system. The system indeed changed in substantial ways. But just as particular Japanese forms of worker organization developed within the labor relations context that the Occupation authorities had attempted to influence, the educational system retained many features specific to Japan's prewar legacy.

In 1946, American education experts advised the Japanese government to adopt a 6–3–3–4 system: six years of elementary schooling and three of middle school became compulsory, and the high school and university levels replaced the complicated prewar secondary and post-secondary tracks (Rohlen 1983). In this system, which continues to the present day, no explicit curricular differentiation exists before the high school level. Mandatory separate tracking of boys and girls prior to high school graduation was also abolished. But the system is not at all a copy of the U.S. system. Comparatively speaking, it represents elements of both American and European systems of schooling. While education through the junior high school level is comprehensive and nonselective, senior high schools are selective and represent different tracks: academic and vocational. "The occupation's reforms were least effective at the high school level," says Rohlen (1983: 69), a view shared by many who have studied the Japanese educational system. As James and Benjamin state:

> Movement from one level of the system to another is much more universal, much less selective than it used to be. However, in light of this vast expansion of educational opportunity, the differentiation within each (post-compulsory) level has become even greater, the status hierarchy even more pronounced—contrary to the initial intent or expectation of the American Occupation. In this sense, the greater the change, the more everything has remained the same.
>
> (James and Benjamin 1988: 19)

The differentiation among Japanese schools at the same level—a kind of hierarchy within each horizontal layer of schooling—is manifested in two ways. The first is a distinction between public and private schools, a distinction that roughly corresponds to high and low "quality" or prestige (the most prestigious schools being in the public sphere). The second is a distinction, at the post–high school level, between men's and women's tracks. These outcomes resulted from the interaction between the demand for education in the postwar period and the way the Japanese government chose to respond to that demand. In effect, prewar de jure sex segregation was replaced by postwar de facto segregation. The story can best be understood by beginning with the extraordinary significance that is now attached to entrance to a prestigious university.

THE LINK BETWEEN EDUCATION AND EMPLOYMENT: EDUCATION AS A LIFE-DETERMINING DECISION

It is difficult for a Westerner to comprehend the intensity of the contemporary Japanese race to acquire human capital in the form of education. Every spring, the weekly news magazines print the names of all students who have passed the entrance examinations to national (the former imperial) universities. These universities occupy the top rungs in the university hierarchy. In contemporary American terms, this would be equivalent to *Time* magazine devoting its late March cover story every year to intense scrutiny of who got into Harvard and other elite universities. Not only are individual Japanese students' names printed but their high school affiliation is listed. Some weekly magazines obligingly print a list that ranks high schools according to the number of students they are sending to each of the top universities. The comparison with the previous year's results is also tabulated.[1] Advertisements for *yobikō* (private tutorial schools for university entrance examinations) line the margins of these magazine pages. The top exam-preparation schools proudly cite the numbers of students they delivered to Tokyo University and other major public and private universities the previous year.[2]

The importance attached to attending a prestigious university is related to historical processes that have linked Japanese schooling with the system of employment. The link between going to a national university and entering employment in the government bureaucracy or a prestigious position in the private sector became well-established prior

[1] In 1984, for instance, Azabu High School had 94 successful applicants to Tokyo University, down 12 from the previous year.

[2] To dispel any lingering doubts in parents' minds that examination preparation schools must be carefully chosen, one advertisement proclaimed, "Even exam preparation schools have their own individuality."

to World War II and did not weaken in the postwar period. Despite a loosening of the standards for establishing new universities and the subsequent proliferation of private ones, the competition for places in the national universities increased. Employers continued to act on their belief that the best employees would come from the elite universities, and families continued to respond to that belief by wanting to send their sons there. In 1957, over 80 percent of the member corporations of the Japan Federation of Employers limited their recruitment of white-collar workers to graduates from a select group of universities. The civil service hired more than half of its new employees from Tokyo University alone (Cummings 1980).

Selective recruitment by university name has continued to be a common procedure used by the government bureaucracy and many large Japanese companies. Rohlen estimates that between one-half and three-quarters of all entry-level career-track positions in the government bureaucracy are filled by Tokyo University graduates (1983). Just as news magazines parade the ratios of graduates from different high schools who enter elite universities, they also frequently run surveys of the top executives of large, prestigious firms to see how graduates of universities are faring in the competition for promotions.

Empirical research on the demand for education in postwar Japan has shown that despite a declining internal rate of return on university education, university application rates have nevertheless risen over time. This nonintuitive result is complemented by the finding that university application rates have risen with the probability of employment in a large firm (Nakata and Mosk 1987).

A 1979 survey showed that about one-half of companies only allowed graduates of particular universities or of particular departments in those universities to take the company entrance examination (Ushiogi 1986). Such examinations, used by the majority of Japanese enterprises, do not test the candidates' expertise in a field, but instead screen for general knowledge, motivation, and attitudes toward work and the company. The consequences of selective recruitment policies are apparent. In 1980, an astounding 95 percent of the graduates from the former imperial universities entered the civil service or firms of 1,000 or more employees. This was three times the rate for graduates of private universities established in the postwar period (Ushiogi 1986).

Selective recruitment by employers is even more common at the high school level (Nakata and Mosk 1987). Some employers have implicit contractual relationships with specific schools in order to recruit their top students year after year. Such employers usually constitute a small proportion of all the employers who recruit from a school, but they dominate in the competition for the best graduates. One survey showed that the set of employers with long-standing relations to high schools hired an average of 50 percent of all work-bound seniors from these schools (Rosenbaum and Kariya 1989).

As a consequence of the institutional links between schools and employers, Japanese students spend little time searching for their first full-time job. A survey of 1984 university graduates showed that 80 percent of students had made the decision of where to work after graduation the following April within the first five days of the recruitment season in the fall (Ushiogi 1986). Over 99 percent of Japanese high school seniors who plan to work after graduation are employed within a month of graduating. This compares to a figure of only 49 percent for American students, and over half of these U.S. students were in part-time jobs they had held during high school (Kariya and Rosenbaum 1987).

In summary, the Japanese public's demand for education, especially at prestigious high schools and universities, is a highly pragmatic one. Entrance into a good high school or university makes life much more predictable because of the recruiting relationships between top employers and those schools. Few students at these schools must search for a job independently as graduation draws near. Employers deal directly with the job-placement offices of high schools and universities, putting school administrators in the position of sponsoring their students for job applications.

THE PRIVATIZATION OF EDUCATION

While a miniscule 1 percent of Japanese elementary school children are enrolled in private schools, the figure rises to 28 percent of high school students, and reaches 76 percent among students in vocational schools, junior colleges, and universities (James and Benjamin 1988). (In fact, a higher proportion of junior college than four-year university students are at private institutions; the respective figures are 90 and 75 percent.)

The figure for private higher education represents a dramatic reversal of the situation one hundred years ago, when students at private post-secondary institutions numbered only 22 percent of the total. Between 1950 and 1980, the number of private universities more than tripled. The number of national and public universities together increased by only 33 percent, making the competition to enter them extremely intense (Nakata and Mosk 1987). More than 30 percent of university entrants each year are *rōnin*, students who have sat out for one to three years while they studied and tried to pass the entrance exam for the school of their (and their parents') choice. This figure rises to over 40 percent for the top public and private universities. Nearly half of the 1.1 million people who wanted to enter universities and colleges in 1989 were not accepted (Japan Institute of Labor 1989); many of these became the *rōnin* of 1990.

The fact that the Japanese higher education system originated in elite universities and was built from the top down has continued to have ramifications for educational competition. The competition for a place in a national university has also been exacerbated by a government policy that has only slightly increased the number of places available in public universities in the postwar period. The Liberal Democratic Party throughout its era of continuous rule has chosen to encourage the proliferation of private universities to satisfy the Japanese public's high demand for education. This way of meeting demand contrasts with the response in the United States and other Western countries after World War II, where demand was met by the public sector. Japan's response was more similar to that of many developing countries (James and Benjamin 1988). And as long as the competitive examination system was maintained and university entrance was merit-based (to the extent that an examination measures merit), the Japanese public has been willing to accept this policy.

The much faster growth of the private over the public sector in higher education has translated both directly and indirectly into higher educational costs that parents must bear. The real costs of education increased sharply between 1960 and 1980. Up until 1970, tuition rose more rapidly at private universities than at public institutions. Tuition at public institutions subsequently increased faster (Nakata and Mosk 1987). In 1989, one year of university education (including tuition and other expenses) cost an average of two million yen ($14,000) (Japan Institute of Labor 1990). The costs of higher education are borne by parents to a greater extent in Japan than in most other industrial countries, as the great majority of young Japanese do not work part-time during high school and therefore do not accumulate any savings for educational expenditures. Scholarship support is also less extensive in Japan than in the United States. While more than half of American students in higher education receive some type of federal assistance, usually in the form of loans, fewer than one-quarter of Japanese students do (U.S. Department of Education 1987). Japanese parents pay on average about 80 percent of their children's higher educational costs (Nakata and Mosk 1987).

Competition at the university level gives rise to competition at the high school level. Since high school is not compulsory, the Japanese government does not have to provide public education to all who desire it. The one-district, one-school U.S. system is rare in Japanese school districts. Instead, each district typically has several schools, finely ranked from the top academic public high school to public night high schools, with private high schools usually in between. The average district has five or six public high schools. Parents and students are keenly aware of which school in their district sends the most graduates to top universities. (Interested parents and students can easily find the figures for high schools nationwide in the pages of weekly news magazines.) Public high school admissions policies are based on entrance examination scores and on grades, with little attention to information about extracurricular activities or personality (Kariya and Rosenbaum 1987). Private high schools also rely principally on examination scores and grades, although some use teacher recommendations as well.

In summary, the structured recruitment from certain universities by top Japanese employers and the civil service funnels downward to the competition for entrance into those universities and the high schools that feed into them. This vertical chain thereby maintains a hierarchy of schools at the university and high school levels in the service of the labor market. Although the first major point of educational selection occurs at entrance to high school, a small number of private senior high schools also have "feeder" junior high schools. In this situation, the entrance examination is at the junior high rather than the high school level. Some of these linked junior and senior high schools are directly connected with prestigious private universities, but even those that have no such institutional connection have a high rate of success in sending their graduates to elite universities. This very highly structured subsystem enrolls a small proportion of Japanese students. In Tokyo in the mid 1980s, about 12 percent of junior high school students were in private schools (Kariya and Rosenbaum 1987). In addition to the vertical linkages to higher levels of schooling, some of these schools also have feeder elementary schools. Competition to enter such elementary schools is intense. Keiō Primary School, for example, admitted 96 of 945 boys (about 10 percent) and 36 of 507 girls (7 percent) who took the admissions test in 1988.[3]

Education for the labor market is hardly unique to Japan, but the consequences for women *are* distinctive. Given that the human capital development system in Japan promotes tight linkage between male students' successful performance in school entrance examinations and coveted permanent employment by a large firm or in the government bureaucracy, it does not make sense for Japanese parents to "invest" in daughters the way they invest in sons. This does not mean that all parents necessarily *spend* less in monetary terms on their daughters' education relative to that of their sons, but investment has largely been in sex-specific higher education throughout the postwar period. Public demand for education and government response have combined to create a peculiarly Japanese outcome: the junior college system for women.

GENDERED TRACKS: JUNIOR COLLEGES AND FOUR-YEAR UNIVERSITIES

Virtually no women received university education prior to World War II, but education was nevertheless viewed as important in enabling daughters to perform their eventual domestic responsibilities well. Only a tiny percentage of married Japanese women were employees in the prewar period; the majority worked instead as unpaid laborers on family farms or in small family businesses. Nonetheless, education was important, especially for upper-class women. Papanek points out the various status-production functions that women in different cultures play in the family: the training of children; activities such as gift-giving that maintain the family's relations with neighbors and relatives; support of the husband's role as breadwinner (through the cooking of meals, ironing of clothes, etc.); and the practice of ritual and religious observances (Papanek 1979). In Japan, women's role as childrearers has always been extremely important. As investors in the human capital of the next generation, women must be well-trained. If anything, it could be argued that this role was *accentuated* by the heightened educational competition in Japan in the 1970s and 1980s. As articulated in a recent article in the *Japan Labor Bulletin*:

[3] *Japan Times*, weekly international edition, 30, no. 22 (June 4–10, 1990).

Women's higher education accrues indirect benefits, leading to higher home investment in children and, down the road, higher earnings for their children. More educated mothers seek to pass on the advantages of their schooling. With the narrowing of job opportunities at the top, the education competition has grown fiercer, extending down to the elementary schools, with mothers devoting substantial energy and household resources to improve their children's future possibilities.

(Japan Institute of Labor 1990: 4)

The labor market incentives that motivate males to acquire higher education have not applied to females. Nor has the Japanese government promoted policies encouraging women to enter four-year universities. Instead, education for its own sake—and especially for the sake of making a good marriage match and of being a good mother—is a strong incentive for women. Chapter 5 showed that a Japanese woman's level of education explains little about her lifetime employment, but education is important for the "marriage market." The correlation between a woman's education and the education of the man she marries is high (in the three-city study, Pearson's $r = .57$, $p <$ .001). For instance, 71 percent of junior high school–educated women in the older cohort in my survey married men who were junior high school graduates; 78 percent of the women who graduated from university married university-educated men. Japanese women's education is life-determining not in the sense of setting them on an employment trajectory but rather in matching them with a male and his employment trajectory.

Over time, one educational track, the junior college system, evolved in Japan to become almost exclusively female. Junior colleges were established on a provisional basis in 1950 (Fujimura-Fanselow 1985). About 200 new ones were established in the 1960s, and by the early 1980s there were over 500 in total, almost all of them private. (Just as the increase in the number of universities was greatest in the private sector, so too was the increase in junior colleges.) Some commentators have argued that the geographical dispersion of junior colleges across the country compared to the higher concentration of four-year universities in urban areas is one factor inspiring parents to encourage junior college as the best educational choice for their daughters. As discussed in the previous chapter, young women who live at home have been considered by good employers to be more worthy of employment than those who live away from their parents.

Figure 6.1. Japanese Men's and Women's Participation in Higher Education
SOURCE: Ministry of Education, Japan, 1988.

HIGHER EDUCATION ENROLLMENT

Sharp gender stratification in Japanese higher education can be seen best in historical and comparative context. Rates of high school graduation are virtually identical for the sexes. In fact, since 1965 the rate of continuation to high school has been slightly higher for Japanese women (currently 95 percent) than for men (93 percent); this sex ratio is similar to that in the United States. Japanese women's rates of attendance at institutions of higher education were very low in 1955; fewer than 3 percent of women attended university, and the rate for junior colleges was similar (Fig. 6.1). By 1988, women's rate of attendance at junior colleges and universities had increased, but the rate of increase at junior colleges had been the more rapid of the two. Figure 6.1 shows the extent to which junior college has become a female track. Men's rate of attendance at such colleges has never exceeded 3 percent, and has shown no net increase since 1955. More than *thirty* times as many men go to university as attend junior college. Conversely, only two-thirds as many women go to universities as attend junior colleges.

The gap between the proportions of male and female high school graduates continuing in school in the United States narrowed between

1962 and 1979 from 12 percentage points to only 2 (with 48 percent of women and 50 percent of men enrolled in post-secondary schools). The difference between the educational gender gap in Japan and the United States is striking when college attendance rates are broken down for two- and four-year institutions. The proportion of American women among the student population at two-year institutions in 1979 was 54 percent, and at four-year institutions, 48 percent. In other words, American men and women were fairly evenly represented relative to each other at junior colleges and universities. In 1980, Japanese women made up 91 percent of the student population at *tandai*, or two-year institutions. By contrast, they constituted only 31 percent of the four-year university student population.

Comparisons with other Western industrial countries yield a similar contrast with Japan. University enrollment rates for men aged 15–24 were higher in Japan in 1980 than in the United States, Canada, France, Italy, Sweden, and Finland. Among these countries, Japan had the second highest male enrollment rate in universities even in 1930, evidencing the high level of education sought by men. In contrast, the proportion of females at four-year universities is by far the lowest in Japan relative to Western industrial nations (Nakata and Mosk 1987).

The courses of study are also quite different at Japanese junior colleges and universities, demonstrating the divergent functions served by the two types of educational institutions. Table 6.1 shows the distribution of the Japanese female junior college population across fields and the distribution for females and males at four-year universities. (Males at junior colleges are not shown because there are so few of them.) Home economics, education, and humanities (literature, history, and philosophy) reign supreme at junior colleges—about 65 percent of the student population are in these three fields. Social sciences, social welfare, art and music, and technical and industrial arts (engineering and other technical fields) make up an additional 30 percent, leaving about 5 percent of women who concentrate in general liberal arts or other areas.

Humanities and education are also major fields of interest for university women (36 and 16 percent respectively), followed by social science (16 percent). But social welfare and home economics assume distant third and fourth places. Thus there is a qualitative jump between junior college and university in terms of what women study: at junior college, the "feminine arts" are the main course, whereas at university there are several entrées. University men are heavily concen-

TABLE 6.1

MAJOR FIELDS OF STUDY IN JAPANESE
JUNIOR COLLEGES AND UNIVERSITIES

| | % of students by major field | | |
| | | Four-year universities | |
Major field	Junior colleges	Women	Men
Home economics	24.3	7.4	0.0
Education	22.6	16.1	4.8
Humanities (literature, history, philosophy)	18.2	35.9	7.4
Social sciences	10.1	16.4	46.3
Social welfare	6.6	9.3	5.7
Technical and industrial arts (including engineering and other technical fields)	6.5	2.3	25.7
Art and music	6.3	6.4	1.2
General liberal arts	2.1	2.1	3.8
Other	3.3	1.7	1.4
Mathematics and science	—	2.4	3.7
Total	100.0	100.0	100.0

SOURCES: Junior colleges—Ministry of Education, Japan, 1984, *Gakkō kihon chōsa* (Basic school statistics). Four-year universities—Ministry of Education, Japan, 1987, *Gakkō kihon chōsa* (Basic school statistics).

trated in the social sciences, including law, and in technical and engineering fields.

Gender stratification in higher education occurs not only by level (junior college versus university) but within the ranks of universities as well. Only a tiny proportion of the students at top Japanese universities are female. Table 6.2 shows the proportions of men and women in the 1984 graduating class at the five original imperial universities and the two most prestigious private universities, Keiō and Waseda. Because admission to university is typically department-specific, figures are shown for two common fields, humanities and law. Humanities is a large field, encompassing language, literature, philosophy, history, and, at some universities, social sciences such as sociology and psychology. Law is also a common area of undergraduate specialization at major universities, and one from which many civil servants and white-collar

TABLE 6.2

SEX DISTRIBUTION OF GRADUATES
FROM MAJOR JAPANESE UNIVERSITIES, 1984

	Graduates			
	Law		Humanities	
University	Men	Women	Men	Women
Former imperial universities				
Tokyo University				
%	95.8	4.2	82.8	17.2
N	(1,005)	(44)	(366)	(76)
Kyoto University				
%	94.7	5.3	77.7	22.3
N	(606)	(34)	(285)	(82)
Tohoku University				
%	94.2	5.8	77.9	22.1
N	(291)	(18)	(152)	(43)
Kyushu University				
%	91.8	8.2	53.9	46.1
N	(303)	(27)	(89)	(76)
Osaka University				
%	88.6	11.4	53.5	46.5
N	(202)	(26)	(76)	(66)
Top private universities				
Keiō University				
%	87.2	12.8	49.7	50.3
N	(1,194)	(175)	(496)	(501)
Waseda University				
%	92.4	7.6	65.2	34.8
N	(1,795)	(147)	(1,005)	(536)

SOURCE: Nihon Recruit Center 1983b.

employees in the major private enterprises are recruited. As shown, men overwhelmingly dominate the law majors at every university, with Tokyo University demonstrating the highest degree of sex segregation: there, men make up 95.8 percent of law graduates. Even in the more general field of the humanities, men constitute about 80 percent of the graduates at Tokyo University and Kyoto University, and more than half of the graduates at all other universities except Keiō. These figures for the top universities show the extent to which men are overrepresented, relative to the general university population. (Figure 6.1

TABLE 6.3

MOTHERS' ATTITUDES TOWARD
CHILDREN'S SOCIALIZATION
(%)

	Sex-based socialization	Egalitarian socialization	Other / don't know
Japan	62.6	34.4	3.0
West Germany	19.9	74.5	5.6
England	20.1	76.3	3.6
United States	31.3	61.9	6.8
Sweden	6.0	92.0	1.9
Philippines	28.1	67.4	4.5

SOURCE: Office of the Prime Minister, Japan, 1982a.
NOTE: The table indicates responses to the question, "Concerning the upbringing of your own children, do you agree with the attitude that 'boys should be raised as boys' and 'girls should be raised as girls,' or do you want to bring up your children in a more similar way?"

showed that men constitute about 70 percent of all university students.)

SEX-ROLE SOCIALIZATION ATTITUDES
AND EDUCATIONAL ASPIRATIONS

Parents' and daughters' perceptions of the disutility of university education for women have been encouraged by employers' policies, but it is also important to look at the dynamics of Japanese families in order to understand how educational decisions are made. For it is inside the family that gender roles crystallize and that expectations form about the obligations of the generations toward each other. Perceptions of the roles of "son" and "daughter" are particularly important in the construction of educational plans.

Most Japanese parents believe that their sons and daughters should be taught the roles specific to their sex rather than be raised in a more gender-neutral way. Table 6.3 places these attitudes in an international context. Over 60 percent of Japanese mothers feel that "boys should be raised as boys" and "girls should be raised as girls." This figure is twice as high as that for American mothers (31 percent) and ten times as high as that for mothers in Sweden. Furthermore, few Japanese mothers (3 percent) are unsure of their views on this topic. This high level of certainty is exceeded only by Swedish mothers, who are as certain of their egalitarianism as Japanese mothers are of their preference for sex-based socialization. Results of other Japanese surveys suggest that an even higher proportion of Japanese fathers favor sex-based socialization. A survey of a random sample of 1,200 adults in Hino city in 1985, for example, indicated that 65 percent of fathers (compared to 45 percent of mothers) wished to raise their sons "as sons" and daughters "as daughters" (Hino Municipal Office 1985). According to a survey in 1979, 73 percent of a national sample of adults felt that "boys should be raised to be masculine, and girls to be feminine" (Office of the Prime Minister, Japan, 1979).

A strong belief in sex-based socialization of children is complemented by sharply different educational aspirations for sons and daughters. As discussed in chapter 2, nearly three-quarters of Japanese mothers would like their sons to go to university, whereas only about one-quarter aspire to this for daughters. Mothers are about equally divided among those who feel that four-year university, junior college, or high school is the most appropriate for a daughter. American mothers differ markedly from this: almost 70 percent have university aspirations for their sons, and a nearly equivalent proportion for their daughters. Japan is the only industrial country where a yawning gap exists between educational aspirations for sons and daughters. This cannot be dismissed as an East Asian phenomenon, for surveys in South Korea indicate that mothers have nearly equal educational aspirations for sons and daughters—88 percent of mothers aspire to university education for sons, and 81 percent for daughters (Korea Survey [Gallup] Polls Ltd. 1987). The divergence in educational aspirations is remarkably robust across other government surveys conducted in Japan.[4]

Japanese parents not only hope for different *levels* of education for sons and daughters, they explicitly state the purpose of education as being different for the two sexes. About two-fifths of the parents who want to send a son to university regard the primary goal as general education, compared to two-thirds for a daughter (Office of the Prime

---

[4] In the Hino city survey cited above, 77 percent of mothers and 78 percent of fathers wanted to send their son to university, compared to 33 and 31 percent, respectively, for daughters. A national opinion survey by the Prime Minister's Office in 1982 found that 45 percent of parents wished to have their son attend university, compared to 19 percent for daughters (Office of the Prime Minister, Japan, 1982b). The absolute figures in the latter survey are lower than in other surveys because of the inclusion of the category "decision is up to son/daughter," which nearly one-third of respondents chose for both sons and daughters.

TABLE 6.4

PARENTAL REASONS FOR WANTING
SONS/DAUGHTERS TO ATTEND UNIVERSITY

	Son	Daughter
To receive a general education		
%	20.6	35.8
N	(90)	(54)
To obtain qualifications that will be useful in a future job		
%	72.9	55.6
N	(318)	(84)
Other		
%	4.4	6.0
N	(19)	(9)
Multiple reasons given		
%	2.1	2.6
N	(9)	(4)
Total	100.0	100.0
	N = 436	N = 151

SOURCE: Office of the Prime Minister, Japan, 1982b.

Minister, Japan, 1982b). Conversely, 27 percent of parents want their son to get a university education for the purpose of obtaining job qualifications, whereas only 16 percent of parents who feel university is important for a daughter cite this as the primary reason. My three-city survey also indicates these divergencies in the motives behind sons' and daughters' university education (Table 6.4).

Parents also differ as to the types of jobs they think are appropriate for their sons and daughters. When asked, "In your opinion, what is the most important thing to consider in a future job for your son/daughter," parents agree on the utilization of the individual's ability (Office of the Prime Minister, Japan, 1982b). Beyond this, the ordering of responses differs depending on the sex of the child. Parents feel that salary considerations and a job where the possibility of unemployment is low are important for their sons. But the priorities for a daughter include a workplace where co-workers are pleasant and a job that ensures leisure and little overtime work. This shows that parents' attitudes toward their sons' future employment stress financial considerations, whereas comfort and social factors are thought more important for daughters.

These survey results are complemented by ethnographic material. Comments from women in their forties illuminate the meaning of a university education when they were growing up. One woman, now a successful tax accountant, told me: "I wanted to study law at university and become a lawyer. But my parents said that if I went to university and became a lawyer, no one would marry me. They refused to help me with university expenses if I chose to study law." Her drastic solution was to run away from home and live with a supportive relative, who helped her finance her studies.

The mixed motives for university education were expressed in the complaints of a young woman finishing her junior year at university in 1985:

> My parents are both university graduates, and ever since I was little, my mother thought I should work. But now that the time is here to think about it seriously, she only wants me to get an office job—to be an *OL* [Japanese slang for "office lady"], a job that is socially respectable for a woman— and put my effort into looking hard for a husband. . . . When I started college, for the first year or so a lot of women were serious about looking for work when they graduated, but as the time approached, the numbers dropped away, and now I look around me and find that I am one of the few serious ones left. It upsets me. It makes me think—what are these university years *for*, anyway?

Another young woman told me anxiously: "I want to go to business school in the United States. But one of my male friends says that if I do, no one will want to marry me." (As a footnote to this, when I returned to Japan three years later, I learned that she had graduated with a bachelor's degree in economics from an elite private university in Japan and had been one of the few women to win a position at the Bank of Japan that year. But within a year and a half, she became engaged to a co-worker and left the bank, and soon afterward she had her first child.)

Socialization of young men and women for different levels of education and different life aspirations stems not just from parents, peers, and eventually co-workers, but also from subtle emphases of the school environment itself. In interviews, several Japanese female teachers explained the ways in which girls were made to feel that they took second place to boys at a public high school. On the class attendance sheet, all boys' names appeared first, followed by the girls' names (rather than a systematic ordering of both sexes based on name). During the physical education period, the third-year boys lined up first, followed

by the second- and first-year boys, then finally by the girls. Other
stories of sex segregation abound. In a survey carried out in a Saitama
prefecture high school in the mid 1980s, nearly 40 percent of female
high school seniors said that they had been told by teachers that it was
not worth it for them to go to four-year universities because if they
did, they would be unable to marry or to find a job. Separation of
male and female roles and giving precedence to males extends even to
PTA rosters and school sports clubs. On the typical PTA members'
sheet, the household head's name appears first, although it is nearly
always the case that mothers rather than fathers are the PTA attendees.
The role of women as caretakers of the family and of domestic functions is even more openly acknowledged in boys' sports teams, which
typically have a female "manager" who washes the team's uniforms.
(Girls' teams do not have such a manager.)

In sum, Japanese parents' socialization attitudes and educational
aspirations for children are strongly linked to the sex of the child, and
this is often mirrored in the school setting as well. Parents are likely
to view university education as job preparation for sons and general
education for daughters. Given that parents and daughters both question the value of a university education for women in the labor market,
how do these perceptions influence parents' actual educational aspirations for children, and what additional role do parents' motivations
and financial resources play?

PARENTS' EDUCATIONAL
ASPIRATIONS FOR CHILDREN

A number of economists have devoted attention to the issue of how
parents decide to allocate resources for human capital development
(education) among their children. Economic theorizing may be especially relevant to the Japanese case, where gender stratification in the
labor market is high and where the competitive educational system
makes educational decision-making particularly strategic.[5]

Gary Becker and Nigel Tomes suggest that in general parental expenditures on each child are positively related to the child's relative
abilities ("endowment"). They argue that this should be true because
the "cost" or "price" of adding to "child quality" is lower for abler
(better-endowed) children. On the other hand, the amount of the be-

_____

[5] Part of this section was published in an earlier form in Brinton 1990.

quest or assets parents give to each child should be negatively related to his or her relative endowment. Parents can compensate their less-talented children by leaving them money rather than investing in their education. In short:

> Two opposing forces are at work: a "wealth" effect that induces parents to compensate less well-endowed children and an efficiency or "price" effect that induces them to reinforce better-endowed children. . . . Our conclusion is that the price effect dominates the wealth effect, that more human capital is invested in better-endowed children. Therefore, parents contribute to the observed inequality in earnings by investing more human capital in children who would receive higher earnings anyway because of their greater endowment. However, since parents invest more nonhuman capital in poorly endowed children, they reduce the inequality in total income relative to that in earnings.
>
> (Becker and Tomes 1976: S154–55)

Not only do parents need to assess their children's skills, they need to figure out the *value* of these skills, which will depend on labor market demand. If a high degree of gender stratification exists in an economy, and parents perceive sex discrimination, it is reasonable to predict that they will view maleness as an important endowment. Being female will be worth less in the labor market, and it will make less sense to invest heavily in daughters' education.

Mark Rosenzweig extends Becker and Tomes's logic to the study of sex-based wage inequality. In his words:

> While it might appear that interfamily differences in available resources and in the (average) genetic endowments of offspring are the major factors underlying individual earnings inequality, such characteristics as birth order and sex are obvious traits that contribute to earnings inequality within families. Indeed, given that the sex of children is randomly distributed across households, it would appear that any aggregate mean differences by sex in acquired human capital may mainly be due to differential sex-specific intra-family allocations of resources devoted to children.
>
> (Rosenzweig 1982: 192–93)

To the extent that males are perceived as being more successful than females in the labor market, parents will seek to invest more in sons' than in daughters' human capital. The maintenance of gender stratification—and alternatively, the possibility of change in it—is therefore at least partially rooted in the family as an allocator of resources.

The three-city data provide a means of seeing how this logic is played out in Japan. Many members of the 40–44 year-old cohort in the survey have adolescent children. They are contemplating potential investments in university education for their children in the not-so-distant future, and it is a good time to catch them as they think concretely about their children's ultimate educational achievement. In parents' thinking, three things are likely to come into play: motivations for education, perceptions of sex discrimination in the labor market, and the resources available for education.

Parents' motivations for children's education no doubt fall into the category of what economists call "psychic" (nonmonetary) returns as well as into the category of material returns. Psychic returns include the feeling that one is a good parent and has done one's best to prepare one's children for adult society. Tangible or material returns might include the financial assistance that better-educated children will be able to give, or the opportunity to live together later in life, when parents are more apt to have financial limitations.

It makes sense for Japanese parents to consider whether they want to rely on a child financially in the future, whether they expect to live with him or her, and whether the amount of education a child receives will serve him or her well in the future. For a son, the more education the better, both for the labor market and for the possibility of finding a good marriage partner. For a daughter, university education has not been perceived in Japan as being very helpful in either the labor market or what economists and sociologists call the "marriage market"—the market for finding a suitable marriage mate.

Parents will be more likely to have university aspirations for a son if they expect to rely financially on him in the future, as they will want to help him succeed in the labor market. If parents expect to rely on a daughter, the story is more complicated. Parents almost certainly expect their daughters to marry, and of course they want them to make "good" marriages. But parents are most likely to rely financially on a son if they rely on any of their children, for daughters marry out of the family and sons stay in. It is more likely that the daughter and her husband will be relied upon by *his* parents. So we might expect the relationship between financial expectations of a daughter and educational expectations for her to be complex and indeterminate.

However, parents will not necessarily have university aspirations for a son if they expect to *live* with him in the future. This is because parents will probably pass on property (the family house or business) to a son with whom they expect to live, which means that he will not have as great a need to amass financial resources through success at his job. This accords with Becker and Tomes's logic about bequests

and investments. The traditional ideal for Japanese parents has been
to live with their eldest son (in what anthropologists term a "stem"
family).[6] Parents thus do better to help their other sons achieve a good
education.

In the case of daughters, if parents expect to live with one of them,
this really means that they expect to live with their future son-in-law.
It will be important to prepare the daughter well for marriage, but too
much education can become a liability for Japanese women in the
marriage market. Thus it is unlikely that expectations of living with a
daughter in old age would significantly affect parents' educational aspirations for her. Another type of reliance on children in parents' old
age is emotional, but since it is not clear how emotional expectations
would have an effect, no predictions are made about them.

Perceptions about the marriage market and the labor market will
not affect parents' aspirations for sons, for it is simply a case of the
more education the better. But parents who perceive little or no sex
discrimination in the labor market will be more likely to have university aspirations for their daughters. Parents will also be more likely to
have university aspirations for a daughter if they feel that it will not
damage her chances of making a good marriage.

Finally, parents' economic resources might affect the likelihood of
their aspiring to a university education for sons and daughters. Public
universities are the most prestigious and are generally cheaper than
private universities, and entrance to one might be facilitated by prior
attendance at *juku* (discussed in more detail below) or, even more
costly, attendance at *yobikō* for one full year before the examination.
So while parents do not necessarily need to have a high income to send
a child to Tokyo University, they might expect it to cost something to
give their child the best chance of passing the entrance examination.
In a study of five high schools in Kobe, Rohlen found that the elite
public schools have a disproportionate representation of students
whose fathers are company employees and are university-educated. "I
can think of no other inclusive social institution in Japan that comes
closer to a simple class structure than the structure of urban high

[6] About 65 percent of Japan's elderly (age 65 or older) live with one of their children
(Office of the Prime Minister, *Kokusei chōsa*, 1985). This involves some type of economic arrangement, with parents either more dependent on their adult children or vice versa.
A 1988 survey showed that in fact about 70 percent of middle-aged Japanese who live
with their parents contribute more than their parents do to household expenses. Most
other middle-aged Japanese contribute equally with their parents. In only a small number of cases do parents pay more (Martin and Tsuya 1989).

schools in cities like Kobe," he says frankly (Rohlen 1983: 129). James and Benjamin (1988) show that there is even greater overrepresentation of students from high-income families at private than at public high schools. But at the university level, the public and the private educational sectors have similar income distributions for their students. In other words, inequality in the public sector *increases* at the university level. Students whose family income is in the top 20 percent of the national distribution are nearly three times as likely to attend university as students in the bottom 20 percent of the income distribution.

Parents with high incomes not only can afford to provide the optimal extra-school environment through tutoring or *yobikō* for their children, but they have an incentive to do so. High income usually means high social status, and high-income parents generally want to maintain their status by having a highly educated son who makes a good marriage match and obtains a good job. Whether high-income parents will desire a university education for their daughter, on the other hand, is less predictable. They will generally only do so if they feel that it will not harm her chances in the marriage and labor markets.

Certain other aspects of a family are also important in influencing the educational aspirations parents have for children. American studies have shown that the level of a mother's education has a greater influence on parents' encouragement of their daughters' education than it does on that of their sons. Having a highly educated father, on the other hand, leads to more parental encouragement of education for both young men and women (Marini 1978). These relationships can also be examined in the Japanese data.

The three cities where the survey was carried out are in different regions of the country, and aspirations for university education are probably higher in cities with highly educated, urban populations because of competition in the labor and marriage markets. This effect is more likely to exist for sons than for daughters. This suggests that parents in Kodaira and Sapporo would be more likely to aspire to university education for their sons than parents in Toyohashi.

In sum, it is easier to predict who will have university aspirations for sons than for daughters because the positive rewards of a good university education are so much clearer for young men. The sibling composition of the family will also play a part in educational decision-making. If the argument of this book with respect to the development of human capital is correct, in that parents "statistically discriminate" against daughters because they perceive the marriage and labor markets to favor daughters who are moderately rather than highly educated, then daughters in families with sons will be particularly disfavored. But a daughter who is an only child or who has sisters but no brothers should be educationally favored compared to girls with brothers. Following the same logic, we should expect parental aspirations to be highest for sons who are only children or who have sisters but no brothers. In contrast, families with sons but no daughters will represent the most competitive environment for a young man.

Appendix Table B.22 shows the means and standard deviations for the variables discussed above. In families in the sample with at least one son, 73.1 percent of parents report having university aspirations for their son. In families with at least one daughter, 27.6 percent of parents hope to send a daughter to university. These figures almost exactly duplicate the national figures for Japan cited earlier, even though the three-city respondents include both mothers and fathers and the national survey respondents include only mothers. Perhaps men and women do not differ in their expectations of children. In fact, virtually the same proportions of mothers (27.5 percent) as fathers (27.7 percent) in my survey aspired to university education for daughters. But more mothers (75.3 percent) than fathers (69.1 percent) hoped for university education for sons. While this difference for sons is not statistically significant, it becomes significant in the causal analyses when other variables are controlled, as will be shown shortly.

In Japanese families with at least one son and one daughter, many more parents (74 percent) expect to rely financially in old age on a son than on a daughter (6 percent), as shown in Table 6.5. More parents expect to live with a son (nearly 40 percent) than with a daughter (fewer than 8 percent). But parents expect their emotional ties with a daughter to be stronger than with a son. The table also shows that parents' needs are ordered for sons and daughters. They are much more likely to anticipate turning to a daughter for emotional than for financial or residential support (this predominance is statistically significant). Likewise, their expectations of sons are clearly ordered from financial help to co-residence and finally to emotional needs. Statistical comparisons among these three expectations of sons show anticipation of financial support to be significantly stronger than for other types of support.

The results of multivariate logistic regression models of university aspirations show that most of the predictions are borne out (Appendix

TABLE 6.5

DIFFERENCES IN PARENTAL
EXPECTATIONS OF SUPPORT FROM SONS
AND DAUGHTERS IN OLD AGE

	Source of help		
Type of assistance	Son (%)	Daughter (%)	t-value
Financial help	74	6	− 19.82***
Joint living arrangement	39	8	− 8.78***
Emotional help	31	44	2.66**

SOURCE: Survey conducted by author.
NOTES: All t-tests are one-tailed. The table is restricted to families with two or more children, where there is at least one son and at least one daughter. The number of respondents is 291. Figures for support from sons and daughters do not necessarily sum to 100 percent because some parents report anticipating help from a combination of children or from none of their children. The critical comparisons for our purposes are the comparison between sons and daughters, and the comparisons among the needs parents expect to have fulfilled by children of each sex.
** t-value significant at .01 level; *** t-value significant at .001 level.

Tables B.23–B.25). Parents are more apt to have university aspirations for a son if they anticipate relying on him financially in old age. As predicted, their anticipation of eventually living with a son is not significantly related to their educational aspirations for him, and neither is anticipation of emotional reliance. Parents with higher household income are more likely to aspire to a university education for their sons. Also, sons who are only children are the most educationally favored, followed by sons who are the eldest in a family of daughters. Parents in these situations can easily focus their high aspirations on a son. Conversely, parents with sons but no daughters are less likely to anticipate sending sons to university, suggesting that there is something like a competitive market for education among sons in such a family.

University aspirations for sons are more common in the two most urban areas, Kodaira and Sapporo, than in Toyohashi. In households where the father is university-educated, parents are more likely to hope for a university education for their sons. In households where the mother has a high school education, parents are also significantly more likely to aspire to sons' university education. Although the effects of other levels of mothers' education are not statistically significant, university aspirations for a son decline as mothers' education continues to rise to junior college and university. Interestingly, mothers are more likely than fathers to have university aspirations for sons. It seems that mothers, especially if they themselves did not go on to higher education, are more likely to invest their aspirations actively in their sons' futures than are fathers. This is consistent with the popular image of the mother-son bond as the strongest one in the Japanese family (Doi 1973; Lebra 1984). It also coincides with the image of the *kyōiku mama* ("education mama") who urges her son on to success in educational competition. This investment of hope in sons makes sense in view of the sex-discriminatory labor market and in view of parental and especially maternal reliance on children in old age. In fact, a mother's reliance on a son in old age is more common than a father's. Not only is the typical Japanese wife younger than her husband, but females' life expectancy exceeds males' by nearly six years (Ministry of Welfare, Japan, 1989).

Given the possible mixed implications of a woman's university education in the marriage and labor markets, factors that lead to higher aspirations for sons do not necessarily have the same effect for daughters (Table B.24). There is no direct measure in the survey of parents' perception of the marriage market, but we can assume that most people have a good general knowledge of how marriage choices are made. About half of all marriages in Japan are arranged (Hodge and Ogawa 1986), meaning in the contemporary context that introductions are provided by relatives, friends, teachers, employers, or other trusted acquaintances of the family. Since marriage is so important in Japan, most families are quite conversant with the "market" value of education and of other achievements and attributes (even including siblings' education, occupations, etc.). The statistical results of Table B.24 can be interpreted with the assumption in mind that Japanese parents generally perceive that a university-educated daughter will have a smaller pool of possible marriage mates than a daughter with a slightly lower level of education.

Expectations of assistance in old age are not related in a statistically significant way to aspirations for a university education for daughters. Nor does household income have a significant effect on expectations for daughters. These results are as expected. The effects of family composition are also as predicted: daughters who are only children or who have sisters but no brothers are educationally favored over daughters with brothers. Parents in Kodaira are also more likely to have university aspirations for daughters than parents in the other two cities. Interestingly, the effects of education of both mother and father exhibit a clearer pattern for aspirations for daughters than for sons: the mother-daughter link is particularly strong. Aspirations for daughters increase with each successive level of mothers' education. But mothers overall are no more likely than fathers to have university aspirations for daughters.

Table B.25 shows the results of a separate analysis of the Toyohashi respondents only. Of the three cities surveyed, only people in Toyohashi were questioned about perceptions of sex discrimination. This happened because the Kodaira and Sapporo surveys were carried out first, before fieldwork had revealed to me the degree of sex discrimination against university-educated women and the importance of asking respondents about their perceptions of it.

The basic results for Toyohashi are similar to the results for all three cities, except that the effects of family composition are not statistically significant. Parents who perceive a high level of sex discrimination in the labor market are less likely to have university aspirations for a daughter. It is not possible conclusively to test the hypothesis that parents in higher-income households have university aspirations for daughters only if they perceive little sex discrimination, because there are too few people in the Toyohashi sample for this statistical test to be reliable. But the idea can be examined in a more exploratory fashion by grouping households into four categories on the basis of their income and looking at the relation between income and aspirations for daughters within collapsed categories of the sex discrimination variable (perceptions of high versus little/no discrimination). Here, income is positively related to university aspirations if people perceive little or no sex discrimination, and is negatively related to university aspirations if they perceive high discrimination. This is consistent with the idea that the household resources—university aspirations relationship is contingent on parents' perceptions of the labor market facing women.

In conclusion, Japanese parents are much more likely to express university aspirations for a son than a daughter, and sons from the following types of households are the most educationally "encouraged": households where the father is highly educated; where income is high; where parents expect a financially interdependent relationship with a son in old age; and where the son is an only child or has sisters but no brothers. University aspirations also seem to be more common in highly urbanized areas. All else being equal, mothers are more likely than fathers to hold high aspirations for sons. By contrast, encouragement of daughters is much harder to predict. Daughters who are only children or who have no male siblings get more encouragement than others. Highly educated parents are more likely to want their daughter to be university-educated. And perceived sex discrimination in the labor market appears to lessen parents' enthusiasm for daughters' university education.

This detailed examination of parents' educational aspirations for children shows how ideas about gendered higher education are shaped in the family and are affected by external circumstances such as sex discrimination. Japanese parents also invest in gender-specific informal, "extra-school" schooling.

EXTRA-SCHOOL SCHOOLING AND TRAINING: THE NATIONAL PICTURE

Despite the popular attention showered in Japan on private tutorial schools and examination-preparation schools, few reliable statistics on the subject exist. These schools operate as private businesses and are therefore outside the compulsory school system. As a result, the Japanese Ministry of Education does not routinely collect statistics on them. The most recent major study of what can be termed "extra-school" schooling is a nationwide survey conducted in 1985 by the National Institute of Education. This report provides a basis for describing elementary and junior high school (but not high school) students' participation in different types of extra-school schools. The survey covered 42,000 households that had an elementary or junior high school student present, and interviewers conducted a survey in 2,000 *juku* (tutorial schools) as well. Comparisons with the most up-to-date prior survey (1976) permit some assessment of the changes in the past ten years.

Table 6.6 shows the proportion of boys and girls in elementary and junior high schools who take part in different types of extra-school schooling. The term *juku* refers to tutorial schools that are either remedial or provide already high-achieving students with extra help in preparing for future school entrance examinations. More and more, parents see *juku* as part of the normal process of schooling. This is shown by the fact that the main reasons parents cite for sending children to *juku* are that children want to attend, that they don't study well by themselves, and that the academic content of the regular school day is so difficult that parents cannot provide much help to children

TABLE 6.6

PERCENTAGE OF STUDENTS
PARTICIPATING IN DIFFERENT TYPES
OF EXTRA-SCHOOL SCHOOLING, BY
EDUCATIONAL LEVEL AND SEX

	Juku	*Katei kyōshi*	*Keikogoto*
1976			
Overall rate	20.2	3.0	51.0
Elementary school boys	13.3	1.8	53.6
Elementary school girls	10.8	1.2	72.4
Junior high school boys	40.6	6.4	14.6
Junior high school girls	35.2	5.8	36.1
1985			
Overall rate	26.3	2.5	55.5
Elementary school boys	17.7	1.0	63.0
Elementary school girls	15.1	1.0	78.8
Junior high school boys	45.9	5.5	15.3
Junior high school girls	43.0	5.2	40.0

SOURCE: Ministry of Education, Japan, 1985.

with their schoolwork (Ministry of Education, Japan, 1985). Other types of extra-school schooling include *katei kyōshi* (private tutoring) and *keikogoto* (lessons such as calligraphy, music, or martial arts). Sex-specific terms exist for the latter: *keikogoto* are lessons for girls and *naraigoto* are lessons for boys. (For convenience, surveys usually refer simply to *keikogoto*.)

Participation in *juku* and in *keikogoto* has risen in the past ten years for all groups (Table 6.6). Moreover, rates of *juku* attendance more than triple between elementary and junior high school, reaching a point where nearly half of all students attend. There is little sex difference in these rates.

In contrast to this, children's participation in special lessons of various types declines with age; this was true in both 1976 and 1985. About two-thirds of boys of elementary school age participated in extracurricular lessons in 1985, compared to only 15 percent of their junior high school counterparts. Girls continue to take extra lessons at a high rate (40 percent) in junior high school, but this is still much lower than the rate (79 percent) for elementary school. Private tutoring is a form of extra-school schooling in which few children take part, although its prevalence goes up in junior high as against elementary school.

By the time students are in junior high school, the overwhelming emphasis in *juku* is on English and mathematics, the two most critical subjects covered in high school and university entrance examinations. Nearly one-third of junior high school students in *juku* spend over two hours per day there, whereas this is true of fewer than 3 percent of students in early elementary and fewer than 15 percent of students in upper elementary grades.

Notwithstanding the general supplementary educational role played by *juku*, attendance rates are highest for children whose parents hold university aspirations for them. Slightly fewer university-bound girls than boys go to *juku*. But despite parents' higher educational aspirations for sons than daughters, the select group of parents who have equivalent aspirations for sons and daughters generally seem to use *juku* in an egalitarian way.

The major limitations of the 1976 and 1985 national surveys of extra-school schooling are two: (1) we can only see what happens up to the high school level, and (2) little attention in the reports is focused on sex differences. (For instance, the reports do not include figures showing whether boys spend more hours than girls in *juku*, commute farther to *juku*, etc.) These are important limitations, because it is during high school that young men's and young women's educational paths start to diverge significantly as they prepare for different future educational and life experiences. These data nevertheless provide important summary information: (1) through the third year of junior high school, young men and women have similarly high rates of attendance at *juku*, but (2) as they move through junior high school, many fewer young men than women are involved in cultural, artistic, or sports-related lessons. Also, the content of these lessons is quite sex-specific. About half of the boys and girls involved in *keikogoto* take calligraphy instruction and about one-third (though slightly fewer for girls) take abacus lessons. But more girls (60 percent) than boys (under 20 percent) in *keikogoto* take music lessons, figures that are almost exactly reversed for sports-related activities such as the martial arts. Thus the sex-role differentiation that occurs at this age is in the context of *keikogoto* rather than in rates of *juku* attendance.

Data from the three-city survey show the total extra-school schooling experiences that young men and women have by the time they finish their education, including a very important one not discussed so far—*rōnin* experience.

SURVEY RESPONDENTS' EXTRA-SCHOOL SCHOOLING AND TRAINING

Nearly equal proportions (about 30 percent) of both men and women in the 25–29 year cohort in the three-city survey attended *juku* at some point in their education. Sex differences do not exist here, but in the prevalence of private tutoring and lessons: 17 percent of young men, but only 8 percent of young women, had a private tutor (statistically significant at the .01 level). Conversely, 46 percent of young men, but 62 percent of young women, had cultural, sports, or artistic lessons (statistically significant at the .001 level). Men and women are equally likely to report that their parents footed the bill for such lessons, but women report a significantly greater *variety* of lessons than men. As one woman in her forties commented: "My parents and I had to think about my qualifications to marry. A tea ceremony license is like a medal. And the more medals I had, the better husband I could get."

The most time- and labor-intensive type of training, *rōnin* experience, is four times more common among males (17 percent) than females (4 percent), a difference that is highly significant statistically ($p < .001$). The percentages of *rōnin* among university graduates are quite a bit higher, but even among this select group, the sex difference remains.[7] One man in his late twenties commented that high school had been a pleasant experience because both he and his parents assumed that he would spend a year afterward as a *rōnin*. Because of that expectation, he was able to relax during high school rather than suffer the *juken jigoku* (examination hell) experienced by many other male students. The male character of *rōnin* experience is mirrored in the statistics of *yobikō*, the private institutions offering preparation for university entrance examinations. In the mid 1980s, males constituted nearly 90 percent of the students enrolled in the year-long university examination preparation course at Yoyogi Seminar, one of the biggest, most renowned *yobikō* in Japan.

These figures on the gender variation in types of extra-school schooling demonstrate again the gradual bifurcation of paths as stu-

---

[7] Among people who went no further than high school, 6 percent of men and no women had *rōnin* experience ($p < .01$).

dents age. The important role of extra-school schooling in the overall Japanese educational system allows parents to "track" their children, paying for more years of arts lessons such as music, tea ceremony, or dance for a daughter and possibly financing a full year of extra study for a son to retake a university entrance examination.

CONCLUSION

Whereas previous chapters focused mainly on Japan's human capital development system from the vantage point of employers hiring, training, and promoting certain types of workers, this chapter has shown how the educational system developed in tandem with the labor market and how parents respond rationally to the strong education–labor market linkage. Although education is typically considered the "supply side" of the labor market, perceptions of the "demand side"—notably employer discrimination—provide input into decision-making and affect the formation of parents' educational aspirations for their children. Parents are guided by their own needs and desires for help from their children later in life, by an awareness of what awaits their children in the labor and marriage markets, and by the resources at their disposal. Perception of sex discrimination in the labor market acts as a discouraging factor in the formation of university aspirations for daughters. Sons and daughters, too, are well aware of the consequences that early educational choices and examination performance have on their lives as adults in Japanese society.

Given this context, it is not surprising that, all else held equal, Japanese mothers are more apt than fathers to aspire to a university education for sons. Mothers can more rationally invest in the labor-market oriented human capital of their sons than in either their own human capital or that of their daughters. While such mothers may be ridiculed as overly fervent, they are simultaneously honored as fulfilling their role as investors in one part of Japan's characteristic human capital development system.

SEVEN

Conclusion

The Japanese economy demonstrates the compatibility between high levels of female labor force participation and highly sex-segregated roles. The human capital development system refined in postwar Japan has facilitated, not impaired, this seeming contradiction. Japan's human capital development system is characterized by highly competitive educational institutions that encourage families' investment of resources early in their children's lives; a family environment that entails a significant amount of intergenerational exchange; and an employment system that rewards continuous work in one organization.

Japanese parents have sharply lower educational aspirations for daughters than for sons. Such aspirations are shaped by the rational decision-making processes by which parents balance the resources available for investment in the education of their children against their expectations that such investment will "pay off." The shaping of life and career goals begins at an early age and occurs within the structure of a very competitive educational system. Extra-school schooling becomes more sex-segregated in adolescence: girls have greater exposure than boys to cultural and artistic lessons, and boys are much more likely than girls to be *rōnin*. The average educational attainment of the sexes differs, with about 33 percent of males completing university compared to 15 percent of females. Sex differences in subjects of study at university are striking, and these differences are even more prominent when junior college females are included in the comparison, as junior college has been equivalent throughout most of the postwar period to finishing school or marriage-preparation school. In sum, when men and women enter the labor market, they have been strongly socialized for sex-segregated work roles.

Employers socialize where parents leave off. Sex serves as a crucial screening device by which to sort out the job applicants and new hires who will remain in the labor force for many years and, if things go well, even remain in the same work organization. Employers' initial judgment and sorting serves as a basis for decisions about on-the-job training and job rotation opportunities for men and women. Women are less apt to enter firm-internal labor markets, and they receive less on-the-job training and job rotation experience. These phenomena are apparent as soon as people enter the work force. By the time they reach their late twenties, men and women differ little in their average number of working years but already have had different experiences on the job. By early middle age, men and women exhibit radically different employment experiences: men have many more years of work experience than women, and if they have left wage employment, it has been with self-employment as a destination. Women are divided among full-time housewives, part-time employees, full-time employees, and self-employed and family enterprise workers.

University-educated Japanese women in particular have experienced difficulties in finding jobs in past decades. Employers have expressed— and practiced—a reluctance to hire them into the same positions as men, fearing that investments made in on-the-job training will be wasted. Japanese women's age at marriage exhibits very low variance in comparison to that of women in other industrialized countries, and strong social norms exist for them to leave the labor force during the early years of childrearing and to spend a concentrated period of time specializing in the roles of wife and mother. These norms coincide neatly with an employment system that rests on the existence of a strong core of permanent workers and a subsidiary, flexible group of employees who move in and out of the system. Further, the emphasis on long-term relations among members of Japanese organizations means that those who remain with the same firm develop a shared culture. The ideology and practice of low interfirm mobility for men only exacerbate women's difficulty in reentering the labor force in early middle age: women returning to work are viewed as outsiders, in an organizational culture where the distinction between outsiders and insiders is extremely important.

Instead of the firm, the household becomes the locus of power and responsibility for most women from their late twenties onward. Women become key "investors" in developing the human capital of their husbands and sons, "for it has been defined as their responsibility to offer the kind of private, domestic support that enables men to make their way in the public world of affairs" (Smith 1987: 3). Women invest especially high aspirations in their sons, thereby playing an indirect role in the economy by supporting men's educational and economic success.

While this summary may again raise the question of whether Japan is on the path to convergence with Western industrial nations, it is important to reiterate that the permanent employment system—an integral component of Japan's human capital development system—is not a carryover from the preindustrial past, but in fact reached its most institutionalized form in the postwar period. Similarly, those aspects of the educational system that either fuel sex-segregated roles or are compatible with them—the junior college system and the extraordinary competition for spaces at Japan's elite public universities—are postwar elaborations. Thus, to argue for convergence between Western and Japanese social and economic institutions governing gender roles is to ignore the historical record of institutional change in Japan.

If Japan is not "lagging behind" the West, does it represent a forerunner of a common East Asian pattern of gender stratification in education and the labor force? This is not likely. Japan and South Korea have similar M-shaped age patterns of female labor force participation, although Japanese women have higher participation rates at almost every age (Fig. 7.1). But Hong Kong, Singapore, and Taiwan show a strikingly different pattern: high labor force participation rates exist among young women, followed by a linear downward trend in participation with age. This represents the "early peak" pattern (Roos 1985) of women's economic participation. Another distinction between Japan and South Korea on the one hand and Hong Kong, Singapore, and Taiwan on the other is that Japanese and Korean women aged 15–19 have lower rates of labor force participation. This is because a higher percentage of them are in school. Current rates of high school advancement in Japan and South Korea are over 90 percent, compared to between 70 and 80 percent in Hong Kong, Singapore, and Taiwan (World Bank 1988). Susan Greenhalgh (1985) and Janet Salaff (1981) have suggested that in the three Chinese societies, lower-class families encourage their daughters to enter the labor force at an early age to help support the family economy for as many years as possible before marriage. This phenomenon has not been reported for Japan and South Korea. But the sharper dip in employment rates for

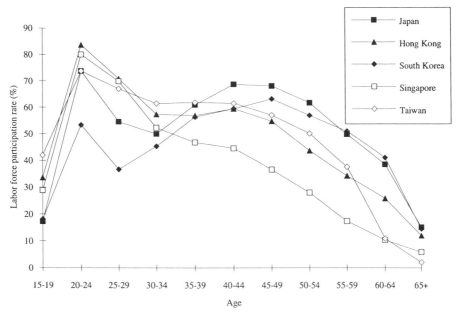

Figure 7.1. Female Labor Force Participation Rates, Japan and Selected Asian Countries

SOURCE: International Labor Organization 1987.

Japanese and Korean women in their twenties and the dramatic upward swing in the late thirties suggests that women are closely coordinating their employment activity with marriage and childrearing responsibilities. By age 45–49, women's rates of employment in these two countries exceed the rates in the other three countries.

Another major difference between Japan and South Korea on the one hand and Hong Kong, Singapore, and Taiwan on the other is that a higher proportion of Japanese and Korean women work as self-employed or family enterprise workers. This is true even when the agricultural labor force is ignored, an important point because the greater size of the agricultural sector in Japan and Korea might account for the discrepancy in the type of economic activity women engage in. Table 7.1 shows that even after restricting the intercountry comparisons to the urban, nonagricultural labor force, the representation of employed women in family enterprises is 2.5 times higher in Japan than in Taiwan, and Korean women's participation is nearly 4 times higher. Hong Kong and Singapore show the lowest rates of such employment. Even controlling for the size of the family enterprise sector in all of these countries, Japan and Korea stand out as having the highest rates

TABLE 7.1
DISTRIBUTION OF URBAN
FEMALE LABOR FORCE AMONG
EMPLOYMENT STATUSES, EAST ASIA
(%)

	Employees	Self-employed	Family enterprise workers	Total
Japan	74.9	11.8	13.3	100.0
South Korea	60.8	19.3	19.9	100.0
Taiwan	83.2	11.6	5.2	100.0
Hong Kong	87.7	6.6	5.7	100.0
Singapore	86.0	8.5	5.5	100.0

SOURCE: International Labor Organization 1988.

of female representation (over 80 percent); men's relative participation in the sector is markedly lower than in the other countries. Comparisons along other dimensions of employment present a complementary picture: Japan and Korea represent a contrast with Taiwan, Singapore, and Hong Kong. The ratio of female to male wages in nonagricultural activities hovers around .50 in Japan and Korea compared to .60 or more in the other countries (Brinton and Ngo 1991). Women's participation in different occupations also shows distinct patterns (Fig. 7.2). In particular, Japanese and Korean women make up fewer than 10 percent of the administrative and managerial workers in their respective countries but constitute a relatively high proportion of the agricultural and service workers.

In sum, there is no case to be made for Japan constituting a prototype of East Asian women's economic role. But could one conclude that Japan is a model of Korea's future? Other evidence suggests a more complex picture. Korean women are "catching up" with men's university attendance rates at a faster pace than Japanese women; so fast, in fact, that by the late 1980s a higher proportion of Korean than Japanese women were entering four-year universities. This is the *reverse* of what one would expect if Japan were to be the model for Korea. Even so, university-educated Korean women have low rates of labor force participation. There also seems to be no evidence of a link between the demand for white-collar workers and women's increasing rates of university advancement in Korea (Lee and Brinton 1991), whereas in Japan there is weak evidence supporting such a link

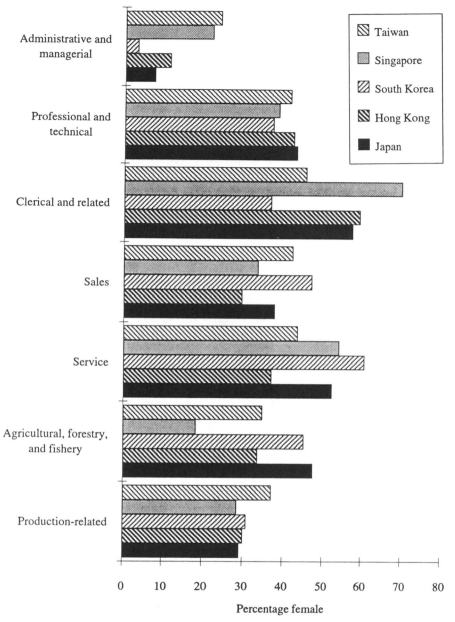

Figure 7.2. Percentage Female in Different Occupations, Japan and Selected Asian Countries

SOURCE: International Labor Organization 1988.

(Brinton and Lee 1991). Korean women's education appears to be driven instead by a different process than one predicted by the narrow model of education for the labor market. One distinction between Japan and Korea that may offer a partial explanation is the educational policy decisions made in the two countries. Whereas the Japanese government has followed the path of restricting the size of entering cohorts at public universities, educational policymakers in Korea have increased the number of spaces available to applicants. This seems to have been both a response and a stimulus to the great demand for university education for both sexes, demonstrated in an extremely high (and sex-egalitarian) level of university aspirations in Korea.

These East Asian comparisons clearly constitute an important arena for testing the theoretical framework of a human capital development system presented in this book. In comparative work, the opportunity to hold constant a range of cultural features is a valuable one, and this can arguably be optimized in research within East Asia. National differences in parts of the human capital development system, such as education and employment institutions, can be examined for their connection to gender stratification patterns and this can further the development of gender stratification theory.

The argument in this book may seem to predict glacially paced change in the roles Japanese men and women play in the economy. If all the elements of Japan's human capital development system point in the same direction—to sex-segregated roles—how will change occur? The answer to this puzzle is that the interdependence of the different parts of Japan's human capital development system paradoxically leads to both stability *and* fragility. Explaining the stability has been the principal task of this book; explaining the fragility is the task of these final pages.

SOURCES OF CHANGE IN GENDER STRATIFICATION

The fragility of the processes maintaining Japanese gender stratification lies in their interconnectedness. Two major recent changes in Japanese society, both largely exogenous to the human capital development system, promise to exert shocks to it. By affecting mainly the operation of the employment system, these two phenomena are likely to set in motion changes in the perception of the utility of women's education and changes in the norms governing age at marriage. In short, the many feedback mechanisms among work institutions, education, and family will be altered in new ways in the future. These alterations may eventually lead to a different equilibrium in the human capital development system. I predict that this will not occur without considerable intervening change and confusion over an extended period of time.

The two changes that are already setting processes in motion are the Equal Employment Opportunity Law ratified by the Japanese Diet in 1985 and, of potentially more far-reaching importance, a labor shortage in Japan that will become even more severe in the twenty-first century.

THE STRUGGLE FOR EQUAL EMPLOYMENT OPPORTUNITY

In the early 1980s, debate over the role of women in Japan's economy and in its households uncharacteristically entered the news media and remained in the national spotlight for a time. The stimulus was the proposed Equal Employment Opportunity Law. In 1980 Japan signed the United Nations Convention on the Elimination of All Forms of Discrimination against Women, which entailed a pledge to enact legislation by 1985 to provide equal employment opportunities to men and women. In response, the Diet passed the Equal Employment Opportunity Law in mid 1985, after intense debate within the Labor Ministry and among labor union representatives, academics, employers' associations, and women's groups.

The law that was finally passed and put into effect one year later (in 1986) is a distinctly Japanese product: it *encourages* employers to refrain from discriminating on the basis of sex in all stages of the employment process, including recruitment, hiring, training, compensation and promotion policies, and retirement. No explicit penalties are imposed on employers who do not conform. This law represents Japan's "administrative guidance" (*gyōsei shidō*) principle at its finest (Johnson 1982; Upham 1987). That is, the appropriate government ministry guides firms in upholding the law but does not penalize them other than by creating public expectations that companies will toe the line. In the midst of the debate in 1984, a Labor Ministry official told me that the most effective enforcement of the law, were it to be passed, would come from its acceptance by the public at large and the corresponding normative pressure on companies to adapt their practices. Similarly, a Japanese labor economist expressed a surprising private view on this subject when the law was approved: "Even though no direct material sanctions will be applied by the government, there is hope. The major corporations have an image to protect, and if it is seen as prestigious to try to be progressive and egalitarian, they will try it. And they, after all, lead the way."

The drafting of the law engendered debate around a number of issues. Should all protective legislation for women be abolished? Critics charged that legal restrictions on overtime work and night work for women (in the Labor Standards Law of the early postwar period) had been convenient excuses for employers not to allow women into certain occupations or not to promote them to managerial rank. Others, especially labor union representatives, argued against the repeal of protective measures for women. Some suggested that the conditions under which Japanese men labored were inhumane, and that it was men's work conditions that should be brought into line with women's. In the end, most protective measures were repealed by the law in the interest of attempting to establish equal starting points for men and women.

The debate reached its highest pitch in the news media with a series of near-hysterical articles published in a number of news and opinion magazines. In an issue of *Chūō Kōron*, Japan's leading intellectual monthly magazine, Hasegawa Michiko attacked the UN convention and the equal employment opportunity bill drafted by the Labor Ministry as un-Japanese. She argued that passage of the bill would threaten the "cultural ecology" of Japanese society by destroying traditional sex roles and demoralizing housewives, who hitherto had held a privileged position. Her argument was strong and vociferous in claiming that Japan had a cultural system that was irrevocably separate from that of the West, and that the latter was characterized by selfishness and individualism of a sort foreign to Japan. In her glorification of housewives, Hasegawa was subsequently accused in writing by Satō Kinko (previously an attorney and then the head of the Women's Bureau of the Labor Ministry) of "speaking from one side of her mouth": notably, Hasegawa is not a housewife, but an associate professor of philosophy.

Less extreme, but no less adamant, positions were taken by several other writers, who claimed that low male unemployment rates would be threatened were the law to pass, and that the Japanese family would crumble as an institution. (Such protests had often been made by employers in cases brought to court by women, beginning in the 1960s.)[1]

---

[1] A series of court cases from the mid 1960s to the mid 1970s challenged forced retirement upon marriage and overt sex discrimination in wage and layoff policies. As

Many commentators based their remarks on the assumption that Japanese women would be driven into the workplace, rather than recognizing that the law simply guaranteed equal opportunity (and with limited enforcement provisions).

Responses to the law by women themselves and by employers were complex. Though the media entertained the fray among public officials and private employers over the law, it would be an exaggeration to say that very many members of the Japanese public, including women themselves, were intensely involved in the discussion. While some women favored passage of the law, others wondered whether it would reinforce women's principal role in the household and subsidiary role in the work organization by demanding that women be more like men in the workplace while continuing to take care of everything at home. Others felt strongly that the law should attempt to humanize men's working lives and worried that it might lead instead to the dehumanization of women's lives.

Many Japanese men and women expressed the view that women represent a stronghold of humanity in a highly regulated, competitive social and economic system. Comments about working hours by doc-

---

Frank Upham writes: "If it is now theoretically possible for female employees to stay on and receive even remotely equal treatment, they have these cases to thank" (1987: 129). Upham divides sex discrimination cases into two groups, those brought to court in the mid 1960s to mid 1970s and those that have come later. The first series of cases emerged from the infamous Sumitomo Cement case of 1966, which was decided in the plaintiff's favor. In 1958, Sumitomo had adopted several regulations governing the hiring of female employees. One of these was that all women were required to sign an agreement that they would retire upon marriage or at age 30, whichever came first (Upham 1987). A challenge to this was brought to court by a woman who had been fired because she refused to resign. The company offered in its defense the following: women were paid at the same rate as men when they were hired, but in order for the company to operate efficiently under such a system, women were required to retire at one of the two time points specified above. Otherwise, the company would be paying the same wages to married women and men. Sumitomo asserted that this did not make sense, because "unmarried women are free from domestic responsibilities and are therefore more productive than married women" (quoted by Upham 1987: 131). Equivalent wages were seen as a gift to female employees for their upcoming marriages.

The court decided against the defendant, stating that there needed to be proof of a decline in women's productivity upon marriage. Since the Sumitomo case, formal mandatory retirement practices have been struck down in a number of other cases. What had been a nearly universal practice among Japanese companies is no longer.

The "second generation" of cases in the past decade has attempted to attack more disguised forms of sex discrimination in the workplace. These cases have dealt with the issues discussed in previous pages—companies' refusal to hire female graduates of four-year universities, the separate tracking of women into dead-end jobs and men into career tracks, and the more stringent requirements for women to be promoted. Some cases have been won, others lost, while yet others remain tangled in the court system.

tors, academics, and other high-status workers could easily be dismissed as the inevitable complaints of professional people in any society. But both the man on the street and statistics collected by the Japanese government and the International Labor Organization attest to the same reality: Japanese work, on average, longer hours than people in other industrial societies (Japan Economic Institute 1990). Japanese men also spend longer hours at the workplace and, significantly, many more work hours outside the office or plant than do women. According to Labor Ministry statistics, men spend an average of nineteen hours every month engaged in work activities outside the workplace, whereas women spend only seven hours (Ministry of Labor 1987c). As one female government bureaucrat pointed out: "The common point for single working women and married part-time working women is that their purpose in life is not only to work. Younger women want to have more free time for leisure and married women want to have more time for household management. I think this lifestyle is more humane than that of men." This common perception that men's working lives are far from ideal may have mitigated the demand for the law. A second factor that may account for a mixed public reaction to the law is the complexity of definitions of equity between the sexes. An insightful view of the mixed feelings about the separate roles of men and women is provided in interviews carried out by Glenda Roberts in her ethnographic study of a Japanese lingerie factory in the mid 1980s. Some female workers in the factory felt that women should be laid off before men, even in the exceptional case where the woman was the only support of her household. Roberts quotes a forty-year-old employee:

> And for women, there are comparatively many places to get a job easily. The opening is wide though shallow. You can get *pāto* work very easily. You start running into a snag when you talk about pay rate. But women are frugal, right? As far as money goes. So, even if she is a single parent, I think it's easier, comparatively, for her to choose a job.
>
> (Roberts 1986: 206)

Roberts describes in detail a speech made by the company president on the anniversary of the founding of the company. The president had prepared his speech on videotape so that employees could watch it as they ate lunch. One theme of the speech was that Japan's economic recovery could be attributed to the strength of the traditional Japanese housewife, who encouraged her husband. The decrease in numbers of this type of women spelled danger for Japan, according to the company president. "In his analogy, the puppeteers, lured by the glitter of the stage, have abandoned their puppets to become actresses themselves. Yet without the puppeteers, the puppets have no strength, no life," Roberts observes (1986: 199) This view expresses the honor attached to women's role as *investors* in the human capital of others in the household, rather than directly in their own human capital and wage-earning power.

The complexities of changing values are also reflected in the comments of the mother whom I quoted earlier in this book, caught between mixed, shifting motives for her daughter's education (see p. 146 above), and those of a well-educated, middle-aged wife I interviewed:

> If a wife and mother puts aside her own desires and endures [*gaman suru*] for years, then when she and her husband are in middle age, her husband says, "what a good wife you are for having put up with all of this"; it is a highly valued virtue to have done this. Great value is put on this type of trait in Japanese culture. This trait in men is valued too. There is value put on dealing with your problems privately. But this is a happy ending to such a story. An unhappy ending is if the couple divorces in middle age; this is occurring more frequently these days than it used to.

It could be argued, then, that the impact of the Equal Employment Opportunity Law will not be significant because many Japanese women do not aspire to bring their working lives into conformity with what they see as the harsh working conditions of men, and because women's indirect role in the economy through their support of men is a time-honored one. Furthermore, the way employers implement the law will be critical to its impact. One accommodation that has been made by many employers is to offer women a choice of tracks when they apply to a company. One is the standard track (*ippan shoku*) where they are expected to quit upon marriage, and the other is the *sōgō shoku* track that almost all men have traditionally entered. A Ministry of Labor survey in 1989 reported that about 40 percent of companies with more than 5,000 employees had adopted a multi-track personnel system; the figure was much lower for smaller companies (Japan Economic Institute 1991). The problem with a multi-track system is that women are forced to choose between two extremes, the traditional women's track that has no promotion possibilities and the traditional men's track that, particularly in large firms, entails virtually total control by the employer over transfers to other parts of the company, including branches in other cities. The inducements for women lie almost entirely in the dead-end track. Why? Some employers offer a lump-sum payment to women who choose this track and eventually quit—a kind of combination retirement payment/dowry. In addition, women who choose the career track are usually warned by their employers that they are putting their prospects of marriage in jeopardy, or that, at best, they risk not having a happy family life if they do manage to marry (Saso 1990).

These new developments point to the continuing inherent conflict for women. As long as training and promotions in the workplace depend mainly on length of service with one company, and as long as incentives are offered to women to exchange this for the opportunity of having a stable marriage and investing time in developing the human capital of their children, change will be slow to occur. However, pressure on employers to adapt to the Equal Employment Opportunity Law is already coming from quite a different direction: the labor shortage in Japan. Stated bluntly, Japanese employers need more workers, and this economic exigency is likely to push them to utilize female labor in other than low-wage, dead-end jobs.

THE IMPACT OF THE LABOR SHORTAGE

The permanent employment system developed in response to a shortage of skilled labor in the early part of the twentieth century. Now, at the end of the century, Japan must again adjust to a shortage of labor. As the country enters the 1990s, it is experiencing a shortage of labor that by all demographic projections promises to become more severe in the coming decades. One indication of the current shortage is the job opening-applicant ratio, which rose from an average of .66 in the early 1980s to 1.25 in 1989, the highest point since 1973 (Japan Economic Institute 1990). Declining birthrates in Japan in recent years mean that the number of young people entering the labor force in coming years will decline. Government concern in 1990 over a birthrate that fell to a low of 1.57 was euphemistically labeled the "1.57 shokku" (the "1.57 shock").

There will be several possible ways of adjusting to a labor shortage, including greater substitution of capital for labor, greater utilization of foreign subsidiaries, greater use of foreign immigrants to Japan, and greater use of female labor. Both of the last two options are problematic for Japanese employers. Given the limited use of foreign labor throughout Japan's history, many employers probably perceive the greater employment of women to be the lesser of two evils. This will inevitably entail more attention on the part of both government and private enterprise to ways of helping women stay in the labor force, including institutional accommodations such as childcare, more flexible work hours, and parental leave policies.[2]

There is nothing in this prognosis for change that is at all incompatible with the social-institutional view of gender stratification offered in this book. In fact, there is an ironic complementarity between the historical processes that shaped the permanent employment system and its exclusion of women and the currently embryonic processes that will ultimately transform the system and create new opportunities for women. In both the historical and current junctures, the response of employers to a limited labor supply may be identified as a key factor in shaping employment policies with fundamental implications for women's working lives. The combination of the Equal Employment Opportunity Law and the labor shortage creates a situation where it will be in more employers' interests to create incentives for women to remain in the labor force.

There are already some signs that the demand for labor and the possibility of higher wages and greater promotional possibilities are having the feedback effects predictable in the institutional framework outlined in this book. That is, the vicious cycle between employers' behaviors and the attitudes and behaviors of young women and their parents appears to be weakening. Newspaper reports in the past few years hint at two transformations. First, a number of women's junior colleges have closed because of dwindling enrollments, and many others are changing their curriculum from home economics and humanities to more technical fare. This suggests that the demand for education is changing in response to the possibility of greater opportunities for highly educated women in the labor market, and for women who have some technical skills (such as in the microelectronics field). Secondly, there are indications that women's age at marriage is on the rise again: 31 percent of women aged 25–29 remained unmarried in 1985, compared to a figure of 21 percent in 1980 (Japan Institute of Labor 1990). One impetus for women to delay marriage is to

---

[2] A Child Care Leave Law was approved by the Diet in 1991. The law urges companies to institute a policy whereby either parent is permitted to take time off from work until a child is one year old. The law initially applies only to companies with at least 30 employees, but it will later be extended to small firms as well. However, there is no guarantee that employees who take advantage of the leave policy will receive pay. See Japan Economic Institute 1991.

accumulate more work experience and "try out" a career. Within the next several years, it will become clearer whether some women are simply delaying marriage and are subsequently finding husbands who will accommodate some relaxation in traditional roles, or whether the apparent marriage-delay behaviors actually represent the choice of more Japanese women *against* marriage.

Japan's declining birthrate, however, in tandem with life expectancies that now exceed those of any other industrial country, may have an effect on women's work patterns that cuts the other way. More and more married women are being exhorted to care for aging parents. Proportionately speaking, more middle-aged Japanese now than ever before are only children or have only one or two siblings. This means that the chances are high that a woman will be called upon to care for an elderly parent or parent-in-law at home. The Japanese preference in human relations for other-oriented human capital investment thus takes on an added twist: middle-aged married women are responsible not just for emotional and psychological investment in their husbands' and children's human capital but for a kind of return investment in elderly parents (especially mothers and mothers-in-law) who sacrificed for *their* children when they were young. The increased longevity of parents makes this traditional expectation salient for more middle-aged wives than ever before.

The Japanese government has been slow to respond with greater public provision of day centers or full-time nursing homes for the elderly, instead seeing this intergenerational relationship as a continuation of Japanese-style intrafamilial ties. Women bear the brunt of this attitude. Thus, just at the point when legislation propounds equal opportunity for men and women, social conditions are promoting strongly unequal time obligations to the family. Some employers have recently introduced policies that allow employees to leave the firm for a time to take care of an ailing parent. This constitutes some recognition that the problem is affecting an increasing number of Japanese families. But to the extent that it is women, not men, who are the primary caretakers and must take time out from their working lives, the effect will not be to reduce gendered work patterns.

In fact, it is changes in the attitudes of men and women toward their family roles that will probably be the slowest to occur. One natural source of change is the gradual retirement of the generations of men raised in pre–World War II Japan who sacrificed their working years to the reconstruction and takeoff of the postwar Japanese economy. In early 1990, a Japanese widow won a court battle with the firm for whom her husband had worked for many years. Her case? That the firm had in effect "worked her husband to death." To the extent that younger Japanese men are beginning to forgo careers in major Japanese corporations in favor of small firms or foreign-owned firms that offer shorter working hours and that expect or even encourage employees to use their vacation time, women may reap some benefits. Direct benefits will be in the form of husbands who are more available to share domestic responsibilities. Indirect benefits will stem from a gradual loosening of the ideology that a good worker is all-sacrificing for the company, and therefore by definition male (since women must likewise be all-sacrificing for husband and family). Increased mobility of men in the labor market would also redound to the benefit of women, because it would loosen the definition of good workers as necessarily being permanent members of the firm, and as such the only truly worthy recipients of on-the-job training. This definition has worked to the detriment of women; a reshaping of it would mean greater opportunities.

Change in Japanese gender stratification is likely to take place to a much greater extent on a cohort or generational basis than has been true in the United States. It can be argued that middle-aged and older Japanese are somewhat less affected than Americans by changes in society, because of the fact that American social institutions allow more fluidity in the choices people make at different ages. Change in gender stratification patterns in Japan will occur mainly as new cohorts move through a human capital development system that itself is undergoing change. In Norman Ryder's terms: "Each fresh cohort is a possible intermediary in the transformation process, a vehicle for introducing new postures. The new cohorts provide the opportunity for social change to occur. They do not cause change; they permit it" (1965: 844). The young women who are now opting, with the support of their parents, for a four-year university education with plans to enter a career-track job are still relatively few in number. If their numbers grow significantly, they will become an identifiable social group— one that is responding to structural change in the employment system. Their educational choices will spur further change in the educational system. Junior colleges will likely suffer from lowered public demand, hastening the changes that are already underway toward a less segregated curriculum. This will affect the next cohort of students.

Change in Japanese gender stratification will not come about mainly as a result of Japanese women protesting discriminatory labor practices. As one middle-aged woman said frankly: "Every social institution in our society is male-dominated, so what good can it do to take our problems to an institution?" This was reiterated to me nearly verbatim on a separate occasion by another woman: "The problem with going to the *rōdō kumiai* [labor union] or to the courts, and so on, to try to solve problems is that even those institutions are pervaded by male dominance. The attitude is 'What are you doing here? Why don't you deal with this yourself?'"

Change in Japan will mainly be produced by the economic necessity for employers to hire and keep good workers. In the decades ahead, more and more of these workers will be women. Perhaps a different miracle will eventually occur.

Research Design for the Three-City Study

The hypotheses of the theoretical model of gender stratification presented in this book involve the behavior of three sets of actors—the individual, parents, and employers. This means that the requirements for a suitable data set are quite formidable. A mail questionnaire (the "Survey on Work Patterns") was designed and executed in three Japanese cities. The cities were Kodaira, a western suburb of Tokyo; Sapporo, the capital of Japan's northernmost island, Hokkaido; and Toyohashi, a city in the Chūbu region, southwest of Tokyo. These cities were chosen for two reasons.

First, the three represent different types of cities. Kodaira is a largely white-collar bedroom community with a significant proportion of its working population commuting to more central areas of Tokyo. Sapporo is a regional metropolis—the largest city in northern Japan, and a "frontier" city in the sense of being newly developed and peopled by a large number of migrants from other parts of the country. As such, it represents a mixture of local industries and is also the regional center for manufacturing, finance, and service institutions that have their headquarters in Tokyo. Toyohashi, on the other hand, is an older industrial city located close to Toyota, a center of the automobile industry. Although these cities do not necessarily represent urban Japan as a whole, they do represent a varied slice in terms of size, industrial structure, and region of the country.

The second criterion used to select sampling sites was personal contacts, for they were essential in obtaining access to the household records from which sampling was carried out. Taking a random sample of men and women in the three cities entailed going to the *shi* (city) or *ku* (ward) offices in each city and using the *senkyonin meibo* (voter registration list) as a sampling frame. This is a complete listing of adults over age 20 registered as residing in the city or, in the case of larger cities such as Sapporo, in each particular *ku* (ward). Voter registration is not voluntary in Japan as it is in the United States. Because Japan has a system in which one is required to register a change of residence within thirty days of moving, records are continuously updated. Names appear in terms of the household unit, with the household head's name, sex, and birthdate appearing first, followed by the same information for the other adult members of the household. Although the voter registration records are legally in the public domain, having a contact in the area who could provide introductions at the city office and assist in obtaining part-time help in sampling was instrumental in getting the job done. The three cities fulfilled this practical requirement, in that I had personal contacts in each of them.

I drew four independent samples in each city: (1) males aged 25–29, (2) females aged 25–29, (3) males aged 40–44, and (4) females aged 40–44. These groups represented a group of men and women who had recently entered the labor market, and a second group who had potential labor market experience of long duration (20–25 years). This permitted the greatest opportunity to test hypotheses concerning parental socialization of and investment in sons and daughters *prior* to their labor force entry, as well as subsequent investment by employers. The 25–29 age group was chosen over the younger five-year cohort (20–24 years of age) in order to minimize the number of respondents who would still be students and who would therefore have no post-schooling labor force experience. The older cohort was chosen on the following bases: (1) members of this cohort received their education in the postwar period, whereas the educational experiences of any older cohort would span the prewar and postwar periods and the accompanying institutional changes in the educational system; and (2) the choice of the younger, 35–39 year-old cohort would have produced a considerably lower labor force participation rate for women, given the age structure of female labor force participation. The 40–44 year-old cohort thus represented the cohort that met the two requirements of having been educated within the postwar system and having a high female labor force participation rate; the latter makes it possible to have a large enough number of working women to be able to run analyses on the determinants of female employment status. Even so, because the proportion of females aged 40–44 in the urban labor force is only 60 percent, I oversampled this group.

A fourteen-page questionnaire was mailed to males in the sample, and a slightly longer, fifteen-page questionnaire was mailed to females. Prior to mailing of the actual questionnaire, a postcard of the University of Washington campus (my home institution) was sent, with a printed message in Japanese on the back explaining that a questionnaire would arrive a few days later. The postcard stated the purpose of the questionnaire and the Japanese institutional affiliation I held (Keiō University). The questionnaire and a stamped return envelope were then mailed, with a requested return date set at about two weeks later. Respondents who were currently students were asked to indicate this on the questionnaire and return it without filling it in. In the case of the Sapporo mailing, carried out in April 1984, a follow-up postcard was sent a few days after the due date reminding nonrespondents to send in their questionnaires. This was followed by telephone contact by a team of undergraduate female students with as many respondents as could be reached, encouraging them to send in the questionnaires. In the next city surveyed, Kodaira, a follow-up postcard was not used, and initial response rates prior to telephoning were only negligibly different from those for the Sapporo sample. Because the follow-up postcard was not judged to be cost-effective, it was not used in Toyohashi. Telephone contact was made with as many nonrespondents as could be reached in Kodaira and Toyohashi asking them to complete the questionnaire.

Sapporo was surveyed in April 1984. This was followed by Kodaira in May, and by Toyohashi in November. Ideally, of course, the survey would have been carried out simultaneously in the three cities. However, given the limited budget and person power with which the survey was conducted, it was necessary to carry it out sequentially. One advantage to this method was that the experiences gained in Sapporo could be used to streamline procedures for the other two cities. The mailing of all three surveys was timed to avoid the major vacation periods in Japan (such as the first week of May and the month of August), when people were likely to be away.

A small number of questionnaires were returned by students, and this number was subtracted from both numerator and denominator in the calculation of the response rate (because students were not intended to be part of the sampling frame). A few questionnaires were also unusable because they had a very high proportion of missing data or had information that was otherwise highly questionable; this number was subtracted only from the numerator. The final response rate of 50.1 percent for the entire sample therefore represents the rate of usable questionnaires that were returned. This compares favorably with the response rates for other mailed questionnaires in Japan. For example, the Ministry of Education survey on extra-school schooling (discussed in chapter 6) was a mailed questionnaire, and had a response rate of 57.3 percent.

The overall response rates for the three cities in the survey were remarkably similar: 50.0 percent (Sapporo), 47.3 percent (Kodaira), and 50.3 percent (Toyohashi). There are two likely explanations for the fact that Kodaira exhibited the lowest response rate. The Tokyo area has been "oversurveyed" by the Japanese government, private companies such as market research organizations, Japanese academic researchers, and foreign academic researchers, and people may quite simply be tired of answering questions. Secondly, the noticeably lower response rate for men in the older cohort is probably related to the relatively long commuting distances faced by men in a bedroom suburb such as Kodaira, and their correspondingly short hours at home. In an attempt to raise the response rate in Kodaira, a team of university students distributed the questionnaires door-to-door to a random sample of the nonrespondents on successive Sundays, when people were most likely to be at home. This effort was not as successful as expected, and refusals tended to be concentrated in the two categories mentioned above: a feeling of invasion of privacy (and/or an unwillingness to fill out a questionnaire not directly connected with one's own life), and an objection on the part of wives or mothers that their husbands or sons were too busy to fill out the questionnaire.

TABLE A.1

LABOR FORCE STATUS OF RESPONDENTS:
COMPARISON OF WEIGHTED SAMPLE
AND 1980 CENSUS DISTRIBUTIONS

| | 25–29 year cohort | | 40–44 year cohort | |
	Males	Females	Males	Females
% in labor force				
Sample	97	53	99	66
Census	97	48	98	59
% not in labor force				
Sample	3	47	1	34
Census	3	52	2	41
Total no. in sample	177	280	251	377

TABLE A.2

EMPLOYMENT STATUS OF CURRENTLY
EMPLOYED RESPONDENTS:
COMPARISON OF WEIGHTED SAMPLE AND
1980 CENSUS DISTRIBUTIONS

| | 25–29 year cohort | | 40–44 year cohort | |
	Males	Females	Males	Females
% employees and managers				
Sample	88	83	77	67
Census	91	84	80	67
% self-employed[a]				
Sample	6	11	22	20
Census	5	6	19	13
% family workers				
Sample	6	6	1	14
Census	4	10	1	20
Total no. in sample	165	141	241	243

[a]Included in the "self-employed" category are pieceworkers and home handicraft workers (naishoku).

Although the response rate is quite respectable for a mail survey, there nevertheless may exist biases that affect statistical results. A number of checks were performed in order to assess the degree of response bias. First, question-naires were categorized into groups as they came in. Once all responses had been received, the four sequential groups were compared with one another on education and employment variables. No significant differences existed among the groups in terms of either educational distribution, industry, or employment status of respondents.

Second, comparisons of the sample as a whole were made with national census data that summarize the characteristics of all urban areas (*shi*) in Japan. Respondents were on average more highly educated than the urban population of Japan: in particular, the sample shows lower proportions of junior high school graduates and higher proportions of university graduates. This is not surprising, given that the questionnaire was fairly demanding in terms of being self-administered and requiring about thirty minutes to complete. The upward bias in education is more pronounced for the female respondents. This, too, is not unexpected if we assume that the demands placed on highly educated males in terms of working and commuting hours are on average greater than for their female counterparts, an issue discussed in chapter 5. The factor of availability of time probably made it easier for highly educated females than males to answer the survey. It may also be the case that females were more interested than males in the content of the survey.

To compute statistics from the sample, weights were applied in order to render the educational distribution of the sample equivalent to the population. Because we are in effect dealing with twelve independently drawn samples (men and women aged 25–29 and 40–44 in three cities), each sample was adjusted independently and the samples were then merged. Statistics reported here and in chapters 5 and 6 are based on the education-adjusted sample.

In order to assess the representativeness of the total education-adjusted sample, it was compared with the general urban population or, where possible, with the three sampled cities. Employment indicators available in published census materials are labor force status, employment status, and industry. As shown in Tables A.1–3, the distributions on the variables are very similar for the respondents and the population overall. Further, the proportions of men and women in the younger cohort (25–29) who entered large firms after leav-ing school are strikingly similar to labor force data collected by the govern-ment. Government statistics for the 20–24 age cohort in 1975 (the cohort most comparable in terms of historical timing of labor market entrance) show that 33.0 percent of men and 35.2 percent of women were employed in large firms. This compares to rates of 32.0 and 35.0 for men and women respec-tively in the younger cohort in our sample.

Statistics computed from this sample also closely match national surveys on a number of attitudinal variables such as perceptions of sex discrimination in the labor market, educational aspirations for sons and daughters, and expec-tations of living with children in old age. These congruencies are discussed in chapters 5 and 6.

TABLE A.3

INDUSTRY OF CURRENTLY EMPLOYED RESPONDENTS:
COMPARISON OF WEIGHTED SAMPLE AND
1980 CENSUS DISTRIBUTIONS

	25–29 year cohort		40–44 year cohort	
	Males	*Females*	*Males*	*Females*
% in agriculture, forestry, and mining				
Sample	6	3	3	7
Census	2	4	4	8
% in construction				
Sample	16	5	12	6
Census	16	4	16	5
% in manufacturing				
Sample	19	13	20	18
Census	19	13	21	21
% in sales				
Sample	21	19	23	27
Census	25	32	23	32
% in finance and real estate				
Sample	0	11	3	4
Census	5	6	4	3
% in transportation and communication				
Sample	5	1	10	3
Census	7	3	10	2
% in utilities and energy services				
Sample	1	1	2	0
Census	1	0	1	0
% in services				
Sample	18	31	14	30
Census	18	36	16	27
% in government (public service)				
Sample	15	16	13	5
Census	7	3	6	2
Total no. in sample	169	144	240	244

NOTE: 1980 census percentages are summed and weighted across the three sampled cities.

THE CONTENT OF THE QUESTIONNAIRE

The questionnaire included a cover page explaining the purpose of the research: to investigate male and female employment patterns in Japanese cities. The cover page also emphasized the ultimate cross-cultural nature of the project. This point was judged by Japanese informants to have some appeal, and so it was stressed. The name of a researcher serving as a contact person in each city, with university address and phone, was also listed. It was felt that the cooperation of a prominent university in each city would both heighten the prestige and legitimacy of the survey and increase the likelihood that people would inquire if they had questions. I served as the contact person in the Faculty of Commerce at Keiō University in Tokyo, and the other contact people were Professors Yamagishi Toshio in the Faculty of Behavioral Science at Hokkaido University in Sapporo and Hino Yoshio in the Faculty of Letters at Aichi University in Toyohashi.

EMPLOYMENT INFORMATION

The following information was collected for the first job held by respondents after they entered the labor force and for current (or most recent) job: employment status; size of firm; full-time, part-time, or temporary position; industry; wages; content of job; period of employment; assessment of promotional possibilities; assessment of the ratio of females to all employees in that position. In addition, information about promotions, the number of establishments where the respondent had been employed, and other questions dealing with the respondent's overall work history were asked. Information drawn from the individual's work history was critical in the construction of composite variables such as the individual's position in an internal labor market, with its advantages of relatively secure employment and placement on a career ladder.

OTHER INFORMATION

In addition to the work history section of the survey, five other sections covered the following: family background and socialization; educational background and experiences; extent and type of training received within the workplace; marital and birth information; and educational aspirations for children and plans for relying on children in old age.

Three characteristics of the questionnaire merit particular attention. First, while focusing on influences from the supply side on work patterns, the questionnaire also asked a number of questions dealing with the demand side (in other words, treatment of the worker by the employer), including, for example, information about on-the-job training and rotation. On these points, the questionnaire sought more detailed information than the large-scale social stratification questionnaires that have been used by Japanese and American researchers to ask questions about social mobility.

A second noteworthy feature of the questionnaire is that it inquired about supply-side variables—family background, socialization, and educational background—in considerable detail. Questions asked about the types of extra-school schooling the respondent had received, and the class ranking of the respondent in high school. The names of schools attended by the respondent since junior high school and their characteristics (regional location, public/private, coeducational/single-sex, regular/evening school) were also asked for in the questionnaire. This facilitated an assessment of the level and quality of education received. This type of detailed information on the socialization influences received by the respondent distinguishes the data set from the government surveys generally used by Japanese labor economists in studying the determinants of labor force participation patterns. Such surveys typically focus more narrowly on demographic variables.

The third significant feature of the questionnaire is that it asked about respondents' educational aspirations for their sons and daughters, and their plans for relying on their children for various needs during old age. This section provides data with which to test a range of theoretical assumptions regarding how parental expectations of reliance on children affect the educational aspirations parents hold for those children.

Supplementary Tables

TABLE B.1

RESPONDENTS' PERCEPTIONS OF SEX
DISCRIMINATION IN THE LABOR MARKET

	In recruitment and hiring	In placement and promotion	In training	In layoff and retirement policies
Percentage whose response is:				
"Considerable"				
%	45.1	60.4	30.7	44.2
N	(152)	(201)	(102)	(146)
"Some"				
%	45.1	32.4	47.0	39.9
N	(152)	(108)	(156)	(132)
"Almost none"				
%	6.6	5.4	20.3	11.9
N	(22)	(18)	(67)	(39)
"None"				
%	3.2	1.9	2.0	3.9
N	(11)	(6)	(7)	(13)
Total				
%	100.0	100.0	100.0	100.0
N	(336)	(333)	(332)	(331)

TABLE B.2

VARIABLES USED IN ANALYSES OF FIRST JOB,
JOB ROTATION, AND EMPLOYER CHANGES

Cohort	Dummy variable (representing historical timing of respondent's entry into the labor market): 0 = respondent 25–29 years of age, 1 = respondent 40–44 years of age.
Father's employment	Series of dummy variables for father's employment status when respondent was 15 years of age: unemployed or absent, self-employed or farm (omitted category), blue-collar, white-collar.
Mother's employment	Dummy variable for mother's employment status outside home when respondent was 15 years of age: 0 = mother was full-time housewife, family enterprise worker, or worked in a home handicraft job; 1 = mother was employed part-time or full-time outside the home.
Ability	Respondent's class rank in senior year of high school, by quintile, scored 1–5. (If respondent did not attend high school, class rank in final year of junior high school is substituted.)
Education	Series of dummy variables for respondent's educational level and, for university, educational quality: junior high school (omitted category), high school, junior college / vocational school, low-ranking university, medium- / high-ranking university.[a]
Work plans	Dummy variable representing women's reported plans in adolescence to work continuously across the life cycle.[b]
Large firm placement	Dummy variable representing initial job placement in the government sector or in a firm employing 1,000 + employees.
Internal labor market placement	Dummy variable representing initial job placement in an internal labor market (see text for details on measurement).
Size of firm (logged)	Natural logarithm of the size of firm in which the respondent began his or her work life. Respondents placed themselves in one of six categories, and the category midpoints were used for the variable construction. Employees in large firms (1,000 or more employees) and government are considered together.

continued on next page

Table B.2 *(continued)*

Industrial sector	Core vs. periphery sector.[c]
White-collar job	White- vs. blue-collar, respondent's first job.
Femaleness of job	Percentage female in the respondent's first job (estimated by respondent). Respondents were asked to indicate this by decile—less than 10 percent, 10–20 percent, etc. A scale was constructed using the midpoints of these categories.
Full-time employee	Dummy variable representing whether the respondent entered the labor force as a full-time employee or not.
Starting wages (logged)	Monthly wages (logged) of starting job. Wages were standardized by the consumer price index.
Finance and insurance, utilities, and wholesale and retail sales industries	Dummy variables representing the industry that the respondent entered in his or her first job.
Job rotation in first workplace	Dummy variable representing whether the respondent had job rotation experience within his or her first workplace.
Employer changes	Dummy variable representing whether the respondent has ever changed employers or not.
Years of labor force experience	Total number of years spent in the labor force.
Ever left the labor force	Dummy variable measuring whether the respondent has ever left the labor force for six months or more.

[a]The scale of university quality was constructed with the cooperation of Professor Nakayama Keiko. Universities were ranked into three groups: the seven former imperial universities, Tokyo Institute of Technology, and Hitotsubashi University (Group 1); a larger group of public and private universities (Group 2); and lower-ranked private universities (Group 3).
[b]The survey question was phrased in the following way: "When you were about 18 years old, what combination of work and family life did you most hope to have in the future?" The proportion of women reporting the expectation of working continuously throughout the life cycle was only 15.9 percent; this category was combined with the category of women who expected that they would quit work temporarily with childbirth and later reenter the work force. The combined category represents 39.6 percent of women.
[c]As explained in the text, industries were scored as being in the core (or monopoly) sector or in the periphery sector according to the classification used by Kawashima and Tachibanaki (1986). Core industries are manufacturing, finance / insurance / real estate, transportation and communication, utilities, and the civil service. Industries in the periphery are agriculture, construction, wholesale and retail sales, and services.

TABLE B.3

MEANS AND STANDARD DEVIATIONS
OF VARIABLES USED IN ANALYSES
OF LARGE FIRM ENTRANCE AND
INTERNAL LABOR MARKET ENTRANCE

	Males (N = 424)		Females (N = 651)	
	Mean	S.D.	Mean	S.D.
Cohort	.587	.493	.570	.495
Father's employment				
Unemployed or absent	.083	.276	.077	.266
Self-employed	.425	.495	.421	.494
Blue-collar	.252	.435	.258	.438
White-collar	.241	.428	.244	.430
Mother's employment outside home	.217	.408	.241	.421
Ability	3.234	1.018	3.315	.899
Education				
Junior high	.160	.367	.137	.344
High school	.373	.484	.471	.500
Junior college / vocational school	.090	.286	.252	.434
Low-ranking university	.226	.419	.094	.292
Medium- / high-ranking university	.151	.358	.046	.210
Work plans (in adolescence)	—	—	.396	.490
Large firm placement	.307	.462	.300	.458
Internal labor market placement	.219	.414	.069	.254

TABLE B.4

LOGIT COEFFICIENTS DESCRIBING THE
EFFECTS OF INDIVIDUAL CHARACTERISTICS
ON ENTRANCE INTO A LARGE FIRM
AFTER LEAVING SCHOOL

	Males	Females	
	Model 1	Model 1	Model 2
Constant	−5.406**	−2.866**	−2.856**
	(.846)	(.517)	(.521)
Cohort	.074	−.234	−.236
	(.254)	(.202)	(.203)
Father's employment			
Unemployed or absent	−.077	.436	.437
	(.488)	(.346)	(.346)
Self-employed	—	—	—
Blue-collar	.281	.058	.059
	(.316)	(.244)	(.244)
White-collar	.497	.309	.310
	(.317)	(.229)	(.229)
Mother's employment outside home	−.268	−.047	−.045
	(.299)	(.232)	(.232)
Ability	.596**	.269*	.269**
	(.130)	(.103)	(.104)
Education			
Junior high	—	—	—
High school	2.525**	1.088**	1.085**
	(.744)	(.380)	(.380)
Junior college / vocational school	2.138**	1.192**	1.190**
	(.838)	(.407)	(.408)
Low-ranking university	2.429**	1.560**	1.604**
	(.765)	(.468)	(.469)
Medium- / high-ranking university	3.283**	2.135**	2.140**
	(.787)	(.539)	(.540)
Work plans in adolescence	—	—	−.032
			(.186)
Maximum likelihood X^2	432.64	754.20	754.16
df	413	640	639

NOTE: All significance tests are one-tailed; *$p < .05$, **$p < .01$. Standard errors are in parentheses.

TABLE B.5

LOGIT COEFFICIENTS DESCRIBING THE
EFFECTS OF INDIVIDUAL CHARACTERISTICS
ON ENTRANCE INTO AN INTERNAL LABOR
MARKET AFTER LEAVING SCHOOL

	Males	Females	
	Model 1	Model 1	Model 2
Constant	−3.414**	−5.991**	−6.310**
	(.523)	(.870)	(.897)
Cohort	−.005	.656*	.738*
	(.274)	(.390)	(.393)
Father's employment			
Unemployed or absent	.332	.215	.153
	(.495)	(.688)	(.694)
Self-employed	—	—	—
Blue-collar	.367	1.022**	.954*
	(.344)	(.439)	(.441)
White-collar	.644*	1.015**	1.013**
	(.338)	(.410)	(.412)
Mother's employment outside home	−.080	−1.283*	−1.325*
	(.315)	(.591)	(.595)
Ability	.453**	.725**	.713**
	(.133)	(.192)	(.194)
Education			
Junior high / high school	—	—	—
Junior college / vocational school	.134	−.325	−.338
	(.500)	(.443)	(.444)
Low-ranking university	.353	.209	.088
	(.327)	(.577)	(.580)
Medium- / high-ranking university	1.176**	.556	.384
	(.354)	(.555)	(.562)
Work plans in adolescence	—	—	.758*
			(.333)
Maximum likelihood X^2	399.62	289.56	284.32
df	414	641	640

NOTE: All significance tests are one-tailed; *$p < .05$, **$p < .01$. Standard errors are in parentheses.

TABLE B.6

MEANS AND STANDARD
DEVIATIONS OF VARIABLES USED IN
ANALYSES OF STARTING WAGES

	Males (N = 142)		Females (N = 208)	
	Mean	S.D.	Mean	S.D.
Education				
Junior high	.020	.142	.050	.218
High school	.347	.478	.404	.492
Junior college / vocational school	.143	.351	.342	.475
Low-ranking university	.286	.453	.158	.366
Medium- / high-ranking university	.204	.404	.046	.210
Ability	3.150	.982	3.283	.948
Size of firm (logged)	5.195	1.849	5.408	1.708
Industrial sector	.224	.419	.292	.455
White-collar job	.422	.496	.796	.404
Femaleness of job	.154	.208	.528	.349
Internal labor market placement	.272	.447	.054	.227
Logged starting wages	11.659	.314	11.473	.449

TABLE B.7

DETERMINANTS OF STARTING WAGES:
JAPANESE FEMALE FULL-TIME EMPLOYEES

	(1)	(2)	(3)
Constant	11.231**	11.115**	11.121**
	(.199)	(.227)	(.238)
Education			
Junior high	—	—	—
High school	−.242	−.262	−.260
	(.187)	(.197)	(.197)
Junior college / vocational school	−.247	−.260	−.258
	(.187)	(.200)	(.201)
Low-ranking university	−.257	−.292	−.290
	(.200)	(.209)	(.210)
Medium- / high-ranking university	−.119	−.124	−.112
	(.235)	(.244)	(.247)
Ability	.141**	.139**	.145**
	(.035)	(.036)	(.037)
Adjusted R^2	.073		
df	202		
Size of firm (logged)		.021	.024
		(.019)	(.020)
Industrial sector		−.112	−.111
		(.073)	(.073)
White-collar job		.076	.964
		(.087)	(.088)
Adjusted R^2		.073	
df		199	
Femaleness of job			−.055
			(.088)
Internal labor market placement			−.092
			(.135)
Adjusted R^2			.068
df			197

NOTE: All significance tests are one-tailed; $^*p < .05$, $^{**}p < .01$. Standard errors are in parentheses.

TABLE B.8
DETERMINANTS OF STARTING WAGES:
JAPANESE MALE FULL-TIME EMPLOYEES

	(1)	(2)	(3)
Constant	10.998**	11.018**	11.004**
	(.189)	(.203)	(.211)
Education			
Junior high	—	—	—
High school	.516**	.525**	.528**
	(.189)	(.171)	(.173)
Junior college / vocational school	.501**	.512**	.517**
	(.177)	(.181)	(.185)
Low-ranking university	.748**	.783**	.782**
	(.170)	(.174)	(.177)
Medium- / high-ranking university	.724**	.769**	.774**
	(.172)	(.177)	(.181)
Ability	.016	.018	.017
	(.026)	(.027)	(.027)
Adjusted R^2	.190		
df	136		
Size of firm (logged)		−.005	−.003
		(.015)	(.018)
Industrial sector		.028	.027
		(.060)	(.061)
White-collar job		−.074	−.073
		(.054)	(.055)
Adjusted R^2		.185	
df		133	
Femaleness of job			.056
			(.123)
Internal labor market placement			−.016
			(.069)
Adjusted R^2			.174
df			131

NOTE: All significance tests are one-tailed; $*p < .05$, $**p < .01$. Standard errors are in parentheses.

TABLE B.9

MEANS AND STANDARD DEVIATIONS
OF VARIABLES USED IN ANALYSES OF JOB
ROTATION AND EMPLOYER CHANGES

	Full sample (N = 749)		Males (N = 314)		Females (N = 435)	
	Mean	*S.D.*	*Mean*	*S.D.*	*Mean*	*S.D.*
Individual characteristics						
Ability	3.284	.931	3.260	.991	3.302	.888
Cohort	.570	.495	.615	.487	.538	.499
Education						
Junior high	.135	.342	.156	.363	.120	.325
High school	.474	.500	.382	.487	.540	.499
Junior college / vocational school	.163	.370	.070	.256	.421	.230
Low-ranking university	.163	.370	.255	.436	.097	.296
Medium- / high-ranking university	.065	.247	.137	.344	.014	.117
Job and workplace characteristics						
Full-time employee	.921	.270	.943	.233	.906	.293
Starting wages (logged)	11.025	.707	10.991	.820	11.050	.611
Size of firm (logged)	5.267	2.006	5.094	2.102	5.392	1.927
Internal labor market placement	.155	.362	.255	.436	.083	.276
Finance and insurance industry	.104	.306	.048	.214	.145	.352
Utilities industry	.025	.157	.029	.167	.023	.150
Wholesale and retail sales industry	.247	.432	.261	.440	.237	.426
Other industries	.624	.484	.662	.474	.595	.491
Work experience variables						
Number of years in labor force	12.401	8.272	16.698	8.657	9.300	6.394
Employer changes	.605	.489	.538	.499	.653	.477
Job rotation in first workplace	.216	.412	.319	.467	.143	.350

TABLE B.10

LOGIT COEFFICIENTS DESCRIBING
THE DETERMINANTS OF JOB ROTATION
IN THE FIRST WORKPLACE

	(1)	(2)
Constant	−4.499**	−6.857**
	(.636)	(2.607)
Individual characteristics		
Sex	.992**	1.078**
	(.207)	(.244)
Cohort	−.043	−.078
	(.200)	(.269)
Ability	.253**	.053
	(.104)	(.114)
Education		
Junior high	—	—
High school	2.025**	1.158*
	(.533)	(.556)
Junior college / vocational school	1.865**	1.306*
	(.584)	(.604)
Low-ranking university	1.868**	1.029*
	(.564)	(.603)
Medium- / high-ranking university	2.986**	1.877**
	(.601)	(.659)
Job and workplace characteristics		
Full-time employee	—	1.093*
		(.628)
Starting wages (logged)	—	.023
		(.219)
Size of firm (logged)	—	.376**
		(.068)
Internal labor market placement	—	.444*
		(.232)
Finance and insurance industry	—	.728**
		(.302)
Utilities industry	—	1.179*
		(.592)
Wholesale and retail sales industry	—	−.029
		(.258)
Other industry	—	—

continued on next page

Table B.10 *(continued)*

	(1)	(2)
Maximum likelihood X^2	696.88	631.56
df	741	734
X^2 change		65.33
df change		7
		$(p < .001)$

NOTE: All significance tests are one-tailed; *$p < .05$, **$p < .01$. Standard errors are in parentheses.

TABLE B.11

LOGIT COEFFICIENTS DESCRIBING THE
DETERMINANTS OF EMPLOYER CHANGES

	(1)	(2)
Constant	1.358	.706**
	(2.013)	(2.060)
Individual characteristics		
Sex	−.811**	−.792**
	(.271)	(.282)
Cohort	−.289	−.400
	(.281)	(.291)
Ability	−.228*	−.208*
	(.104)	(.107)
Education		
Junior high	—	—
High school	−.418	−.246
	(.346)	(.353)
Junior college / vocational school	−.210	.033
	(.397)	(.406)
Low-ranking university	−.258	−.085
	(.410)	(.419)
Medium- / high-ranking university	−.260	.224
	(.499)	(.518)
Years in the labor force	.081**	.100**
	(.019)	(.020)
Job and workplace characteristics		
Full-time employee	.152	.276
	(.362)	(.366)
Starting wages (logged)	−.077	−.075
	(.173)	(.177)
Size of firm (logged)	−.056	.006
	(.050)	(.052)
Internal labor market placement	.099	.249
	(.229)	(.239)
Finance and insurance industry	−.182	−.006
	(.312)	(.325)
Utilities industry	.970*	1.298*
	(.577)	(.598)
Wholesale and retail sales industry	.661**	.691**
	(.226)	(.233)
Job rotation in first workplace	—	−1.387**
		(.253)

continued on next page

Table B.11 *(continued)*

	(1)	(2)
Maximum likelihood X^2	697.76	664.76
df	535	534
X^2 change		33.00
df change		1
		$(p < .001)$

NOTE: All significance tests are one-tailed; $*p < .05$, $**p < .01$. Standard errors are in parentheses.

TABLE B.12
VARIABLES USED IN ANALYSIS
OF WOMEN'S LABOR FORCE BEHAVIOR
AT TIME OF MARRIAGE

Ability	Measured as explained in Table B.2.
Education	Series of dummy variables for respondent's educational level: junior high school (omitted category), high school, junior college / vocational school, university.
Entered the labor force as an employee	Dummy variable representing whether the respondent originally entered the labor force as an employee (as opposed to a self-employed or family enterprise worker).
Size of firm, initial employment	Series of dummy variables representing the size of firm the respondent initially entered: small firm of 1–99 employees, medium-sized firm of 100–999 employees, large firm of 1,000 or more employees, or government service.
Age at marriage	Age at first marriage.
Husband's university education	Dummy variable representing whether husband is university-educated or not.

TABLE B.13

MEANS AND STANDARD DEVIATIONS OF
VARIABLES USED IN ANALYSIS OF WOMEN'S
LABOR FORCE BEHAVIOR AT TIME OF MARRIAGE
($N = 300$)

	Mean	S.D.
Ability	3.360	.872
Education		
Junior high	.190	.393
High school	.543	.499
Junior college / vocational school	.173	.379
University	.093	.291
Entered the labor force as an employee	.793	.406
Size of firm, initial employment		
Small firm	.500	.501
Medium-sized firm	.197	.398
Large firm	.170	.376
Government service	.133	.341
Age at marriage	24.273	2.891
Husband's university education	.307	.462
Left the labor force within one year of marriage	.480	.500

TABLE B.14

LOGIT COEFFICIENTS DESCRIBING THE
DETERMINANTS OF WOMEN'S LABOR FORCE
BEHAVIOR AT TIME OF MARRIAGE

Constant	$-2.872**$
	(1.182)
Ability	$-.046$
	(.148)
Education	
Junior high	—
High school	.601*
	(.332)
Junior college / vocational school	.456
	(.448)
University	.690
	(.585)
Entered the labor force as an employee	.616*
	(.311)
Size of firm, initial employment	
Small firm	—
Medium-sized firm	$-.061$
	(.327)
Large firm	.172
	(.350)
Government service	$-.899*$
	(.406)
Age at marriage	.073*
	(.043)
Husband's university education	$-.007$
	(.315)
Maximum likelihood X^2	398.28
df	289

NOTE: All significance tests are one-tailed; $*p < .05$, $**p < .01$.
Standard errors are in parentheses.

TABLE B.15

VARIABLES USED IN ANALYSES
OF EMPLOYMENT STATUS

Ability; education; internal labor market placement	Measured as explained in Table B.2.
Father's self-employment	Dummy variable representing whether the respondent's father is a nonagricultural self-employed worker or not.
Years of labor force experience	Measured as explained in Table B.2.
Husband's university education	Measured as explained in Table B.12
Husband's employment status	Dummy variable representing whether husband is self-employed or not.
Age of youngest child 12 or under	Dummy variable representing whether youngest child is age 12 or under.
Type of household	Dummy variable representing the respondent's household structure: 0 = nuclear in structure (parents and children), 1 = extended (parents, other adult relatives, and children).
Entered the labor force as an employee[a]	Dummy variable representing whether the respondent entered the labor force as an employee or not.
Started as self-employed	Dummy variable representing whether respondent entered the labor force as a self-employed worker or not.
Size of firm, initial employment	Measured as explained in Table B.12.
Self-employment	For men, dummy variable representing whether respondent is currently self-employed or not.
Employment status	For women, variable representing whether respondent is a full-time housewife (0), self-employed worker (1), part-time employee (2), or full-time employee (3).

[a]"Employee" is used here as the reference category by which to describe women's initial employment experience, whereas "self-employment" is used to describe men's experience. The reason for this is that self-employment for women is more heterogeneous than it is for men. Moreover, some women are family enterprise workers. Therefore, it is "cleaner" to make a dummy variable out of the flip side of the employment status concept—"employee" status—and make the residual category self-employed, piecework, and family enterprise workers.

TABLE B.16

MEANS AND STANDARD
DEVIATIONS OF VARIABLES USED
IN ANALYSES OF EMPLOYMENT STATUS

	Males (N = 226)		Females (N = 260)	
	Mean	S.D.	Mean	S.D.
Father's self-employment	.274	.447	—	—
Ability	3.358	1.041	3.339	.827
Education				
Junior high	.239	.427	.182	.386
High school	.358	.481	.551	.498
Junior college / vocational school	.053	.225	—	—
Low-ranking university	.217	.413	—	—
Medium- / high-ranking university	.133	.340	—	—
Junior college / vocational school; university	—	—	.267	.443
Internal labor market placement	.230	.422	—	—
Husband's university education	—	—	.360	.481
Husband's employment status	—	—	.165	.372
Type of household	—	—	.309	.463
Age of youngest child 12 or younger	—	—	.492	.501
Started as self-employed	.093	.291	—	—
Entered the labor force as an employee	—	—	.831	.376
Size of firm, initial employment				
Small firm	—	—	.576	.495
Medium-sized firm	—	—	.212	.410
Large firm	—	—	.199	.400
Government service	—	—	.127	.334
Self-employment	.217	.413	—	—
Employment status	—	—	1.381	1.155

NOTE: As explained in the text, different variables are used in the analysis of men's and women's employment status. Thus, the means and standard deviations of only those variables relevant for each analysis are shown here.

TABLE B.17

LOGIT COEFFICIENTS DESCRIBING
THE DETERMINANTS OF OLDER
MEN'S SELF-EMPLOYMENT

Constant	$-.700$
	$(.639)$
Father's self-employment	$.519$
	$(.376)$
Ability	$-.351^*$
	$(.188)$
Education	
Junior high	—
High school	$.548$
	$(.466)$
Junior college / vocational school	$.286$
	$(.889)$
Low-ranking university	$.655$
	$(.533)$
Medium- / high-ranking university	$-.333$
	$(.858)$
Started in internal labor market	-1.288^*
	$(.647)$
Started as self-employed	1.818^{**}
	$(.531)$
Maximum likelihood X^2	202.24
df	217

NOTE: All significance tests are one-tailed; $^*p < .05$, $^{**}p < .01$. Standard errors are in parentheses.

TABLE B.18

LOGIT COEFFICIENTS DESCRIBING
THE DETERMINANTS OF OLDER
WOMEN'S EMPLOYMENT STATUS

	Housewives vs. self-employed or family workers	Housewives vs. part-time employees	Housewives vs. full-time employees
Constant	−.114 (1.224)	.758 (.966)	−1.625 (1.197)
Ability	.075 (.293)	−.020 (.237)	.315 (.252)
Education			
Junior high	—	—	—
High school	−.152 (.681)	−.669 (.528)	−.782 (.568)
Junior college / vocational school; university	.517 (.867)	−.869 (.680)	−.030 (.697)
Husband's university education	−1.031 (.629)	−.980* (.462)	−1.459** (.520)
Husband's employment status	2.401** (.584)	−1.285* (.741)	−.931 (.700)
Type of household	1.780** (.530)	.718* (.423)	.785* (.444)
Age of youngest child 12 or under	−.983* (.509)	−.429 (.378)	−.827* (.402)
Entered the labor force as an employee	−1.481** (.581)	.017 (.532)	1.387* (.828)
Size of firm, initial employment			
Small firm	—	—	—
Medium-sized firm	.207 (.671)	.812 (.506)	.476 (.569)
Large firm	−.730 (.730)	.062 (.478)	−.179 (.526)
Government service	−.967 (.962)	−.018 (.657)	.528 (.587)
Maximum likelihood X^2	524.29		
df	248		

NOTE: All significance tests are one-tailed; $*p < .05$, $**p < .01$. Standard errors are in parentheses. The analysis is restricted to currently married women with children.

TABLE B.19

VARIABLES USED IN ANALYSIS
OF OLDER MEN'S CURRENT WAGES

Ability; education	Measured as explained in Table B.2.
Internal labor market placement	Measured as explained in Table B.2.
Years of labor force experience (logged)	Natural logarithm of total number of years spent in the labor force.
Proportion of work years spent as full-time employee	Proportion of years in the labor force spent as full-time employee.
Size of firm where currently employed (logged)	Natural logarithm of the size of firm where the respondent works. Respondents placed themselves in one of six categories, and the category midpoints were used for the variable construction. Employees in large firms (1,000 or more employees) and government are considered together.
Current yearly wages (logged)	Natural logarithm of current before-tax yearly wages, including bonuses.

TABLE B.20

MEANS AND STANDARD DEVIATIONS
OF VARIABLES USED IN ANALYSIS
OF OLDER MEN'S CURRENT WAGES
($N = 171$)

	Mean	S.D.
Current yearly wages (logged)	15.372	.375
Ability	3.474	1.008
Education		
Junior high	—	—
High school	.339	.475
Junior college / vocational school	.058	.235
Low-ranking university	.216	.413
Medium- / high-ranking university	.164	.371
Internal labor market placement	.287	1.001
Years of labor force experience (logged)	3.082	.283
Proportion of work years spent as full-time employee	.852	.275
Size of firm where currently employed (logged)	5.634	1.840

TABLE B.21

DETERMINANTS OF OLDER
MEN'S CURRENT WAGES

	(1)	(2)	(3)	(4)
Constant	15.099**	15.129**	14.201**	14.088**
	(.099)	(.096)	(.366)	(.354)
Ability	.018	.008	.001	.003
	(.029)	(.028)	(.028)	(.027)
Education				
Junior high	—	—	—	—
High school	.206**	.149*	.176**	.153*
	(.075)	(.075)	(.075)	(.072)
Junior college / vocational school	.147	.094	.149	.146
	(.125)	(.123)	(.122)	(.117)
Low-ranking university	.257**	.194*	.303**	.273**
	(.083)	(.083)	(.092)	(.089)
Medium- / high-ranking university	.466**	.369**	.446**	.417**
	(.093)	(.095)	(.102)	(.098)
Internal labor market placement		.205**	.186**	.114*
		(.062)	(.061)	(.062)
Years of labor force experience (logged)			.245*	.210*
			(.105)	(.102)
Proportion of work years spent as full-time employee			.178*	.116
			(.096)	(.094)
Size of firm where currently employed (logged)				.054**
				(.015)
Adjusted R^2	.143	.192	.223	.279

NOTE: All significance tests are one-tailed; $*p < .05$, $**p < .01$. Standard errors are in parentheses.

TABLE B.22

MEANS AND STANDARD DEVIATIONS
OF VARIABLES USED IN ANALYSIS
OF UNIVERSITY ASPIRATIONS

	Families with sons (N = 501)		Families with daughters (N = 491)	
	Mean	*S.D.*	*Mean*	*S.D.*
Sex of respondent	.353	.478	.338	.474
Household characteristics				
Wife's education				
Junior high	.210	.468	.198	.399
High school	.522	.500	.532	.500
Junior college / vocational school	.169	.374	.163	.370
University	.077	.267	.081	.274
Husband's education				
Junior high	.220	.414	.216	.412
High school	.389	.488	.399	.490
Junior college / vocational school	.046	.209	.041	.198
University	.325	.469	.322	.468
Household income (logged)	15.645	.525	15.569	.517
Region				
Toyohashi	.373	.484	.370	.483
Sapporo	.294	.456	.298	.458
Kodaira	.333	.472	.332	.471
Expectations for old-age assistance				
Expect financial help from a son [daughter]	.657	.475	.191	.394
Expect emotional help from a son [daughter]	.417	.494	.436	.496
Expect to live with a son [daughter]	.325	.469	.134	.341
Family composition				
Only child—son [daughter]	.103	.304	.079	.271
More than one child—all sons [daughters]	.198	.399	.147	.354

continued on next page

Table B.22 *(continued)*

	Families with sons (N = 501)		Families with daughters (N = 491)	
	Mean	*S.D.*	*Mean*	*S.D.*
More than one child—son [daughter] is youngest or middle in a mixed-sex set	.416	.493	.495	.500
More than one child—son [daughter] is oldest in a mixed-sex set	.282	.451	.277	.448
Perception of sex-egalitarianism in the labor market	—	—	1.542	.648
University aspirations for son [daughter]	.731	.444	.276	.447

NOTES: All independent variables in the model are dummy variables scored as "0" or "1" with the exception of two variables: the logged income variable and the perception of sex discrimination in the labor market. Logged income is the natural logarithm of current yearly before-tax income, including bonuses. Perceptions of sex discrimination were originally measured on a four-point scale, with a score of "1" representing perception of considerable sex discrimination and a score of "4" representing perception of no sex discrimination. Scores of "3" and "4" were so infrequent that the two were combined, so that the three categories are: (1) perception of considerable sex discrimination, (2) perception of some sex discrimination, and (3) perception of almost none or no sex discrimination.

The dependent variable in the model is a dummy variable scored as "1" or "0" according to whether the respondent had university aspirations for a son (daughter) or not.

TABLE B.23

DETERMINANTS OF PARENTS'
UNIVERSITY ASPIRATIONS FOR A SON

Constant	−8.100**
	(3.542)
Sex of respondent	−.531*
	(.242)
Household characteristics	
Wife's education	
Junior high	—
High school	.681**
	(.304)
Junior college / vocational school	.600
	(.405)
University	.105
	(.532)
Husband's education	
Junior high	—
High school	.389
	(.316)
Junior college / vocational school	.807
	(.588)
University	1.147**
	(.385)
Household income	.465*
	(.230)
Region	
Toyohashi	—
Sapporo	.703**
	(.292)
Kodaira	.473*
	(.279)
Expectations for old-age assistance	
Expect financial help from a son	.550*
	(.297)
Expect emotional help from a son	.248
	(.762)
Expect to live with a son	.155
	(.274)

continued on next page

Table B.23 *(continued)*

Family composition	
Only child—son	1.141**
	(.485)
More than one child—all sons	.067
	(.362)
More than one child—son is youngest or middle in a mixed-sex set	—
More than one child—son is oldest in a mixed-sex set	.528*
	(.284)
Maximum likelihood X^2	510.30
df	487

NOTE: All significance tests are one-tailed; *$p < .05$, **$p < .01$. The analysis was restricted to households with at least one son. Standard errors are in parentheses.

TABLE B.24

DETERMINANTS OF PARENTS' UNIVERSITY
ASPIRATIONS FOR A DAUGHTER

Constant	−9.548**
	(4.081)
Sex of respondent	.121
	(.264)
Household characteristics	
Wife's education	
Junior high	—
High school	1.028**
	(.461)
Junior college / vocational school	1.582**
	(.506)
University	2.436**
	(.603)
Husband's education	
Junior high	—
High school	.423
	(.455)
Junior college / vocational school	1.578**
	(.658)
University	1.315**
	(.462)
Household income	.381
	(.263)
Region	
Toyohashi	—
Sapporo	.067
	(.315)
Kodaira	.763**
	(.291)
Expectations for old-age assistance	
Expect financial help from a daughter	.149
	(.431)
Expect emotional help from a daughter	−.159
	(.298)
Expect to live with a daughter	−.354
	(.399)

continued on next page

Table B.24 *(continued)*

Family composition	
Only child—daughter	1.241**
	(.505)
More than one child—all daughters	1.524**
	(.440)
More than one child—daughter is youngest or middle in a mixed-sex set	—
More than one child—daughter is oldest in a mixed-sex set	.385
	(.308)
Maximum likelihood X^2	446.25
df	474

NOTE: All significance tests are one-tailed; $*p < .05$, $**p < .01$. The analysis was restricted to households with at least one daughter. Standard errors are in parentheses.

TABLE B.25

DETERMINANTS OF PARENTS'
UNIVERSITY ASPIRATIONS FOR A DAUGHTER,
TOYOHASHI SAMPLE

	(1)	(2)
Constant	3.672	.234
	(8.097)	(8.686)
Sex of respondent	.297	.198
	(.557)	(.576)
Household characteristics		
Wife's education		
Junior high	—	—
High school	2.128**	2.291*
	(1.174)	(1.189)
Junior college / vocational school	3.246**	3.530**
	(1.236)	(1.270)
University	3.136**	3.328**
	(1.396)	(1.432)
Husband's education		
Junior high	—	—
High school	.550	.287
	(.845)	(.862)
Junior college / vocational school	1.759	1.750
	(1.297)	(1.306)
University	1.617*	1.592*
	(.879)	(.894)
Household income	−.541	−.395
	(.532)	(.558)
Expectations for old-age assistance		
Expect financial help from a daughter	1.612	1.623
	(1.355)	(1.362)
Expect emotional help from a daughter	−1.101	−1.074
	(.744)	(.745)
Expect to live with a daughter	.609	.633
	(1.246)	(1.263)
Family composition		
Only child—daughter	−.137	−.008
	(1.519)	(1.512)
More than one child—all daughters	.799	.869
	(1.249)	(1.224)
More than one child—daughter is youngest or middle in a mixed-sex set	—	—

continued on next page

Table B.25 *(continued)*

	(1)	(2)
More than one child—daughter is oldest in a mixed-sex set	.399 (.599)	.369 (.614)
Perception of sex-egalitarianism in the labor market	—	.717* (.387)
Maximum likelihood X^2	115.38	111.94
df	150	149

NOTE: All significance tests are one-tailed; $*p < .05$, $**p < .01$. Standard errors are in parentheses. The analysis was restricted to households with at least one daughter. Because the question on perceptions of sex discrimination was asked of Toyohashi respondents only, this analysis is limited to them.

References

Abegglen, James C. 1958. *The Japanese Factory: Aspects of Its Social Organization.* Glencoe, Ill.: Free Press.

Abegglen, James C., and George Stalk, Jr. 1985. *Kaisha: The Japanese Corporation.* New York: Basic Books.

Arrow, Kenneth. 1973. "The Theory of Discrimination." In *Discrimination in Labor Markets*, edited by Orley Ashenfelter and Albert Rees, 3–33. Princeton, N.J.: Princeton University Press.

———. 1976. "Economic Dimensions of Occupational Segregation: Comment I." *Signs* 1, 3 (pt. 2): 233–37.

Atsumi, Reiko. 1979. "*Tsukiai*—Obligatory Human Relationships of Japanese White-Collar Employees." *Human Organization* 38, 1: 63–70.

Bae, Kyu Han, and William Form. 1986. "Payment Strategy in South Korea's Advanced Economic Sector." *American Sociological Review* 51, 1: 120–31.

Barnes, William F., and Ethel B. Jones. 1974. "Differences in Male and Female Quitting." *Journal of Human Resources* 9, 4: 439–51.

Becker, Gary. 1964. *Human Capital.* New York: National Bureau of Economic Research.

———. 1985. "Human Capital, Effort, and the Sexual Division of Labor." *Journal of Labor Economics* 3, 1 (pt. 2, supplement): S33–58.

Becker, Gary, and Nigel Tomes. 1976. "Child Endowments and the Quantity and Quality of Children." *Journal of Political Economy* 84, 4 (pt. 2): S143–62.

Beechey, Veronica. 1978. "Women and Production: A Critical Analysis of Some Sociological Theories of Women's Work." In *Feminism and Materialism: Women and Modes of Production*, edited by Annette Kuhn and AnnMarie Wolpe, 155–97. London: Routledge & Kegan Paul.

Ben-Porath, Yoram. 1980. "The F-Connection: Families, Friends, and the Organization of Exchange." *Population and Development Review* 6, 1: 1–30.

Berk, Richard A., and Sarah Fenstermaker Berk. 1979. *Labor and Leisure at Home*. Beverly Hills, Calif.: Sage Publications.

Bernstein, Gail Lee. 1983. *Haruko's World: A Japanese Farm Woman and Her Community*. Stanford: Stanford University Press.

Bielby, Denise D., and William T. Bielby. 1988. "She Works Hard for the Money: Household Responsibilities and the Allocation of Work Effort." *American Journal of Sociology* 93, 5: 1031–59.

Bielby, William, and James Baron. 1984. "A Woman's Place Is with Other Women: Sex Segregation within Organizations." In *Sex Segregation in the Workplace*, edited by Barbara Reskin and Patricia Roos, 27–55. Washington, D.C.: National Academy Press.

Blaug, Mark. 1976. "The Empirical Status of Human Capital Theory: A Slightly Jaundiced Survey." *Journal of Economic Literature* 14, 3: 829–55.

Blood, Robert O. 1967. *Love Match and Arranged Marriage*. New York: Free Press.

Boserup, Ester. 1970. *Woman's Role in Economic Development*. New York: St. Martin's Press.

Bowen, William G., and T. Aldrich Finegan. 1969. *The Economics of Labor Force Participation*. Princeton, N.J.: Princeton University Press.

Brinton, Mary C. 1988. "The Social-Institutional Bases of Gender Stratification: Japan as an Illustrative Case." *American Journal of Sociology* 94, 2: 300–334.

———. 1989. "Gender Stratification in Contemporary Urban Japan." *American Sociological Review* 54, 4: 549–64.

———. 1990. "Intrafamilial Markets for Education: An Empirical Example." In *Social Institutions: Their Emergence, Maintenance, and Effects*, edited by Michael Hechter, Karl-Dieter Opp, and Reinhard Wippler, 307–30. New York: Aldine.

———. 1992. "Christmas Cakes and Wedding Cakes: The Social Organization of Japanese Women's Life Course." In *Japanese Social Organization*, edited by Takie Sugiyama Lebra. Honolulu: University of Hawaii Press.

Brinton, Mary C., and Hang-yue Ngo. 1990. "The Age Structure and Sex Segregation of Occupations." Working paper.

———. 1991. "Occupational Sex Segregation in Comparative Perspective." Working paper.

Brinton, Mary C., and Sunhwa Lee. 1991. "Women's Education and the Labor Market in Japan and South Korea." Working paper.

Broadbridge, Seymour. 1966. *Industrial Dualism in Japan*. Chicago: Aldine.

Burawoy, Michael. 1983. "Factory Regimes under Advanced Capitalism." *American Sociological Review* 48, 5: 587–605.

Caves, Richard E., and Masu Uekusa. 1976. *Industrial Organization in Japan*. Washington, D.C.: Brookings Institution.

Clark, Rodney C. 1979. *The Japanese Company*. New Haven, Conn.: Yale University Press.

Cohn, Samuel. 1985. *The Process of Occupational Sex Typing*. Philadelphia: Temple University Press.

Cole, Robert E. 1971a. *Japanese Blue-Collar*. Berkeley and Los Angeles: University of California Press.

———. 1971b. "The Theory of Institutionalization: Permanent Employment and Tradition in Japan." *Economic Development and Cultural Change* 20, 1: 47–70.

———. 1973. "Functional Alternatives and Economic Development: An Empirical Example of Permanent Employment in Japan." *American Sociological Review* 38, 4: 424–38.

———. 1979. *Work, Mobility, and Participation: A Comparative Study of American and Japanese Industry*. Berkeley and Los Angeles: University of California Press.

Cole, Robert E., and Ken'ichi Tominaga. 1976. "Japan's Changing Occupational Structure and Its Significance." In *Japanese Industrialization and Its Social Consequences*, edited by Hugh Patrick, 53–96. Berkeley and Los Angeles: University of California Press.

Coleman, Samuel. 1983. *Family Planning in Japanese Society*. Princeton, N.J.: Princeton University Press.

Coleman, James. 1988. "Social Capital in the Creation of Human Capital." *American Journal of Sociology* 94 (supplement): S95–120.

Condon, Jane. 1985. *A Half Step Behind: Japanese Women of the '80s*. New York: Dodd, Mead.

Cook, Alice, and Hiroko Hayashi. 1980. *Working Women in Japan: Discrimination, Resistance, and Reform*. Ithaca, N.Y.: New York State School of Industrial and Labor Relations.

Crawcour, Sydney. 1978. "The Japanese Employment System." *Journal of Japanese Studies* 4, 2: 225–45.

Cummings, William K. 1980. *Education and Equality in Japan*. Princeton, N.J.: Princeton University Press.

Dalby, Liza Crihfield. 1983. *Geisha*. New York: Vintage Books.

Davis, Kingsley. 1984. "Wives and Work: The Sex Role Revolution and Its Consequences." *Population and Development Review* 10, 3: 397–417.

Degler, Carl. 1980. *At Odds: Women and the Family in America from the Revolution to the Present*. Oxford: Oxford University Press.

Doeringer, Peter B., and Michael J. Piore. 1971. *Internal Labor Markets and Manpower Analysis*. Lexington, Mass.: D. C. Heath.

Doi, Takeo. 1973. *The Anatomy of Dependence*. Tokyo: Kodansha International.

Dore, Ronald. 1973. *British Factory, Japanese Factory: The Origins of Diversity in Industrial Relations*. Berkeley and Los Angeles: University of California Press.

Edwards, Richard. 1979. *Contested Terrain: The Transformation of the Workplace in the Twentieth Century*. New York: Basic Books.

Engels, Friedrich. 1975. *The Origin of the Family, Private Property, and the State*. 1884. New York: International Publishers.

England, Paula. 1979. "Women and Occupational Prestige: A Case of Vacuous Sex Equality?" *Signs* 5, 2: 252–65.

————. 1982. "The Failure of Human Capital Theory to Explain Occupational Sex Segregation." *Journal of Human Resources* 17, 3: 358–70.

————. 1984. "Wage Appreciation and Depreciation: A Test of Neoclassical Economic Explanations of Occupational Sex Segregation." *Social Forces* 62, 3: 726–49.

England, Paula, George Farkas, Barbara Kilbourne, and Thomas Dou. 1988. "Explaining Occupational Sex Segregation and Wages: Findings from a Model with Fixed Effects." *American Sociological Review* 53, 4: 544–58.

Fruin, W. Mark. 1978. "The Japanese Company Controversy." *Journal of Japanese Studies* 4, 2: 267–300.

Fujimura-Fanselow, Kumiko. 1985. "Women's Participation in Higher Education in Japan." *Comparative Education Review* 29, 4: 471–89.

Garon, Sheldon. 1987. *The State and Labor in Modern Japan.* Berkeley and Los Angeles: University of California Press.

Goldin, Claudia. 1983. "The Changing Economic Role of Women: A Quantitative Approach." *Journal of Interdisciplinary History* 13, 4: 707–33.

Goldscheider, Calvin, and Francis K. Goldscheider. 1987. "Moving Out and Marriage: What Do Young Adults Expect?" *American Sociological Review* 52, 2: 278–85.

Gordon, Andrew. 1985. *The Evolution of Labor Relations in Japan: Heavy Industry, 1853–1955.* Cambridge, Mass.: Council on East Asian Studies, Harvard University.

Granovetter, Mark. 1984. "Small Is Bountiful: Labor Markets and Establishment Size." *American Sociological Review* 49, 3: 323–34.

Greenhalgh, Susan. 1985. "Sexual Stratification: The Other Side of 'Growth with Equity' in East Asia." *Population and Development Review* 11, 2: 265–314.

Gronau, Reuben. 1988. "Sex-related Wage Differentials and Women's Interrupted Labor Careers—the Chicken or the Egg." *Journal of Labor Economics* 6, 3: 277–301.

Grusky, David B., and Robert Hauser. 1984. "Comparative Social Mobility Revisited: Models of Convergence and Divergence in 16 Countries." *American Sociological Review* 49, 1: 19–38.

Halaby, Charles N. 1979. "Sexual Inequality in the Workplace: An Employer-Specific Analysis of Pay Differences." *Social Science Research* 8, 1: 79–104.

Hamilton, Gary G., and Nicole Woolsey Biggart. 1988. "Market, Culture, and Authority: A Comparative Analysis of Management and Organization in the Far East." *American Journal of Sociology* 94 (supplement): S52–94.

Hartmann, Heidi. 1976. "Capitalism, Patriarchy, and Job Segregation by Sex." In *Women and the Workplace: The Implications of Occupational Segregation,* edited by Martha Blaxall and Barbara Reagan, 137–70. Chicago: University of Chicago Press.

Hashimoto, Masanori, and John Raisian. 1985. "Employment Tenure and Earnings Profiles in Japan and the United States." *American Economic Review* 75, 4: 721–35.

Hazama, Hiroshi. 1976. "Historical Change in the Life Style of Industrial Workers." In *Japanese Industrialization and Its Social Consequences,* edited by Hugh Patrick, 21–51. Berkeley and Los Angeles: University of California Press.

Higuchi Yoshio. 1982. "Kikon joshi no rōdō kyōkyū kōdō" (The movement of the labor supply of married women). *Mita Shōgaku Kenkyū* 25, 4: 28–59.

———. 1983. "Joshi rōdōryoku shinshutsu no sekaiteki dōkō to bunseki riron" (The analysis of world trends in female labor). *Nihon Rōdō Kyōkai Zasshi* 25, 11: 27–36.

Higuchi Yoshio and Hitoshi Hayami. 1984. "Joshi rōdō kyōkyū no nichibei hikaku" (A Japan–U.S. comparison of female labor supply). *Mita Shōgaku Kenkyū* 27, 5: 30–50.

Hill, M. Anne. 1983. "Female Labor Force Participation in Developing and Developed Countries—Consideration of the Informal Sector." *Review of Economics and Statistics* 65, 3: 459–68.

———. 1984. "Female Labor Force Participation in Japan: An Aggregate Model." *Journal of Human Resources* 19, 2: 280–87.

Hill, Martha S. 1978. "Self-Imposed Limitations on Work Schedule and Job Location." In *Five Thousand American Families: Patterns of Economic Progress*, vol. 6, edited by Greg Duncan and James Morgan, 151–93. Ann Arbor: University of Michigan, Institute for Social Research.

Hino Municipal Office. 1985. *Hino-shi fujin ni kansuru ishiki chōsa* (Hino city opinion survey concerning women). Hino, Japan: Hino Municipal Office.

Hobsbawm, Eric. 1983. "Introduction: Inventing Traditions." In *The Invention of Tradition*, edited by Eric Hobsbawm and Terence Ranger, 1–14. Cambridge: Cambridge University Press.

Hodge, William, and Naohiro Ogawa. 1986. "Arranged Marriages, Assortative Mating, and Achievement in Japan." Tokyo: Nihon University Population Research Institute, Research Paper Series, no. 27.

Hogan, Dennis P., and Takashi Mochizuki. 1985. "Demographic Transitions and the Life Course: Lessons from Japanese and American Comparisons." Paper presented at the annual meeting of the American Sociological Association, Washington, D.C.

Hosoi Wakizo. 1925. *Jokō aishi* (The sad history of factory girls). Tokyo: Iwanami.

International Labor Organization. Various years. *Yearbook of Labor Statistics*. Geneva: ILO.

Ishihara Osamu. 1914. *Jokō to kekkaku* (Factory girls and tuberculosis). Cited in *Jokō to kekkaku*, edited by Kagoyama Takashi. 1970. Tokyo: Koseikan.

Jacobs, Jerry. 1989. *Revolving Doors: Sex Segregation and Women's Careers*. Stanford: Stanford University Press.

Jacoby, Sanford. 1979. "The Origins of Internal Labor Markets in Japan." *Industrial Relations* 18, 2: 184–96.

James, Estelle, and Gail Benjamin. 1988. *Pubic Policy and Private Education in Japan*. New York: St. Martin's Press.

Japan Economic Institute. 1990. *Japan Economic Institute Report*, no. 11a. Washington, D.C.

———. 1991. *Japan Economic Institute Report*, no. 33a. Washington, D.C.

Japan Institute of Labor. 1989. *Japan Labor Bulletin* 28, 9.
———. 1990. *Japan Labor Bulletin* 29, 4.
Johnson, Chalmers. 1982. *MITI and the Japanese Miracle: The Growth of Industrial Policy.* Stanford: Stanford University Press.
Kalleberg, Arne L., and James R. Lincoln. 1985. "Work Organization and Workforce Commitment: A Study of Plants and Employees in the U.S. and Japan." *American Sociological Review* 50, 6: 738–60.
———. 1988. "The Structure of Earnings Inequality in the United States and Japan." *American Journal of Sociology* 94 (supplement): S121–53.
Kamata, Satoshi. 1983. *Japan in the Passing Lane.* New York: Pantheon Books.
Kariya, Takehiko, and James Rosenbaum. 1987. "Self-Selection in Japanese Junior High Schools: A Longitudinal Study of Students' Educational Plans." *Sociology of Education* 60, 3: 168–80.
Kaufman, Robert L., and Seymour Spilerman. 1982. "The Age Structures of Occupations and Jobs." *American Journal of Sociology* 87, 4: 827–51.
Kawashima, Yōko. 1983. "Wage Differentials between Women and Men in Japan." Ph.D. diss., Stanford University.
Kawashima, Yōko, and Toshiaki Tachibanaki. 1986. "The Effect of Discrimination and of Industrial Segmentation on Japanese Wage Differentials in Relation to Education." *International Journal of Industrial Organization* 4: 43–68.
Koike, Kazuo. 1983a. "Internal Labor Markets: Workers in Large Firms." In *Contemporary Industrial Relations in Japan*, edited by Taishiro Shirai, 29–62. Madison: University of Wisconsin Press.
———. 1983b. "Workers in Small Firms and Women in Industry." In *Contemporary Industrial Relations in Japan*, edited by Taishiro Shirai, 89–116. Madison: University of Wisconsin Press.
Kondo, Dorinne K. 1990. *Crafting Selves: Power, Gender, and Discourses of Identity in a Japanese Workplace.* Chicago: University of Chicago Press.
Korea Survey (Gallup) Polls Ltd. 1987. "Life Style and Value System of Housewives in Korea." Seoul: Korea Survey.
Koshiro, Kazutoshi. 1983a. "Development of Collective Bargaining in Postwar Japan." In *Contemporary Industrial Relations in Japan*, edited by Taishiro Shirai, 205–57. Madison: University of Wisconsin Press.
———. 1983b. "Labor Relations in Public Enterprises." In *Contemporary Industrial Relations in Japan*, edited by Taishiro Shirai, 259–93. Madison: University of Wisconsin Press.
———. 1983c. "The Quality of Work Life in Japanese Factories." In *Contemporary Industrial Relations in Japan*, edited by Taishiro Shirai, 63–88. Madison: University of Wisconsin Press.
Kuhn, Annette. 1978. "Structures of Patriarchy and Capital in the Family." In *Feminism and Materialism: Women and Modes of Production*, edited by Annette Kuhn and AnnMarie Wolpe, 42–67. London: Routledge & Kegan Paul.
Kurosaka, Yoshio. 1989. "The Japanese Economy and the Labor Market." *Japanese Economic Studies* 17, 3: 3–40.

Landes, Elizabeth M. 1977. "Sex Differences in Wages and Employment: A Test of the Specific Capital Hypothesis." *Economic Inquiry* 15, 4: 523–38.

Lapidus, Gail. 1978. *Women in Soviet Society: Equality, Development, and Social Change.* Berkeley: University of California Press.

Lazear, Edward. 1979. "Why Is There Mandatory Retirement?" *Journal of Political Economy* 87, 6: 1261–84.

Lebra, Joyce, Joy Paulson, and Elizabeth Powers. 1976. *Women in Changing Japan.* Boulder, Colo.: Westview Press.

Lebra, Takie Sugiyama. 1981. "Japanese Women in Male-Dominant Careers: Cultural Barriers and Accommodations for Sex Role Transcendence." *Ethnology* 20, 3: 291–306.

———. 1984. *Japanese Women: Constraint and Fulfillment.* Honolulu: University of Hawaii Press.

Lee, Sunhwa, and Mary C. Brinton. 1991. "The Expansion of Secondary and Higher Education in South Korea." Working paper.

Leibowitz, Arleen. 1975. "Education and the Allocation of Women's Time." In *Education, Income, and Human Behavior,* edited by F. Thomas Juster, 171–97. New York: McGraw-Hill.

Leonard, Sheldon. 1968. *Education and Ecstasy.* New York: Dell.

Levine, Solomon, and Hisashi Kawada. 1980. *Human Resources in Japanese Industrial Development.* Princeton, N.J.: Princeton University Press.

Lincoln, James R., Mitsuyo Hanada, and Kerry McBride. 1986. "Organizational Structures in Japanese and U.S. Manufacturing." *Administrative Science Quarterly* 31, 3: 338–64.

Lincoln, James R., and Kerry McBride. 1987. "Japanese Industrial Organization in Comparative Perspective." *Annual Review of Sociology* 13: 289–312.

Lipman-Blumen, Jean. 1976. "Toward a Homosocial Theory of Sex Roles: An Explanation of the Sex Segregation of Social Institutions." In *Women and the Workplace: The Implications of Occupational Segregation,* edited by Martha Blaxall and Barbara Reagan, 15–31. Chicago: University of Chicago Press.

Lloyd, Cynthia, and Beth Niemi. 1979. *The Economics of Sex Differentials.* New York: Columbia University Press.

Loscocco, Karyn, and Arne L. Kalleberg. 1988. "Age and the Meaning of Work in the United States and Japan." *Social Forces* 67, 2: 337–56.

McLaughlin, Steven, Barbara D. Melber, John O. G. Billy, Denise M. Zimmerle, Linda D. Winges, and Terry R. Johnson. 1988. *The Changing Lives of American Women.* Chapel Hill: University of North Carolina Press.

McLendon, James. 1983. "The Office: Way Station or Blind Alley?" In *Work and Lifecourse in Japan,* edited by David W. Plath, 156–82. Albany: State University of New York Press.

Marini, Margaret Mooney. 1978. "The Transition to Adulthood: Sex Differences in Educational Attainment and Age at Marriage." *American Sociological Review* 43, 4: 483–507.

———. 1984. "Age and Sequencing Norms in the Transition to Adulthood." *Social Forces* 63, 1: 229–44.

————. 1988. "Sociology of Gender." In *The Future of Sociology*, edited by Edgar F. Borgatta and Karen S. Cook, 374–93. Newbury Park, Calif.: Sage.

Marsh, Robert M., and Hiroshi Mannari. 1976. *Modernization and the Japanese Factory*. Princeton, N.J.: Princeton University Press.

Martin, Linda G., and Noriko O. Tsuya. 1989. "Interactions of Middle-Aged Japanese with Their Parents." Paper presented at the 1989 annual meeting of the Population Association of America, Baltimore.

Mead, George Herbert. 1934. *Mind, Self, and Society*. Chicago: University of Chicago Press.

Milkman, Ruth. 1987. *Gender at Work: The Dynamics of Job Segregation by Sex during World War II*. Urbana: University of Illinois Press.

Mincer, Jacob. 1974. *Schooling, Experience, and Earnings*. New York: National Bureau of Economic Research.

Ministry of Education, Japan. 1984. *Gakkō kihon chōsa* (Basic school statistics). Tokyo: Ministry of Education.

————. 1985. *Jidō, seito no gakkōgai gakushū katsudō ni kansuru jittai chōsa* (Survey of extra-curricular study activities of youth). Tokyo: Ministry of Education.

————. 1987. *Gakkō kihon chōsa* (Basic school statistics). Tokyo: Ministry of Education.

————. 1990. *Gakkō kihon chōsa* (Basic school statistics). Tokyo: Ministry of Education.

Ministry of Labor, Japan. 1981. *Joshi rōdōsha no koyō kanri ni kansuru chōsa* (Survey of employment administration of female employees). Tokyo: Women's Bureau, Ministry of Labor.

————. 1983. *Joshi rōdōsha no koyō kanri ni kansuru chōsa* (Survey of employment administration of female employees). Tokyo: Women's Bureau, Ministry of Labor.

————. 1985a. *Joshi rōdōsha no koyō kanri ni kansuru chōsa* (Survey of employment administration of female employees). Tokyo: Women's Bureau, Ministry of Labor.

————. 1985b. *Pāto-taimu rōdō jittai chōsa* (Survey of the situation of part-time workers). Tokyo: Statistics Bureau.

————. 1987a. *Chingin kōzō kihon tōkei chōsa* (Basic survey of wage structure). Tokyo: Government Printing Office.

————. 1987b. *Joshi rōdōsha no koyō kanri ni kansuru chōsa* (Survey of employment administration of female employees). Tokyo: Women's Bureau, Ministry of Labor.

————. 1987c. *Maitsuki kinrō tōkei chōsa* (Monthly labor survey). Tokyo: Government Printing Office.

————. 1988. *Fujin rōdō no jitsujō* (Status of women workers). Tokyo: Government Printing Office.

Ministry of Welfare, Japan. 1989. *Jinkō dōtai tōkei* (Vital statistics). Tokyo: Government Printing Office.

Mizuno, Asao. 1988. "Wage Flexibility and Employment Changes." *Japanese Economic Studies* 16, 2: 38–73.

Moe, Terry. 1984. "The New Economics of Organization." *American Journal of Political Science* 38: 739–77.

Morgan, S. Philip, and Kiyosi Hirosima. 1983. "The Persistence of Extended Family Residence in Japan: Anachronism or Alternative Strategy?" *American Sociological Review* 48, 2: 269–81.

Morgan, S. Philip, Ronald Rindfuss, and Allan Parnell. 1984. "Modern Fertility Patterns: Contrasts between the United States and Japan." *Population and Development Review* 10, 1: 19–40.

Mouer, Ross, and Yoshio Sugimoto. 1986. *Images of Japanese Society.* London: KPI.

Murakami, Yasusuke. 1984. "*Ie* Society as a Pattern of Civilization." *Journal of Japanese Studies* 10, 2: 281–363.

Murakami Yasusuke, Kumon Shunpei, and Satō Seizaburō. 1979. *Bunmei to shite no Ie shakai* (*Ie* society as a pattern of civilization). Tokyo: Chūōkōronsha.

Naito, Norikuni. 1983. "Trade Union Finance and Administration." In *Contemporary Industrial Relations in Japan*, edited by Taishiro Shirai, 145–59. Madison, Wisconsin: University of Wisconsin Press.

Nakamura, Takafusa. 1981. *The Postwar Japanese Economy: Its Development and Structure.* Tokyo: University of Tokyo Press.

Nakane, Chie. 1970. *Japanese Society.* Berkeley and Los Angeles: University of California Press.

Nakata, Yoshifumi, and Carl Mosk. 1987. "The Demand for College Education in Postwar Japan." *Journal of Human Resources* 22, 3: 377–404.

National Institute of Employment and Vocational Research, Japan. 1988. *Seinen ishiki chōsa* (Survey of youth attitudes). Tokyo: National Institute of Employment and Vocational Research.

Niemi, Beth. 1974. "The Female-Male Differential in Unemployment Rates." *Industrial and Labor Relations Review* 27, 2: 331–50.

Nihon Recruit Center. 1983a. "Daigakusei (danshi, joshi) no shūshoku dōki chōsa" (Job-seeking behavior of male and female university graduates). Tokyo: Nihon Recruit Center.

———. 1983b. *Daigaku sōran* (A general survey of universities). Tokyo: Nihon Recruit Center.

———. 1984. "Joshi gakusei wa nani o kangaete iru ka" (What do women students think?). Tokyo: Nihon Recruit Center.

———. 1985. "Shinyū shain wa nani o kangaete iru ka" (What do new employees think?). Tokyo: Nihon Recruit Center.

Noguchi, Paul. 1983. "Shiranai Station: Not a Destination but a Journey." In *Work and Lifecourse in Japan*, edited by David W. Plath, 74–95. Albany: State University of New York Press.

Office of the Prime Minister, Japan. 1938. *Dainippon teikoku tōkei nenkan* (Statistical yearbook of Japan). Tokyo: Statistics Bureau.

———. 1971. *Shūgyō kōzō kihon chōsa* (Basic survey of employment structure). Tokyo: Statistics Bureau.

———. 1973. *Sekai seinen ishiki chōsa hōkokusho* (Report on the world youth attitude survey). Tokyo: Youth Policy Office.

―――. 1979. *Fujin ni kansuru ishiki chōsa* (Opinion survey concerning women). Tokyo: Office of the Prime Minister.

―――. 1980. *Shūgyō kōzō kihon chōsa* (Basic survey of employment structure). Tokyo: Statistics Bureau.

―――. 1982a. *Fujin mondai ni kansuru kokusai hikaku chōsa* (Comparative survey of women's problems). Tokyo: Office of the Prime Minister.

―――. 1982b. *Kyōiku ni kansuru yoron chōsa* (Opinion survey on education). Tokyo: Office of the Prime Minister.

―――. 1983. *Kakei chōsa nenpō* (Annual report on the family income and expenditure survey). Tokyo: Statistics Bureau.

―――. 1987a. *Josei ni kansuru yoron chōsa* (Opinion survey concerning women). Tokyo: Government Printing Office.

―――. 1987b. *Shūgyō kōzō kihon chōsa* (Basic survey of employment structure). Tokyo: Statistics Bureau.

―――. Various years. *Kokusei chōsa* (Population census). Tokyo: Statistics Bureau.

―――. Various years. *Nihon tōkei nenkan* (Japan statistical yearbook). Tokyo: Statistics Bureau.

―――. Various years. *Rōdōryoku chōsa* (Survey of the labor force). Tokyo: Statistics Bureau.

Ohkawa, Kazushi, and Henry Rosovsky. 1973. *Japanese Economic Growth: Trend Acceleration in the Twentieth Century.* Stanford: Stanford University Press.

Oi, Walter. 1983. "The Fixed Employment Costs of Specialized Labor." In *The Measurement of Labor Cost*, edited by Jack E. Triplett, 63–122. Chicago: University of Chicago Press.

Ono, Tsuneo. 1980. "Postwar Changes in the Japanese Wage System." In *The Labor Market in Japan*, edited by Shunsaku Nishikawa, 145–76. Tokyo: University of Tokyo Press.

Osako, Masako Murakami. 1978. "Dilemmas of Japanese Professional Women." *Social Problems* 26, 1: 15–25.

Osawa, Machiko. 1984. "Women's Skill Formation, Labor Force Participation, and Fertility in Japan." Ph.D. diss., Southern Illinois University.

―――. 1985. "The Feminization of Clerical Work in the U.S. and Japan: Education and the Changing Occupational Structure." Working paper.

―――. 1987. "Trends and Characteristics of Working Women in Japan." Paper presented to the Association of Asian Studies, Boston, Mass.

―――. 1988a. "Changing Role of Education and Women Workers in Japan." *Keiō Business Review* 24: 87–101.

―――. 1988b. "Working Mothers: Changing Patterns of Employment and Fertility in Japan." *Economic Development and Cultural Change* 36, 4: 623–50.

Ouchi, William. 1981. *Theory Z.* Reading, Mass.: Addison-Wesley.

Pampel, Fred C., and Kazuko Tanaka. 1986. "Economic Development and Female Labor Force Participation: A Reconsideration." *Social Forces* 64: 599–619.

Papanek, Hanna. 1979. "Family Status Production: The 'Work' and 'Non-Work' of Women." *Signs* 4, 4: 775–81.

Patrick, Hugh, and Thomas Rohlen. 1987. "Small-Scale Family Enterprises." In *The Political Economy of Japan*, vol. 1, edited by Kozo Yamamura and Yasukichi Yasuba, 331–38. Stanford: Stanford University Press.

Peck, Merton, and Shūji Tamura. 1976. "Technology." In *Asia's New Giant*, edited by Hugh Patrick and Henry Rosovsky, 525–85. Washington, D.C.: Brookings Institution.

Pharr, Susan. 1981. *Political Women in Japan: The Search for a Place in Political Life*. Berkeley and Los Angeles: University of California Press.

———. 1984. "Status Conflict: The Rebellion of the Tea Pourers." In *Conflict in Japan*, edited by Ellis Krauss, Thomas Rohlen, and Patricia Steinhoff, 214–40. Honolulu: University of Hawaii Press.

Phelps, Edmund. 1972. "The Statistical Theory of Racism and Sexism." *American Economic Review* 62, 4: 659–61.

Polachek, Solomon. 1975. "Discontinuous Labor Force Participation and Its Effects on Women's Market Earnings." In *Sex, Discrimination, and the Division of Labor*, edited by Cynthia Lloyd, 90–122. New York: Columbia University Press.

———. 1979. "Occupational Segregation among Women: Theory, Evidence, and a Prognosis." In *Women in the Labor Market*, edited by Cynthia Lloyd, 137–57. New York: Columbia University Press.

———. 1981. "Occupational Self-Selection: A Human Capital Approach to Sex Differences in Occupational Structure." *Review of Economics and Statistics* 68, 1: 60–69.

———. 1985. "Occupational Segregation: A Defense of Human Capital Predictions." *Journal of Human Resources* 20, 3: 437–40.

Roberts, Glenda. 1986. "Non-Trivial Pursuits: Japanese Blue-Collar Women and the Life-Time Employment System." Ph.D. diss., Cornell University.

Rohlen, Thomas P. 1974. *For Harmony and Strength*. Berkeley and Los Angeles: University of California Press.

———. 1975. "The Company Work Group." In *Modern Japanese Organization and Decision-Making*, edited by Ezra F. Vogel, 185–209. Berkeley and Los Angeles: University of California Press.

———. 1977. "Is Japanese Education Becoming Less Egalitarian? Notes on High School Stratification and Reform." *Journal of Japanese Studies* 3, 1: 37–70.

———. 1979. "'Permanent Employment' Faces Recession, Slow Growth, and an Aging Workforce." *Journal of Japanese Studies* 5, 2: 235–72.

———. 1980. "The *Juku* Phenomenon: An Exploratory Essay." *Journal of Japanese Studies* 6, 2: 207–42.

———. 1983. *Japan's High Schools*. Berkeley and Los Angeles: University of California Press.

Roos, Patricia. 1985. *Gender and Work: A Comparative Analysis of Industrial Societies*. Albany: State University of New York Press.

Roos, Patricia, and Barbara Reskin. 1984. "Institutional Factors Contributing to Sex Segregation in the Workplace." In *Sex Segregation in the Workplace*, edited by Barbara F. Reskin, 192–232. Washington, D.C.: National Academy Press.

Rosaldo, Michelle Zimbalist. 1974. "Woman, Culture, and Society: A Theoretical Overview." In *Woman, Culture, and Society*, edited by Michelle Zimbalist Rosaldo and Louise Lamphere, 17–42. Stanford: Stanford University Press.

Rosenbaum, James, and Takehiko Kariya. 1989. "From High School to Work: Market and Institutional Mechanisms in Japan." *American Journal of Sociology* 94, 6: 1334–65.

Rosenzweig, Mark R. 1982. "Wage Structure and Sex-Based Wage Inequality: The Family as Intermediary." *Population and Development Review* 8 (supplement): 192–206.

Ryder, Norman. 1965. "The Cohort as a Concept in the Study of Social Change." *American Sociological Review* 30, 6: 843–61.

Sacks, Karen. 1974. "Engels Revisited: Women, the Organization of Production, and Private Property." In *Woman, Culture, and Society*, edited by Michelle Zimbalist Rosaldo and Louise Lamphere, 207–22. Stanford: Stanford University Press.

Sakuma, Ken. 1988. "Change in Japanese-Style Labor-Management Relations." *Japanese Economic Studies* 16, 4: 3–48.

Salaff, Janet. 1981. *Working Daughters of Hong Kong: Filial Piety or Power in the Family?* Cambridge: Cambridge University Press.

Sano Yōko. 1972. *Joshi rōdō no keizaigaku* (The economics of female labor supply). Tokyo: Japan Institute of Labor.

Saso, Mary. 1990. *Women in the Japanese Workplace*. London: H. Shipman.

Saxonhouse, Gary R. 1976. "Country Girls and Communication among Competitors in the Japanese Cotton-Spinning Industry." In *Japanese Industrialization and Its Social Consequences*, edited by Hugh Patrick, 97–125. Berkeley and Los Angeles: University of California Press.

Seiyama, Kazuo, and Yuji Noguchi. 1984. "Kōkōshingaka ni okeru gakkōgai kyōiku tōshi no kōka" (The effects of investment in extra-school schooling on advancement to high school). *Kyōiku Shakaigaku Kenkyū* 39: 113–26.

Semyonov, Moshe. 1980. "The Social Context of Women's Labor Force Participation: A Comparative Analysis." *American Journal of Sociology* 86, 3: 534–50.

Shimada, Haruo. 1981. *Earnings Structure and Human Investment: A Comparison between the United States and Japan*. Tokyo: Kogadusha.

———. 1983. "Japanese Industrial Relations—A New General Model? A Survey of the English-Language Literature." In *Contemporary Industrial Relations in Japan*, edited by Taishiro Shirai, 3–27. Madison: University of Wisconsin Press.

Shimada, Haruo, and Yoshio Higuchi. 1985. "An Analysis of Trends in Female Labor Force Participation in Japan." *Journal of Labor Economics* 3, 1 (pt. 2): S355–74.

Shinotsuka Eiko. 1982. *Nihon no joshi rōdō* (Female labor in Japan). Tokyo: Toyo Keizai.

Shirai, Taishiro. 1983. "A Supplement: Characteristics of Japanese Managements and Their Personnel Policies." In *Contemporary Industrial Relations
in Japan*, edited by Taishiro Shirai, 360–82. Madison: University of Wisconsin Press.

Smith, James P., and Michael P. Ward. 1984. *Women's Wages and Work in the
Twentieth Century*. Report prepared for the National Institute of Child
Health and Human Development, Rand Publication Series.

———. 1985. "Time-Series Growth in the Female Labor Force." *Journal of
Labor Economics* 3: S59–90.

Smith, Robert J. 1987. "Gender Inequality in Contemporary Japan." *Journal
of Japanese Studies* 13, 1: 1–25.

Smith, Robert J., and Ella Lury Wiswell. 1982. *The Women of Suye Mura*.
Chicago: University of Chicago Press.

Spitze, Glenna, and Linda Waite. 1980. "Labor Force and Work Attitudes:
Young Women's Early Experiences." *Sociology of Work and Occupations*
7, 1: 3–32.

Stacey, Judith. 1983. *Patriarchy and Socialist Revolution in China*. Berkeley
and Los Angeles: University of California Press.

Steinmetz, George, and Erik Olin Wright. 1989. "The Fall and Rise of the
Petty Bourgeoisie: Changing Patterns of Self-Employment in the Postwar
United States." *American Journal of Sociology* 94, 5: 973–1018.

Stevenson, Harold. 1989. "The Asian Advantage: The Case of Mathematics."
In *Japanese Schooling: Patterns of Socialization, Equity, and Political Con-
trol*, edited by James J. Shields, Jr., 85–97. University Park: Pennsylvania
State University Press.

Taira, Koji. 1970. *Economic Development and the Labor Market in Japan*.
New York: Columbia University Press.

Takezawa, Shin'ichi, and Arthur M. Whitehill. 1981. *Work Ways: Japan and
America*. Tokyo: Japan Institute of Labor.

Tanaka, Kazuko. 1987. "Women, Work, and Family in Japan: A Life Cycle
Perspective." Ph.D. diss., University of Iowa.

Tilly, Louise, and Joan W. Scott. 1978. *Women, Work, and Family*. New York:
Holt, Rinehart & Winston.

Tominaga Ken'ichi. 1979. "Shakai kaisō to shakai idō no sūsei bunseki" (A
trend analysis of social class and social mobility). In *Nihon no kaisō kōzō*
(The structure of Japanese social stratification), edited by Tominaga
Ken'ichi, 33–87. Tokyo: Tokyo University Press.

Treiman, Donald. 1977. *Occupational Prestige in Comparative Perspective*.
New York: Academic Press.

Treiman, Donald, and Heidi Hartmann. 1981. *Women, Work, and Wages:
Equal Pay for Jobs of Equal Value*. Washington, D.C.: National Academy
Press.

Tsurumi, E. Patricia. 1990. *Factory Girls: Women in the Thread Mills of Meiji
Japan*. Princeton, N.J.: Princeton University Press.

Turner, Ralph. 1960. "Modes of Social Ascent through Education: Sponsored
and Contest Mobility." *American Sociological Review* 25, 6: 121–39.

United Nations. 1982a. *Demographic Yearbook*. New York: United Nations.
————. 1982b. *Statistical Yearbook*. New York: United Nations.
————. 1988. *Demographic Yearbook*. New York: United Nations.
U.S. Bureau of the Census. 1979. *Current Population Survey* (May). Washington, D.C.: Government Printing Office.
————. 1984. *1980 Census of Population*, vol. 1, *Characteristics of the Population*. PC80–1-D1-A. Washington, D.C.: Government Printing Office.
————. Various years. *Statistical Abstract of the United States*. Washington, D.C.: Government Printing Office.
U.S. Bureau of Labor Statistics. 1980. *Employment and Earnings* 27, 9. Washington, D.C.: Government Printing Office.
U.S. Department of Education. 1987. *Japanese Education Today*. Washington, D.C.: Government Printing Office.
Upham, Frank K. 1987. *Law and Social Change in Postwar Japan*. Cambridge, Mass.: Harvard University Press.
Ushiogi, Morikazu. 1986. "Transition from School to Work: The Japanese Case." In *Educational Policies in Crisis: Japanese and American Perspectives*, edited by William K. Cummings, 197–209. New York: Praeger.
Van Wolferen, Karel. 1988. *The Enigma of Japanese Power*. New York: Random House.
Vanek, Joann. 1974. "Time Spent in Housework." *Scientific American* 231: 116–20.
Vogel, Ezra F. 1967. *Japan's New Middle Class*. Berkeley and Los Angeles: University of California Press.
————. ed. 1975. *Modern Japanese Organization and Decision-Making*. Berkeley and Los Angeles: University of California Press.
————. 1979. *Japan as No. 1: Lessons for America*. New York: Harper & Row.
Walby, Sylvia. 1986. *Patriarchy at Work: Patriarchal and Capitalist Relations in Employment*. Minneapolis: University of Minnesota Press.
Walker, K. E., and M. Woods. 1976. *Time Use: A Measure of Household Production of Family Goods and Services*. Washington, D.C.: American Home Economics Association.
Walters, Pamela Barnhouse. 1988. "Sex and Institutional Differences in Labor Market Effects on the Expansion of Higher Education, 1952 to 1980." *Sociology of Education* 59, 4: 199–211.
Whitehill, Arthur, and Shin'ichi Takezawa. 1968. *The Other Worker*. Honolulu: East-West Center Press.
Wolf, Margery. 1985. *Revolution Postponed: Women in Contemporary China*. Stanford: Stanford University Press.
World Bank. 1988. *World Development Report*. New York: Oxford University Press.
Woronoff, Jon. 1980. *Japan: The Coming Social Crisis*. Tokyo: Lotus Press.
————. 1983. *Japan's Wasted Workers*. Totowa, N.J.: Allanheld, Osmun.
Yamamura, Kozo, and Susan B. Hanley. 1975. "Ichi hime, ni Taro: Educational Aspirations and the Decline in Fertility in Postwar Japan." *Journal of Japanese Studies* 2, 1: 83–125.

Yashiro, Naohiro. 1981. "Women in the Japanese Labor Force." Ph.D. diss.,
    University of Maryland.
————. 1983. *Joshi rōdō no keizai bunseki.* Tokyo: Nihon Keizai Shinbunsha.
Yasuba, Yasukichi. 1976. "The Evolution of Dualistic Wage Structure." In
    Japanese Industrialization and Its Social Consequences, edited by Hugh
    Patrick, 249–98. Berkeley and Los Angeles: University of California Press.
Yokoyama Gennosuke. 1898. *Nihon no kasō shakai* (The lower strata of Jap-
    anese society). Tokyo: Iwanami Bunken. Reprinted by Iwanami Shoten,
    1949.

Index

Abegglen, James C., 13, 111
Absenteeism, 109–10
Administration. *See* Managerial occupations
Administrative guidance, 229
Administrative support occupations. *See* Clerical sector
Age structure, 24, 46–49, 70, 81, 237; and employment status, 175–80; in occupations, 59, 62–69; and wages, 44–46, 47. *See also* Life cycle
Agriculture, 7–8, 53; women's role in, 7–8, 25–29
American Occupation, 122, 192
Arrow, Kenneth, 98

Becker, Gary, 208–9
Birth rates, 11n, 25, 31, 236
Blaug, Mark, 76
Blue-collar occupations: age patterns in, 64–67; gender stratification in, 35–36, 64, 66, 67
Bonus system, 133n
Britain, 29
Businesses. *See* Work organizations

Capitalism, 25–26n; and patriarchy, 17, 71, 73–74, 76. *See also* Industrialization
Childrearing, 91–93, 238n. *See also* Domestic sphere

Clark, Rodney C., 109
Clerical sector, 34–36, 44, 151; age structure in, 67–69; pink-collar work, 61, 67; service sector jobs, 24–25, 146; sex segregation in, 67–69; white-collar work, 44, 175
Cole, Robert E., 2, 35, 124, 130
Commuting, 180–81
Corporations. *See* Work organizations

Daughters. *See* Family; Human capital investment; Sex roles
Divorce, 99. *See also* Marriage
Domestic sphere: childrearing, 91–93, 238n; household duties, 179–80, 223–24, 236–37; motherhood, 44, 73. *See also* Family; Marriage
Dualism: in light and heavy industries, 119–20, 129, 129n, 133; within organizations, 130

East Asian economies, status of women in, 224–28
Economic role of women, 36, 135, 137–39; cross-cultural comparisons, 9–11, 19, 24, 32–33, 34–37, 44; direct, 69–70; dual, 11–13, 30–32, 72–73, 75n; indirect, 89, 91–95, 233
Economy: as a model for other countries, 13–14; and productivity, 110; system compared to U.S., 59–61,

Compositor:	Recorder Typesetting
Text:	10/13 Sabon
Display:	Sabon
Printer:	Maple-Vail Book Mfg. Group
Binder:	Maple-Vail Book Mfg. Group